W9-BIR-259

PLAY DIRECTOR'S
Survival Kit

A Complete Step-by-Step Guide to Producing Theater in Any School or Community Setting

JAMES W. RODGERS
University of Kentucky
Lexington, Kentucky

WANDA C. RODGERS
Woodford County High School
Versailles, Kentucky

Graphics and Illustrations by
RUSSELL JONES
University of Kentucky
Lexington, Kentucky

JOSSEY-BASS
A Wiley Imprint
www.josseybass.com

Published by Jossey-Bass
A Wiley Imprint
989 Market Street, San Francisco, CA 94103-1741   www.josseybass.com

Jossey-Bass books and products are available through most bookstores. To contact Jossey-Bass directly call our Customer Care Department within the U.S. at 800-956-7739, outside the U.S. at 317-572-3986 or fax 317-572-4002.

Jossey-Bass also publishes its books in a variety of electronic formats. Some content that appears in print may not be available in electronic books.

Library of Congress Cataloging-in-Publication Data
Rodgers, James W.
      Play director's survival kit : a complete step-by-step guide to
producing theater in any school or community setting / James W.
Rodgers, Wanda C. Rodgers ; graphics and illustrations by Russell
Jones.
    p. cm.
    Includes bibliographical references.
    ISBN 0-87628-565-5
    1. Amateur theater—Production and direction. I. Rodgers, Wanda
C. II. Title.
PN3155.R54   1995
792'.0222'0233—dc20   94-43944

FIRST EDITION
PB Printing 10 9 8 7 6 5 4 3

Dedication

To our daughters, Julie and Jennifer,
the two best productions we have ever collaborated on.

Acknowledgments

We see this book as an opportunity to pass on some of the knowledge we have received from so many gifted individuals who have taught and worked with us over the years. They are too numerous to name, but to all of them we say a heartfelt "thank you." We hope that this resource will lead our readers to creative and artistic experiences that give them the same joy we have so often experienced throughout our careers.

We are especially grateful to Trish Clark, Jeff Fightmaster, Pat Foran, Marie Henderson, Matt Merrill, and Mary Stephenson for reading early drafts of selected chapters; to Norman Hart for his specific and most helpful suggestions; to our close friends John Higgins, Roger Leasor, and Russ Jones for their very specific involvement; and to our editor, Connie Kallback, for her trust, support, and encouragement.

About the Authors

JAMES W. RODGERS, Ph.D., is currently a full professor at the University of Kentucky. For twenty-seven of his more than thirty-five years of teaching experience, Dr. Rodgers has served as a department chair, first at Fairview High School in Dayton, Ohio, and then at the University of Detroit in Michigan, William Paterson State College in New Jersey, and the University of Kentucky. During his career he has directed over one hundred fully mounted productions in a variety of venues including professional, community, university, summer stock, and high school theaters. Dr. Rodgers is also a published playwright.

WANDA C. RODGERS has taught in five states and in a variety of schools. She currently teaches Drama, English, and Communications at Woodford County High School in Versailles, Kentucky, where she has been named "Outstanding High School Teacher of the Year" for Woodford County. In her first year in Kentucky she inherited a drama budget nine dollars in the red, an open stage positioned between the cafeteria and gymnasium, and no equipment—lights, sound, or sets. Although much of this has improved, the facilities are still primitive. It has, however, served as the site of many quality productions including several highly complicated and technically challenging musicals—proof that theater can be a positive and successful experience even under adverse circumstances.

Contents

ACT TWO: PRE-PRODUCTION CONSIDERATIONS

ACT THREE: REHEARSALS AND PERFORMANCES

ACT FOUR: AUDIENCE DEVELOPMENT

EPILOGUE: DIRECTORY

Prologue

"WELCOME TO THE THEATER"

What You Can Expect from This Resource

We have written this resource, first, for individuals who have an interest in theater but only limited experience and little or no formal training. You may be a high school math or history teacher with a minor in theater or an amateur actor who has been coerced into directing the next community theater production. We expect you to be more than a little overwhelmed; that's only natural. If at the same time you are enthusiastic about the prospect of directing and have a strong desire to create the best production possible, then we would say without reservation, this guide is for you.

The guide might also be of interest to high school or community theater directors who are looking for a refresher course. It is easy to get "burnt out" or discouraged in our profession; sometimes you need to be reassured or to rethink the way you have been handling certain aspects of the job. It is our contention that there is no one "right" way to deal with the process; in fact, as with acting, there are probably as many methods to directing as there are directors. In this resource we are simply sharing the way that has worked best for us over the years. It is our hope that the guide will renew or even affirm your approach.

We have viewed our role as professional consultants. We both hold advanced degrees in theater and each of us has been actively pursuing the craft for over thirty years. We have directed more than one hundred twenty full-length plays or musicals for high schools, universities, communities, and even professional theater organizations, so we feel we have something to offer.

We have imagined that you are sitting in our living room asking questions and we are responding in what we hope is a clear, straightforward manner. Whenever possible, we have listed important issues in an outline form so you can find and follow ideas easily. This guide has not been written to be read at one sitting, but rather, to be kept on your desk or bedside table as a reference guide. Throughout, we have tried to be brief and succinct. Our objective is to give you as much information as possible and to make your job easier. After all, theater should be fun.

The guide has been laid out in what we feel is a logical order. It is our hope that if you follow it chapter by chapter, you will have a satisfying experience during every phase of the rehearsal process. That, at any rate, is our objective.

Throughout the resource, we have given examples from Oscar Wilde's brilliant classic comedy, *The Importance of Being Earnest.* We suggest that you obtain a copy from either your local bookstore or library and keep it close at hand for clarity and reference.

A word about the song titles which we have used as headings for each chapter. While we hope you will have some fun matching their significance to the content in each chapter, the real reason for their inclusion is to remind you of the great popularity of theater and the contribution it has made throughout the ages. Since before the fifth century B.C. the theater has been the source of both entertainment and enlightenment. Its popularity can be attributed at least in part to the fact that theater is a celebration of life. Every time we watch a play we are learning more about ourselves. The stage becomes a laboratory that continually investigates and reflects on the possibilities and limitations of the human spirit. The most successful efforts are always highly imaginative and thought-provoking. Here's hoping that your efforts will be, too.

Welcome to the theater!

Act One
PLAY SELECTION

1 Understanding Your Role as Director

"Magic to Do"

from Pippin.
Music and lyrics by Stephen Schwartz;
book by Roger O. Hirson (Bob Fosse uncredited).

Opened in New York, October 23, 1972; ran 1,944 performances. Ben Vereen, John Rubinstein, Ann Reinking, and Irene Ryan were in the cast.

Almost everyone has heard of the term *director,* but surprisingly few people know exactly what stage directors do. Perhaps that is because their presence is never seen, only felt. As artists, they are relatively new to the profession. Actors have been around since before the fifth century B.C., but directors, not until late in the nineteenth century. It was in Germany that the initiator, George II, Duke of Saxe-Meiningen, stepped apart from his troupe and called himself their director. Until that time, plays had been overseen by playwrights or, more often than not, by leading actors in a company.

The "Duke," as he was affectionately called, felt that the play, not a player, should be the focus of attention, and he went about to make it so. He turned the whole rehearsal process around and gave attention to all actors, not just the leading player. He rehearsed a play for weeks, not just days, and took time to make sure that every movement and every gesture added something to the meaning. He also concerned himself with scenic detail; nothing escaped his attention. The Duke literally revolutionized the way theater was put together and brought new meaning to performance.

Today, directors continue to be special people, constantly struggling to find better ways of turning illusion into a form of reality. They are frequently thwarted by obstacles but find great satisfaction in discovering new and creative ways of working out solutions. Although it cannot be denied that all directors take certain pride in a finished, well-executed product, for them greater satisfaction comes from working through the process and dealing with the day-to-day maze of details.

James Agate, the novelist, defined directors as "people engaged by the management to conceal the fact that the players cannot act." The observer has a limited view. It is true that skilled directors can help untrained actors look good and that untrained directors can make good actors look bad. The trade has far more to it than the casual observer might perceive. The best in the business are individuals with keen eyes, sharp ears, an intuitive sensitivity, and a wide range of gifts to draw upon:

- Like painters, they can manipulate line, mass, balance, composition, light, shade, and color to achieve visual meaning.
- Like musicians, they can use rhythm, volume, pitch, and tone to bring out nuances.
- Like choreographers, they can move bodies through space to communicate both subtle meanings and complicated ideas.
- Like coaches, they can take diverse individuals and inspire them to play as a team.

In short, directors are an amalgam; they synthesize ideas, inspiration, and intuitions into meaning and form. They come in all shapes and sizes. They are not limited by their age or gender. They do, however, have three things in common:
they are all...

intuitive,

enthusiastic, and

gregarious.

Ideas come easily to them, they love their craft, and they enjoy being with people. These are the key elements of their personalities; everything else is individual and transitory—

except, perhaps, one other mutual characteristic. Directors are all a little mad. Like Don Quixote, they are always on a quest and are willing to tilt at windmills to achieve an objective. They don't always succeed, but the adventures they undergo are worth the efforts.

If you, too, are a bit daring, willing to step out in faith, and not afraid to appear a little mad, read on. We have "foibles and fables to portray," and indeed, "magic to do."

2 How to Get Started

"One Brick at a Time"

from Barnum.
Music by Cy Coleman,
lyrics by Michael Stewart,
and book by Mark
Bramble.

Opened in New York, April 30, 1980; ran 854 performances. The original cast included Jim Dale as P. T. Barnum, the creator of "The Greatest Show on Earth," and Glenn Close as his wife, Mrs. Barnum.

It's time to start. You've accepted the job, taken on the risk, and now it is time to step out in faith. Where to begin? Many directors start by looking for a play to direct. We feel that this is putting the cart before the horse. You have literally thousands of plays to choose from, but unless you analyze your particular situation, you can easily become overwhelmed reading through catalog descriptions. We would argue that it is best, first, to assess your limitations. By doing so you will narrow your options and make your search more focused. As the title character sings in the Cy Coleman musical, *Barnum*, it is better to take it "One Brick at a Time."

FACING YOUR LIMITATIONS

We have found that the best way to assess limitations is to seek answers to questions we have labeled *who, what, where, when, how, why,* and *to whom:*

- *Who* can help me?
- *What* kind of talent do I have to work with?
- *Where* is the play I am to direct to be presented?
- *When* am I supposed to have the production ready?
- *How* much money do I have to work with?
- *Why* have I decided (or been asked) to present this play?
- *To whom* is the play being presented?

WHOM DO I HAVE TO HELP ME?

Theater is a team sport. It takes more than just talent to produce a successful production. In fact, you will probably end up with more people on the Production Staff—those who contribute as designers, technicians, heads of committees, assistants, and members of crews—than you will have actors on the stage. It is essential, therefore, that you find bright, organized, and committed people to assist on the production so you can concentrate your time and efforts on directing the play.

We suggest, as a first step, that you seek out three major assistants. They can all be students or volunteers; they do not need previous experience. In fact, we have found that it is best when these individuals are eager but inexperienced. They follow direction better and are more willing to do it your way. The only important prerequisite for these three helpers is that they all be "TEDs": Tactful, Energetic, and Dependable.

Needed, Three TEDs

Stage Manager: Perhaps the most important and widely acknowledged of these three key assistants is the individual who will be responsible for supervising the actors, the stage manager. This person will prepare the rehearsal space, assist with scheduling "calls" (when an actor is needed), keep a record of your direction (blocking) in a prompt book, and be in complete charge of running dress rehearsals and performances. We consider the stage manager's role so important to the success of your production that we have dedicated a whole chapter to discussing the specific responsibilities of this job. (See Chapter 13.)

Production Coordinator: Sometimes listed in programs as an Assistant to the Director or a Production Stage Manager, this individual will be the liaison between you and all the personnel assigned to the design and technical areas of production (set, properties, lighting, costumes, makeup, sound, and special effects). This person's specific duties will be to keep workers in these areas on schedule and informed of any changes. (See Chapters 7 through 12.)

Director of Audience Development and Services: This individual will be responsible for overseeing all the volunteers needed to work on ticket sales, program design and underwriting, advertising, poster layout and distribution, promotional campaigns, newspaper releases, and front-of-house management and organization (house manager, ushers, coat check, and concessions operators). (See Chapters 23 through 27.)

Professional Assistants

In every production you will find seven specialized design areas:

- Set
- Properties
- Lighting
- Costuming
- Makeup
- Sound
- Special Effects

Most organizations cannot afford to hire seven specialists, so in many school and community situations these seven responsibilities are combined and handled—or at least supervised—by two specialists:

- The first specialist designs and constructs the sets, properties, and special effects; designs and hangs the lights; and supervises the recording of all music and sound effects.
- The second specialist designs, constructs, borrows, or rents all the costumes; orders and designs all the makeup; and orders and styles wigs. In most situations this individual is also responsible for designing the actors' hair styles.

The point we are trying to make is that, in addition to your contributions, you will need to recruit the services of at least two trained and skilled designers. Screen these individuals carefully. If you can link up with two or more creative, proficient, and enthusiastic people, you will be well on your way to realizing a highly successful production.

Have your design team lined up before you audition your play. If no one in your school or organization has the expertise to handle these jobs, reach out into the community for help. Contact the closest university; an advanced student might be looking for a project. If this approach fails, you might try contacting other arts organizations. They might keep a list of individuals professionally trained in these areas who are interested in working in small school or community operations.

You must be prepared to offer a stipend to your key designers. Their work requires considerable time, talent, and effort. Don't expect these specialists, even if you recruit university students, to donate their time and talent. If they have been professionally trained and have had experience, expect to pay for their service and expertise.

Operators, Crews, and Volunteers

Your Production Coordinator and Director of Audience Services can help you recruit resourceful and responsible people within your school or organization to operate the lighting and sound equipment and to work on the following crews:

Property Crew: in charge of locating set properties (tables, chairs, etc.), hand props (glasses, bottles, a small glass blown unicorn, etc.), and items needed for stage decor (pictures, books to fill a bookcase, etc.).

Stage Crew: in charge of constructing and painting scenery and building set pieces.

Running Crew: in charge of working backstage during productions, changing sets, moving set pieces, flying in scenery.

Wardrobe Crew: in charge of organizing and maintaining costumes, and assisting actors during quick changes.

Makeup Crew: in charge of organizing and maintaining all makeup paraphernalia and assisting actors in putting on makeup and styling hair and wigs.

Lighting Crew: in charge of assisting in the hanging and focusing of all lighting instruments.

Assistants to the Director of Audience Development and Services: in charge of selling advertising; distributing posters, flyers, handbills, and other display materials; and following through on other promotional ideas.

Front-of-House Personnel: includes house manager, ushers, and individuals in charge of selling tickets and concessions, plus, in season, checking hats and coats.

At the end of this chapter we have prepared a reproducible form that you can use as a checklist when you start recruiting operators, crews, and volunteers for your production.

WHAT KIND OF TALENT DO I HAVE TO WORK WITH?

Another important consideration before you start looking for a specific play is how much talent and interest you have in your school or community. One way to determine this is to schedule an acting workshop. Bring in an acting specialist, if at all possible. If not, design a sixty- to ninety-minute class using exercises, improvisations, and theater games. Two excellent resources are Viola Spolin's *Improvisation for the Theatre* and *Theater Games for Rehearsal*. (See Chapter 36.)

WHERE WILL THE PLAY BE PRESENTED?

Find out as much as you can about the auditorium or hall where your play will be presented. Keep asking until you get specific answers to the following questions. Use the reproducible page at the end of this chapter to keep track of your own situation. (See 2.4.)

How Large Is the Stage?

If the actual playing area of your stage is small, you may want to consider plays with limited technical requirements and no more than eight to ten characters.

How Large Is the Backstage Area?

If you have limited storage space behind and/or on either side of the stage, you will want to be cautious about choosing a play with multiple settings.

How Large Is the Auditorium?

Determine the acoustics in the auditorium. This is a critical factor especially when you are working with inexperienced actors. If the auditorium is large, consider a bright, broad comedy over a quiet, intimate drama. More intense character studies are better suited to small auditoriums.

How Sophisticated Is the Lighting and Sound Equipment?

Get an inventory of all lighting instruments and sound equipment. Make sure that everything is standard equipment, is in good working order, and meets all safety codes. If you discover that you have a limited supply of lighting instruments, you may want to avoid plays that require area lighting or special effects.

How Often Can I Use the Auditorium?

This is probably your most important question. You need to find out immediately how many classes or other activities are scheduled in the space. Ideally you want the space free and open for your exclusive use. When this is the case and you are not rehearsing, your designers and crews can work on the set.

The amount of time you have in the auditorium is a major consideration in choosing a play. If the auditorium has already been scheduled for other events, it is imperative that you at least have exclusive use of the space one full week before opening. You need this much time to move in the set, dress it, hang lights, set cues, and run dress rehearsals. Don't accept anything less. If the administration cannot or will not cooperate, it is best to reschedule your event or move to an alternative space. The less time you have in your performance space, the more important it is to find a script that can be staged with minimal technical requirements.

WHEN AM I SUPPOSED TO HAVE THE PRODUCTION READY?

The total amount of time you have to both plan and rehearse your play is another important consideration. It is best when you have at least one full month to search and prepare for your production and two full months for rehearsal. If your rehearsal time is limited, we suggest that you choose a play with an average size cast—six to ten characters—and with few special staging problems, like crowd scenes or stage fights. Chapter 33 contains a list of contemporary plays that are fairly straightforward in their requirements and therefore somewhat easier to direct.

HOW MUCH MONEY DO I HAVE TO WORK WITH?

It is impossible to produce a play without a budget. If you are working with a school and the administration wants a theater activity, they should support it with a budget of at least $1,000 annually (double if they expect you to produce a musical). If this is not possible, the administration should at least advance you monies against income from potential ticket sales and other sources of revenue such as advertisements, sponsorships, and fundraising events. The same holds true for community theaters. Don't accept a job without a realistic budget.

The following is a breakdown of where your money will be spent. Develop your own budget and then use the information to argue for backing. A reproducible form for this purpose can be found at the end of this chapter.

Royalties

Allow an average of $50 for the first performance, $40 for additional performances. Royalties for musicals are based on the size of the house and the number of performances. They are always considerably higher than for plays.

Scripts

Allow $5.00 per copy to cover handling and shipping as well as the cost of the script itself. Make sure you purchase additional copies for yourself, your three assistants (Stage Manager, Production Coordinator, and Director of Audience Services), and all designers and crew heads (set, lighting, sound, costume, makeup, properties). Take note that you will need the scripts for you and your designers at least one month before auditions are scheduled.

Set Construction

Include the cost of tools, space and equipment rentals, and all materials. Get a realistic estimate; remember, lumber is expensive.

Lighting

Include both rental and purchase expenses for replacement parts.

Properties

In addition to purchase and rental expenses, include the added cost of replacing perishables, of renting a truck (for transporting large furniture pieces), and mileage (for designers and crew members who drive around and look for properties). You may also need to include the cost of insurance to cover damage and loss. **Warning:** Antiques are fragile and expensive to replace. **Suggestion:** Seek out reproductions; from the audience, you can't tell the difference. Take out an insurance policy against damages.

Sound

Include the cost of recording tapes, the rental of recording equipment and speakers, and stage mikes, which are sometimes needed to help project the actors' voices. **Warning:** If you are working on a budget for musicals, you may need to include the expense of renting body mikes.

Costumes and Accessories

If you rent costumes, don't forget to include handling and shipping expenses. If you borrow, don't forget to include washing and dry-cleaning expenses. **Warning:** Don't forget accessories; you need to include all undergarments, hats, gloves, shoes, stockings, canes, umbrellas, purses, handkerchiefs, scarves, rings, pins, and any other personal props that might be required in the script.

Makeup, Wigs, and Hairpieces

Along with makeup include the cost of cleansing tissues, brushes, liners, sponges, and so on. **Warning:** Wigs and hairpieces can be expensive and need to be styled and set.

Programs

Don't forget to include the cost of layout as well as the cost of printing. This can be an income item if you sell advertising. Programs are discussed in detail in Chapter 26. **Suggestion:** Find someone who knows computers and try desktop publishing.

Tickets

You need to be accountable! Have your tickets numbered and printed professionally. Tickets are one of the first impressions a patron has of your organization; let it be impressive. (See Chapter 23.)

Posters, Handbills, Flyers

Quantity is as important as quality with these items. Since they are "throw-away" items, our advice is to not spend too much money on them. If they are going to be truly effective pieces, however, you will need to saturate your community with them. (See Chapter 24.)

Services

Under this heading include the cost for janitorial services and security guards.

Rent

Some schools, churches, and recreational centers will impose a rental charge on any facilities used after hours. **Warning:** You may have to pay rent for a space to build and store sets and for a truck to transport the scenery to your auditorium.

Salaries

If your budget is large enough, you may want to hire some professional help: set, lighting, or costumer designers, or a movement or vocal coach.

Contingencies

It is prudent to budget in a reserve for emergencies.

At the end of this chapter we include a worksheet that you can use as a checklist when you draw up your first budget.

ASSESSING YOUR SITUATION

Now that you have considered all your limitations, it is time to make a list of your strengths and to recognize your weaknesses. Answer the following questions as a first step in deciding what kind of play will be most appropriate for your situation:

Assessment Checklist

1. How many people can I expect to audition for the play?

2. What might be the ratio of men to women?

3. Do I have competent help in the following areas?
   a. Set Design
   b. Set Construction
   c. Lighting
   d. Costumes
   e. Makeup
   f. Sound

4. How do I assess the space where I will present the play?
   a. How large is the stage?
   b. How large is the backstage area?
   c. How well-equipped is the theater?
      —Lighting equipment?
      —Sound equipment?
   d. How large is the auditorium?
   e. How are the acoustics?
   f. How often can I use the stage for rehearsal?

5. How long do I have to rehearse the play?

6. What kind of conflicts can I anticipate?

7. How much money do I have to work with?

8. Do I have TEDs for the following three key positions?
   a. Stage Manager
   b. Production Coordinator
   c. Director of Audience Development and Services

9. Do I have enough volunteers to work backstage?
   a. Stage crew
   b. Property crew
   c. Light board operator
   d. Sound board operator
   e. Wardrobe crew
   f. Makeup crew

10. Do I have enough volunteers to handle publicity and front-of-house operations?
    a. Publicity crew
    b. Box Office
    c. House Manager
    d. Ticket Takers and Ushers
    e. Volunteers to work concessions and cloak room

TO WHOM AM I PRESENTING THIS PLAY?

Another great way of narrowing your options is to analyze your audience. Who will be coming to this play? What are their expectations? How sophisticated are their tastes? What kind of play do you need to produce to draw a large crowd? The more you know about your audience, the more intelligent the choice you will make when selecting a play.

All audiences want to be entertained. It doesn't naturally follow, however, that you have to limit your options to a comedy. In fact, sometimes it is difficult for inexperienced actors to master the technical skills necessary to play comedy well. Mysteries and some serious plays can entertain as well. Agatha Christie's "potboiler," *The Mousetrap,* and Thornton Wilder's drama, *Our Town,* have been long-time favorites with high school and community theater audiences. Both of these plays have some humor, but both have an overall serious tone. Nevertheless, they tell compelling stories and are very popular with audiences. If you want to stretch your actors and challenge your audience, you might consider a classic, like Shakespeare's *A Midsummer Night's Dream,* or a contemporary play with many challenging roles like *The Diary of Anne Frank* by Frances Goodrich and Albert Hackett.

We have devoted an entire chapter to directing period plays, Chapter 20, and have included a list of suggested titles that we recommend for school and community directors working with inexperienced actors. Two other chapters might also prove helpful while you are deliberating on an appropriate play: Chapter 31 offers a detailed description of theater forms (Tragedy, Heroic Drama, Domestic Drama, Melodrama, Thesis Play, Farce, Domestic Comedy, and Satire), and Chapter 33 offers a list of contemporary plays that are especially appropriate for the beginning director. You have many options to consider; the choice is yours. Step out in faith but know your limitations.

PROPOSED ORGANIZATIONAL STRUCTURE FOR THEATER DIRECTORS

DIRECTOR

Stage Manager

Production Coordinator

Director of Audience Development and Services

Performers:

actors
singers
dancers

Designers:

set
lighting
special effects
properties
sound
costumes
makeup
hair
wigs

Front-of-House Personnel:

house manager
box office manager
box office staff
ticket takers
ushers
concessions
publicity
promotion
layout and design
advertisement/
   sponsorships

crew heads
board operators
working crews
running crews

A DIRECTOR'S CHECKLIST
OF RESPONSIBILITIES

Six months to one year	Schedule dates for performances.
	Reserve auditorium.
	Clear dates for production week.
	Try to clear dates for all rehearsals.
	Hold workshop.
	Clear availability of script with publisher.
Three months	Order scripts.
	Recruit Stage Manager.
	Recruit Production Coordinator.
	Recruit Director of Audience Development.
	Line up Production Staff: Designers (Set, Lights, Props, Sound, Special Effects, Costumes, Makeup).
	Announce auditions.
	Analyze the play.
	Lay out the rehearsal schedule.
	Hold production meetings with designers.

MUSICALS

Eight weeks

Hold auditions.
Cast the musical.
Start rehearsal process.
Hold weekly production meetings.
Organize promotional campaign.

STRAIGHT PLAYS

Five to Six weeks

Hold auditions.
Cast the play.
Start rehearsal process.
Hold weekly production meetings.
Organize promotional campaign.

Four weeks	Write releases.
	Start publicity designs for posters.
	Start advertising solicitations.
	Order tickets.
	Establish front-of-house policies.
Three weeks	Talk to media; set up stories and interviews.
	Put up posters.
	Start promotion campaign.
Two weeks	Solicit ushers, ticket takers, etc.
	Open box office.
One week	Tech week.
	Performances.

OPERATORS, CREWS, AND VOLUNTEERS

YOU ARE NEEDED!

The following is a list of positions that need to be filled by resourceful and responsible people for our upcoming production of _____.

Please indicate your support and interest by signing up below.

PROPERTY CREW (Number of people needed: _____)

_____   _____

_____   _____

_____   _____

STAGE CREW (Number of people needed: _____)

_____   _____

_____   _____

_____   _____

_____   _____

RUNNING CREW (Number of people needed: _____)

_____   _____

_____   _____

_____   _____

_____   _____

WARDROBE CREW (Number of people needed: _____)

_____   _____

_____   _____

_____   _____

_____   _____

2.3 continued

MAKEUP CREW (Number of people needed: _____)

_____   _____

_____   _____

_____   _____

_____   _____

LIGHTING CREW (Number of people needed: _____)

_____   _____

_____   _____

_____   _____

_____   _____

ASSISTANTS TO THE DIRECTOR OF AUDIENCE DEVELOPMENT AND SERVICES
Need to assist in selling advertising, distributing posters, etc. (Number of people needed: _____)

_____   _____

_____   _____

_____   _____

_____   _____

HOUSE MANAGER (One person needed)

_____   _____

USHERS (Number of people needed: _____)

_____   _____

_____   _____

_____   _____

_____   _____

TICKET SELLERS (Number of people needed: _____)

_____   _____

_____   _____

CONCESSION SELLERS (Number of people needed: _____)

_____   _____

_____   _____

OTHER NOTES

_____

_____

_____

_____

_____

_____

_____

_____

_____

_____

_____

_____

_____

_____

_____

_____

_____

_____

_____

_____

_____

CHECKLIST TO HELP YOU DETERMINE WHERE BEST TO PRESENT YOUR PLAY

1. **How large is the stage?**

   Width of playing area: _____

   Depth of playing area

       from curtain line to back of stage: _____

       depth of apron (forestage) _____

2. **How large is the backstage area?**

   Stage left:_____   Stage right: _____

   Upstage behind the acting area: _____

3. **How large is the auditorium?**

   Number of feet from the stage to back of auditorium: _____

   Number of seats in the auditorium

       Main floor: _____

       Balcony: _____

4. **How sophisticated is the lighting and sound equipment?**

   Condition of the lighting board: _____

   Number of dimmers: _____

   Number of lighting instruments: _____

   Condition of the sound equipment: _____

5. **How often can I use the auditorium?**

   During the week: afternoons: _____

                       evenings: _____

   Saturdays—Times: _____

   Sundays—Times: _____

2.5

BUDGET CHECKLIST

Projected Income:

Ticket Sales $_____

Programs $_____

Concessions $_____

Sponsorships $_____

Patrons $_____

Total Projected Income: $_____

Projected Outlay:

Royalties $_____

Play scripts

     handling and shipping $_____

Setting: $_____

     designer (salary) $_____

     materials $_____

     building space (rental) $_____

     equipment (rental) $_____

     Transportation (rental) $_____

     storage $_____

Total Projected Outlay: $_____

Lighting: $_____

     designer (salary) $_____

     equipment (rental) $_____

       lighting board $_____

       instruments $_____

     purchases $_____

       replacement bulbs $_____

       colored gelatin $_____

       gobos $_____

Total Lighting: $_____

Properties:

     purchases $_____

     rentals $_____

     transportation (rental) $_____

     insurance $_____

Total Properties: $_____

Sound: $_____

     equipment (rental) $_____

       sound board $_____

       speakers $_____

2.5 continued

microphones	$_____	
purchases	$_____	
records	$_____	
tapes	$_____	
recording expenses	$_____	
Total Sound:		$_____

Costumes and Accessories:
purchases	$_____	
rentals		
handling and shipping	$_____	
cleaning		
dry-cleaning	$_____	
washing	$_____	
Total Costumes and Accessories:		$_____

Makeup, Wigs, and Hairpieces:
purchases	$_____	
services	$_____	
Total Makeup, Wigs, and Hairpieces:		$_____

Programs:
layout	$_____	
printing	$_____	
Total Programs:		$_____

Tickets		$_____

Promotional Materials (posters, flyers):
layout	$_____	
printing	$_____	
Total Promotional Materials:		$_____

Space:
rental	$_____	
maintenance		
(janitorial services)	$_____	
security		
(security guards)	$_____	
Total Space:		$_____

Contingency:		$_____

TOTAL:		$_____

© 1995 by John Wiley & Sons, Inc.

CHECKLIST FOR ASSESSING YOUR SITUATION

Answer the following questions as a first step in deciding what kind of play will be most appropriate for your situation.

1. How many people can I expect to audition for the play?
2. What might be the ratio of men to women?
3. Do I have competent help in the following areas?
   a. Set design
   b. Set construction
   c. Lighting
   d. Costumes
   e. Makeup
   f. Sound
4. How do I assess the space where I will present the play?
   a. How large is the stage?
   b. How large is the backstage area?
   c. How well equipped is the theater?
      —Lighting equipment
      —Sound equipment
   d. How large is the audience?
   e. How good are the acoustics?
   f. How often can I use the stage for rehearsals?
5. How long do I have to rehearse the play?
6. What kind of conflicts can I anticipate?
7. How much money do I have to work with?
8. Do I have TEDs for the following three key positions?
   a. Stage Manager
   b. Production Coordinator
   c. Director of Audience Development and Services
9. Do I have enough volunteers to work backstage?
   a. Stage crew
   b. Property crew
   c. Light board operator
   d. Sound board operator
   e. Wardrobe crew
   f. Makeup crew

2.6 continued

10. Do I have enough volunteers to handle publicity and front-of-house operations?
    a. Publicity crew
    b. Box Office
    c. House Manager
    d. Ticket Takers and Ushers
    e. Volunteers to work concessions and cloak room

NOTES:

_____

_____

_____

_____

_____

_____

_____

_____

_____

_____

_____

_____

_____

_____

_____

_____

_____

3 Other Options

"Open a New Window"

from Mame.
Music and lyrics by Jerry Herman;
book by Robert E. Lee and Jerome Lawrence.

Opened in New York, May 24,1966; ran 1,508 performances. Angela Lansbury and Beatrice Arthur starred in the first production. Ginger Rogers starred in London, and Lucille Ball made the film version.

Now you hold a clearer picture of your particular situation, and you have a more definite understanding of your limitations. If, at this point, you feel that you don't have the financial support, the technical expertise, or quite the number of people you need to tackle a full stage production, you might consider another option.

CHILDREN'S PLAY

One of the best ways to build a reputation, establish good will, and have fun—all at the same time—is to produce a small, imaginative play for children and then tour it to local grade schools. Even though your play or musical will run under an hour in length, you will still have to solve all the problems you will eventually encounter when you tackle your first full-length play, but on a smaller, less intimidating scale. You still need to select the right play, unravel its meaning, lay out a rehearsal schedule, work through all the design problems—set, lighting, sound, special effects, costumes, and makeup— train a stage manager, conduct auditions, decide on a cast, rehearse, help actors develop characterizations, and run a smooth performance. In addition, you will learn how to tour a small production.

Play Selection

Since we are suggesting that you tour your production, you might want to look for a play or musical with no more than eight to ten players and with limited technical requirements. In our opinion, the best listing of children's plays can be found in catalogues from the following three sources:

Anchorage Press
Box 8067
New Orleans, Louisiana 70182

Dramatic Publishing Company
311 Washington Street
P.O. Box 129
Woodstock, Illinois 60098

Pioneer Drama Service
2172 South Colorado Blvd.
P.O. Box 22555
Denver, Colorado 80222

Rehearsal Schedule

You will want to allow at least four weeks to rehearse. You don't want to over-rehearse, but if all of you have had relatively little experience, you might want to allow a week or two more. Chapter 6 goes into all the details you need to set up a rehearsal schedule.

Design Considerations

You will have to decide if you want to present your play in the school's auditorium (if they have one), in the gym (if they don't), or in a classroom. We encourage you to opt for the classroom. You don't have as many technical demands if you design your production to be presented in a limited, intimate space. You can create magic with a few blocks that can be moved around or stacked, a simple backdrop, and a prop or two. Remember, in theater, less often says more.

As far as costumes are concerned, you can adapt some discarded clothing, add suggestive pieces to a basic leotard or sweat suit, rent the entire show, paint details on a simple muslin pattern, or follow the example of the professional children's theater group known as The Paper Bag Players and build all your wardrobe out of large sheets of heavy butcher paper. Children love to use their imagination; don't forget to use yours.

Directing the Play

Chapters 13 through 19 of this guide give you suggestions and guidelines on how to handle various aspects of auditioning, casting, and directing your play. Also covered is what your stage manager needs to know to help you run a smooth production.

The main thing you and your actors must remember when you work on a children's play is "to believe." You can't play "at" the characters; you've got to "become" the characters and totally commit to their action. Tell your actors that they need to find the child within themselves and allow that person to perform rather than the sophisticated, reserved, and conservative individuals most of them have become. Incorporate a lot of improvisations during rehearsals. (See Viola Spolin's books listed in Chapter 36.) The important thing is to constantly use your imagination and have fun.

Touring Your Production

You will want to pay attention to the special needs of touring. Make a contact and firm up performance dates before you announce your auditions. That way you can be very specific with your cast about dates and times they need to be excused from classes or work. Finalize all arrangements for transportation early. Let the size of your performing space and the size of the van determine how much scenery and how many props you can work into the design of your production. Have your stage manager work out all the logistics about travel, parking, dressing rooms, setup time, equipment, food, and the like. Plan ahead and ask plenty of questions.

Study Guide

Instead of a program, you may want to prepare a study guide that discusses the themes of the play and offers games and activities that can be used both to prepare the children for the performance and to follow through on the experience after the play has been presented. Study guides are an excellent way of involving more people. The following is a list of contents most commonly found in study guides:

1. Plot summary
2. Background material on the play/story
3. Background material on the playwright/author
4. Background material on the time and place settings
5. Vocabulary used in the play
6. Suggested activities before and after the play such as discussion questions, creative writing exercises, performing activities, creative problem-solving activities
7. Study aids such as crossword puzzles, cutouts, pages to color, follow the dots, treasure maps, riddles, matching games, hidden pictures, word searches, and recipes
8. Bibliography of related books and audio and visual materials
9. General theater etiquette procedures
10. Evaluation form
11. Information on performing organization (philosophy, objectives, policies)

If you do create a study guide, make sure that it is written in clear, concise language and that the overall look of the guide is aesthetically pleasing. Direct the study guide to the teacher, not to the students. Don't let the content overwhelm or be too sophisticated; write to the level of the children who will see your performance. Again, your imagination is your best guide.

For more information on children's theater, we recommend *Theatre for Young People: A Sense of Occasion* by Helane S. Rosenberg and Christine Prendergast (Holt, Rinehart and Winston, 1983).

CONTEST PLAY

Many states offer one-act play competitions for schools and community theaters. Although we don't feel theater should be competitive, district, state, and regional gatherings offer an excellent opportunity for teachers, students, and community players to exchange ideas and learn from each other.

Like touring children plays, you must consider length, technical requirements, and size of cast when you select plays for contests. Performances are timed, usually between thirty to forty-five minutes, and you are often given only ten to twenty minutes to set up before the performance and break down after the performance.

Our suggestion is to choose a play that has equal opportunities for from five to twelve actors. Be sure you write and receive permission and pay appropriate royalties to the publishing company before you officially enter the competition. Be especially cautious about doing a cutting from a full-length play; permission is usually restricted, or a full royalty payment is required.

COFFEE HOUSE THEATER

One of the best ways to build audiences and generate future support from your administration or community is to sponsor an evening of selected scenes or one-acts, a reader's theater piece, a "staged reading" of an original play, or revue material in a coffee house setting. You can create a coffee house theater setting in a school gym, cafeteria, library, or even a large classroom. In the community, you can use the fellowship hall of a church or a meeting room in a community center.

If you want to accommodate between fifty to one hundred people, we suggest that you place a raised 16-by-12-foot or 24-by-16-foot platform at one end of a room and stagger the placement of tables and chairs on three sides of the platform. If a more intimate environment is desired, you can mark off a space for a playing area in the center of a room, and place tables and chairs around all sides of the playing area, leaving ample space for entrances at all corners. This layout of space is called arena staging or theater-in-the-round, and can be especially appropriate when you have a small budget and very little technical support. (For a diagram and description of alternative theater arrangements, see Chapter 30.)

Directing in the round is not as difficult as it might seem at first. You just have to make sure actors don't play too long to one side of the house and that they realize the greatest number of people can see their faces when they are playing away from center and with their backs to one of the entrances. Beginning actors will find it disconcerting to have the audience so close to them, but if they concentrate, stay in the moment, and relate directly to their partners, they will not be distracted.

Lighting is the most critical design element in arena staging. You don't have to create many effects, but it is best when you can raise and lower the lights on the stage area and keep the audience in relative darkness during the performance. You need to consult with a theater lighting expert for ideas on how to rig special equipment. Also make sure that the space has been wired to support it.

If you offer coffee house theater, keep the menu simple. A variety of coffees, soft drinks, lemonade, popcorn, pretzels, and sweets (brownies, cookies, slices of cake) are all you need to serve. The emphasis should be on the entertainment, not on the menu.

CHECKLIST FOR SELECTING A CHILDREN'S PLAY

Play Title: _____

Author: _____

Publishing company: _____

Royalties: _____

Number of characters:

   Men: _____   Women: _____

   Comment on how many roles could be played by either sex:

_____

_____

Design Considerations:

   Number of sets: _____

   Number of costumes: _____

   List of props needed:

_____ _____ _____

_____ _____ _____

_____ _____ _____

_____ _____ _____

   List of special effects:

_____

_____

_____

Appropriateness and other comments:

_____

_____

_____

_____

STAGE MANAGER'S CHECKLIST FOR TOURING PRODUCTIONS

Date of Tour: _____

Time of Performance: _____

Distance to Travel: _____

Departure Time: _____

Destination: _____

Contact Person: _____

Travel Directions:

_____

_____

_____

_____

Parking Location:

_____

Location of Costume and Makeup Room(s):

_____

Performing Area:

_____Auditorium _____Gymnasium _____Classroom

Location:

_____

_____

Special Instructions:

_____

_____

_____

Setup Time: _____

STAGE MANAGER'S CHECKLIST FOR LOADING A TOURING PRODUCTION

Play Title: _____

Date of Performance: _____

Time of Departure: _____

Location: _____

Names of People Going on Tour:

_____   _____

_____   _____

_____   _____

_____   _____

_____   _____

_____   _____

_____   _____

Equipment:

Sets—Number of pieces: _____

Lighting Equipment—Number of pieces: _____

Costumes—Number of pieces: _____

Makeup—Number of pieces: _____

Properties—Number of pieces: _____

Sound Equipment—Number of pieces: _____

Other—List separately:

_____

_____

_____

_____

CHECKLIST FOR STUDY GUIDES

The following is a list of items that could be included in a study guide:

1. Plot summary
2. Background material on the play/story
3. Background material on the playwright/author(s)
4. Background material on the time and place settings
5. Special vocabulary used in the play
6. Suggested activities before and after the play such as discussion questions, creative writing exercises, performing activities, and creative problem-solving activities
7. Study aids such as crossword puzzles, cutouts, pages to color, follow the dots, treasure maps, riddles, matching games, hidden pictures, word searches, and recipes
8. Bibliography of related books and audio and visual materials
9. General theater etiquette procedures
10. Evaluation form
11. Information on performing organization (philosophy, objectives, policies)

NOTES

_____

_____

_____

_____

_____

_____

_____

_____

4 How to Select the Right Play

"*Something Sort of Grandish*"

from Finian's Rainbow. *Music by Burton Lane; lyrics by E. Y. Harburg; book by E. Y. Harburg and Fred Saidy.*

Opened in New York, January 10, 1947; ran 725 performances. The original cast included David Wayne, and the 1968 film version starred Fred Astaire, Petula Clark, and Tommy Steele.

If you have assessed your situation and all signals are go for presenting a full-length production, then your next step is to select the "right" play for your particular situation. At first, you might think that selecting a script is like going on a shopping spree—so many wonderful plays to choose from. True, there are literally thousands of scripts on the market, but you need to select one that best fits the profile of your organization as you determined in the ten-point assessment checklist near the end of Chapter 2. Even after you have narrowed your options—what type of play you want to direct (domestic comedy, farce, melodrama); the number of sets, costumes, and other design factors you can handle; the approximate cast size, and the breakdown of men's and women's roles you want to look for—the actual selection of a specific play can still be an awesome task.

We encourage you not to rush the process. Selecting a play should be like choosing a mate: you need to carefully assess all strengths and weaknesses before making a commitment. If you don't, you'll spend your entire rehearsal period in conflict with your script, making compromises you never intended to make. You will need to deal with enough unexpected obstacles during the rehearsal process; contending with a poorly chosen play should not be one of them. To protect against this possibility, we are going to show you how to analyze plays so you can ultimately pick the one that is, indeed, "Something Sort of Grandish" for your situation.

WHERE TO FIND SCRIPTS

First, you have to know where to look for scripts. A score of publishing houses specialize in plays. In our opinion, however, three offer the most worthwhile selections. Each company holds the rights to an impressive number of Broadway hits plus a number of other plays that are especially appropriate for school and community theater organizations.

Samuel French, Inc. has been serving both professional and nonprofessional theater for over one hundred sixty years. It has seven central offices located throughout the English-speaking world, including the U.S.A., England, Canada, and Australia. Since its home office is in London, it holds the rights to most British plays. It has recently added a growing list of musicals to its acquisitions and offers a limited number of budget plays. Their catalog has a number of special sections, including listings of children's plays, holiday plays, and contest plays.

Dramatist Play Service, Inc. is strictly an American house. It was founded in 1936 "by playwrights for the benefit of playwrights." It holds the rights to an impressive list of prize-winning Broadway plays. Their catalog also includes an index of suggested plays for high schools and similar groups.

Dramatic Publishing Company is another American publishing house. Their catalog carries a large selection of plays and musicals especially appropriate for high schools and community theaters.

Each of the companies will send you a catalog upon request. Do it now! They will become your bible for a couple of weeks. Actually, the catalogs are fairly interesting reading. They give you a great deal of information. The following is a typical entry taken from the Samuel French catalog:

> CHARLEY'S AUNT, (All Groups.) Farce. Brandon Thomas. 6m., 4f. Ext., 2 int. World-famous farce which has moved millions to tears of laughter. Jack Chesney loves Kitty Verdun, and Charles loves Miss Spettigue. They invite the ladies to meet Charley's wealthy aunt from Brazil. But alas, the millionaire aunt sends word that she will have to defer her visit for a few days. What is to be done? The dear young things must not be compromised—no, never!—but neither will the youths give up the opportunity of declaring their love. The problem is solved by forcing another Oxford undergraduate into a black satin skirt, a lace fichu, a pair of mitts, and old-fashioned cap and wig. As Charley's Aunt then, this old frump is introduced to the sweethearts, to Jack's father and Stephen Spettigue, Miss Spettigue's guardian. The sweethearts hug and kiss Charley's dear old aunt; the two men make love to her. The real aunt turns up, assumes another name. In the comic confusion which results, young Lord Babberley, posing as the aunt, tricks Stephen Spettigue into agreeing to the marriage of his ward to Charley, the real aunt marries Jack's father, Jack gets Miss Verdun and "Charley's Aunt" regains the fortune he lost at gambling and the girl he loves. In its many stage and motion picture revivals, this play has reached a wide and eager audience. $4.75. (Royalty, $50-$25.) (No Royalty in Canada.) Publicity Kit and Posters.

> (from Samuel French , Inc. Basic Catalog)

From this brief entry you learn the title of the play (*Charley's Aunt*), the group it is best suited to (all groups), the kind of play it is (farce), the author's name (Brandon Thomas), the cast breakdown (six males and four females), the number of settings and their locations (1 exterior, 2 interiors), a brief summary of the play, the cost of an acting script ($4.75), the royalty costs ($50 for the first performance; $25 for each subsequent performance; no royalty in Canada), plus additional information (publicity kit and posters available at an additional charge). The description of the story line even gives you a flavor of the play. Some more recent entries include critics' comments. (Don't be too influenced by the quotes. They are taken out of context and do not always reflect the critics' true reaction.)

The range for royalties varies. Plays in public domain, like *The Importance of Being Earnest,* require no royalty, while more recent releases can cost as high as $60 for the first public performance. Royalties for musicals can be five to ten times this amount (see Chapter 21). Subsequent performances for straight plays can be less. They range from between $25 to $50 a performance.

GUIDELINES FOR SELECTING A PLAY

Never select a play based on the catalog entry alone. Instead, send for a copy and read it through carefully. As you are reading, ask yourself the following questions:

- Is this play within our budget? Consider royalties, sets, costumes, and special effects.

- Are the roles within the range of our actors? Consider distribution of lines, and range of emotions.

- Is the language in the play appropriate for our audience? Consider ethnic slurs as well as vulgarity.

- Is the message of the play too controversial for our audience? Consider social and political issues.

- Can we handle the vocal requirements of the play? Consider dialects and accents and singing requirements.

- Can we handle the special movement requirements in this play? Consider period movement, fight scenes, dances, and so on.

- Can we handle the technical requirements of the play? Consider number of sets, the lighting, and sound and special effects.

- Is the play worth doing? Consider subject matter, theme, timeliness, and universality of the play.

- Does this play excite me?

This last item is the key. Even if a play seems worth doing and meets all the limitations, never choose to direct it unless you can get excited about it. Let someone else direct the "worthy play" on another occasion. You hold out for a play that speaks to you, a play you know you would enjoy working on. After all, you are going to have to live with the script you choose for two months or more. You can't expect to get others interested in the project unless you are genuinely excited yourself.

Another warning: You have an ethical responsibility to the playwright. Don't select a play that requires major editing or rewriting. Legally you are at risk. In some more recent plays, copyright requirements clearly state that no alterations of any kind may be made without written consent. This restriction is implied even when it does not appear in print. It is true that some older plays are dated and judicious cuts and word changes might be needed to make the play work. If you feel this is your situation, read the copyright restrictions carefully. The important guideline is to make sure that you do not alter the playwright's intent. If you feel a great deal of cutting or rewriting is necessary, find another script or, in the case of adapted material, seek permission to do your own. In our opinion one of your major obligations is to the playwright. As director, you are an interpreter, not a creator; be careful that you do not abuse your privilege.

CHECKLIST FOR SELECTING A PLAY

1. *Does the play meet the basic goals I have set for this production?* Consider type of play (comedy, drama, melodrama, farce, etc.), size of cast (including break down of men and women roles), number of sets, costumes, and other design factors.

2. *Is this play within our budget?* Consider royalties, sets, costumes, and special effects.

3. *Are the roles within the range of our actors?* Consider distribution of lines, and range of emotion.

4. *Is the language in the play appropriate for our audience?* Consider ethnic slurs as well as vulgarity.

5. *Is the message of the play too controversial for our audience?* Consider social and political issues.

6. *Can we handle the vocal requirements of the play?* Consider dialects and accents and singing requirements.

7. *Can we handle the special movement requirements in this play?* Consider period movement, fight scenes, dances, and so on.

8. *Can we handle the technical requirements of the play?* Consider number of sets, the lighting, and sound and special effects.

9. *Is the play worth doing?* Consider subject matter, theme, timeliness, and universality of the play.

10. *Does this play excite me?*

Act Two

PRE-PRODUCTION
CONSIDERATIONS

5

How to Unravel a Play's Meaning

"A Puzzlement"

from The King and I. *Music by Richard Rodgers, lyrics & book by Oscar Hammerstein II.*

Opened in New York, March 29, 1951; ran 1,246 performances. Gertrude Lawrence and Yul Brynner starred in the original production. Before he died, Brynner had played the role 4,625 times.

When you were a child, did you enjoy taking things apart to see how they worked? Perhaps you still enjoy tinkering with cars or appliances. That is what we are inviting you to do in this chapter—get under the hood of your play, so to speak, and see how it has been put together and what makes it tick. It's a fascinating exercise, and you will find that the exploration is quite revealing. By getting beyond the printed words you'll begin to have a clearer understanding of the play and its parts: plot, character, thought, language, music, and spectacle. You'll be able to figure out why characters have been included in the cast, and even why your playwright was compelled to write the play. All this information for taking a little time to snoop around—what more can you ask?

What practical benefits will you reap from this exercise? You will be able to make more intelligent choices when you cast your play, and you will be more perceptive when you need to help actors interpret the meaning of a line or find the motivation behind an action. You'll have a clearer vision about how the play should look—what the setting, the lighting, and the costumes should say to an audience. You will know how a play should sound, and how fast or how slow scenes should be paced. All this essential information can be found in the play itself. The object of this chapter is to clear up the "puzzlement" and put the right information into place.

TITLES OF PLAYS

When we start analyzing plays, we like to start by examining the title. Quite often titles can reveal the playwright's dominant theme. Take Lorraine Hansberry's *A Raisin in the Sun* as an example. The central character, Mama Younger, dreams of moving her family into a decent home. She is afraid that if she doesn't get them away from the negative influences of tenement life, like grapes, they will wither to raisins in the sun.

Likewise, Tennessee Williams was quite insightful with his title, *A Streetcar Named Desire*. *Desire* is the malady as well as the motivation behind every action of his central character, Blanche DuBois. Like a streetcar, she is on a track headed for self-destruction. In the first scene of the play she subtly reveals this fact when she states, "They told me to take a streetcar named Desire, and then transfer to one called Cemeteries and ride six blocks and get off at—Elysian Fields!"

Oscar Wilde's *The Importance of Being Earnest* is another clever title that works on several levels. Early on in the story we learn that John (Jack) Worthing passes himself off as Ernest in the city. He is in love with Gwendolen, and Gwendolen is in love with the name of Ernest. She would never consider marrying a man named Jack. Wilde also uses the word *Earnest* on another level. Jack states at the end of the play, "I've now realized for the first time in my life the vital Importance of Being Earnest." The play on words in the title suggests the script's overall use of wit and intellectual fun.

Even relatively simple titles can be revealing. For example, titles can tell us the names of central characters: *Macbeth, The Country Wife, The Foreigner,* and, when there are two central characters, titles can signal which character the playwright focused on: *The Miracle Worker* (Anne Sullivan, not Helen Keller), *'Night, Mother* (the daughter, not the mother), *The Lion in Winter* (King Henry II, not Eleanor of Aquitaine).

COPYRIGHT DATE

Another way of uncovering meaning is to get a better understanding of what motivated the playwright. Plays are usually a reflection of their times, so you might get a clue if you look at the date the play was first presented. You'll usually find it listed on an inside page near the beginning of the script. Ask yourself what was happening in the playwright's world during the time the play was written. The information can be revealing. For example, our country was still reeling from the McCarthy investigation of "un-American activities" when Arthur Miller wrote his impressive dramatization of the Salem witch-hunt, *The Crucible*. The parallels are obvious.

Another example is *Of Mice and Men*. Our country was still in the throes of the depression when John Steinbeck wrote his powerful drama about the invisible minority, the migrant workers, who were displaced and lived on dreams.

Oscar Wilde wrote *Earnest* in 1895, at the height of the Victorian age. His play can be read as a mocking comment on this society that, in his opinion, was elitist, artificial and took itself much too earnestly.

THE NAMES OF CHARACTERS

We always have a great deal of fun looking at the names in the cast of characters lists. Quite often they reveal character traits or personalities. This was the rule rather than the exception until the twentieth century, especially with English writers. In Richard Sheridan's *The Rivals,* for instance, major roles are characterized by their names: Sir Anthony Absolute, Sir Lucius O'Trigger, Mrs. Malaprop, and Lydia Languish. In *Earnest,* Wilde named many of his characters quite fittingly: Jack Worthing, Gwendolen Fairfax, Lady Bracknell, Miss Prism, and The Reverend Canon Chasuble.

Twentieth-century playwrights have not always followed the practice, but when they do they are a lot more subtle. For example, you have to be alert to catch the cleverness of Arthur Miller when he named his central character Willy Loman (low man). Only astute critics realized Edward Albee's highly symbolic use of names in his prize-winning drama, *Who's Afraid of Virginia Woolf.* To show the disintegration of the "American family tradition" Albee referred to the two central characters as George and Martha.

THE FUNCTIONS OF CHARACTERS

It helps in casting the play to understand why characters have been included. It gives you a clearer understanding of the qualities an actor must have to interpret the role effectively.

One and sometimes two characters are the central catalyst for the action. They are called *protagonists*. In these roles you need to find actors that can sustain our interest and win our sympathy.

The character who opposes the protagonist is called the *antagonist*. In mysteries and melodramas this character is always the villain; in more sophisticated dramas, the antagonist may be more sympathetic. In either case, the antagonist is quite often the best written role and needs to be played by a strong actor.

The *confidant* is created so that the protagonist will have someone to confide in. Whomever you cast in this role needs to be a good listener.

The *foil* is a character who stands in contrast to the protagonist. One of the two may be comic if the other is overly serious; one may be stupid, to set off the other's intelligence; or one may be shrewd in contrast to the other's naïveté. Make sure to play up the contrast when you cast these roles.

The *raisonneur* is a character who speaks for the dramatist and is the voice of reason. He or she is always alert, composed, and intelligent. The actor who is cast in this role must be able to convey this as a first impression.

Stock characters are clearly defined characters that function as types (stereotypes) rather than uniquely defined individuals. Again, it is best if the persons you cast look their roles.

Utility characters are functionaries whose only purposes are to set the tone, establish atmosphere, and deliver messages. Maids, butlers, and party guests are examples of this type. Make sure you cast actors who blend into an ensemble.

SPEECHES

Speeches themselves offer important clues to both character and meaning. This is especially true of soliloquies, monologues, and asides. All three reflect inner thoughts not intended to be overheard by any other characters in the play. They have another aspect in common; they are all truthful and, consequently, insightful.

Shakespeare was a master of writing soliloquies: "To be or not to be; that is the question." "Is this a dagger I see before me?" and "O Romeo, Romeo, wherefore art thou Romeo?" are all key moments that offer great insight into both character and meaning.

Most playwrights today write monologues instead of soliloquies. Monologues sometimes take the form of a direct address to the audience. The speech at the end of Tennessee Williams's *A Glass Menagerie,* where Tom tells Laura to blow out her candles, is an excellent example. In other plays people can be present when a character drifts off into a monologue but their presence is not felt or acknowledged. This is the case when Mrs. Tyrone gives her beautiful monologue at the end of the play in Eugene O'Neill's *A Long Day's Journey Into Night.*

Monologues can be comic as well as serious and still convey meaning. Thornton Wilder's *The Matchmaker* includes many good examples. Throughout the play several characters step out of the scene, cross downstage, and directly address the audience. These extended speeches offer some of the best humor in the play.

Asides, like soliloquies and monologues, are inner thoughts not intended for other characters to hear. They are always short and often funny. Oscar Wilde includes a number of witty and insightful asides in *Earnest.* For example, in the second act, Cecily

Cardew muses aloud, "Miss Fairfax! I suppose one of the many good elderly women who are associated with Uncle Jack in some of his philanthropic work in London. I don't quite like women who are interested in philanthropic work. I think it is so forward of them."

PLAYWRIGHT'S INTENT

Another way to find meaning is to consider the playwright's intent. Sometimes the playwright's only objective is to entertain; on other occasions the intent may be to inform, or enlighten, or even urge us on to action.

When dramatists write plot-driven plays like mysteries or farces, the intent is to entertain and little more. The plot is usually farfetched, the characters are stereotypical, and the themes are usually over-worked clichés. But who cares? If the production is well staged, the action energetic, and the actors engaging, the play works and the audience has a grand time. Agatha Christie's classics, *Ten Little Indians* and *The Mousetrap*, London's longest-running play, and Michael Frayn's popular farce, *Noises Off*, are three excellent examples of plot-driven plays.

Character dramas take themselves more seriously. They aim to enlighten us while they entertain. Alfred Uhry's *Driving Miss Daisy* and Jason Miller's *That Championship Season* are two Pulitzer Prize-winning examples of plays that emphasize character rather than plot.

On occasion, the playwright's intent is to move us to action. In these plays the statement is paramount in the playwright's mind. The scripts are called propaganda or thesis plays and the action is always intense. Playwrights using this form see the stage as a soap box and try to raise our social consciousness. In 1844, W. H. Smith was able to do just that with his temperance melodrama, *The Drunkard, or The Fallen Saved*. It had a run of over 7,500 performances and reportedly more than 10,000 people came forward and took the Abstinence Pledge after seeing the play. More recently, Larry Kramer's searing drama, *The Normal Heart*, moved many to become more informed about AIDS and to get involved in the fight against indifference.

STRUCTURAL ANALYSIS

Understanding how a play has been put together can help a director recognize what moments should be stressed in a production and how scenes should build to a climax. Analyzing a play reveals the subtleties and mysteries of the piece and gives insight into the strengths and weaknesses of the play's structure.

The French Scene

One of the best ways to analyze a script is to break it down into motivational units. Classic French playwrights used this approach when they wrote. The entrance or exit of a major character was the signal for a change of motivation and was noted in the script as a change in scene. Some classic French dramas were divided into as many as thirty to forty scenes and yet, in production, they played uninterrupted in two, three, or four acts. Since so many contemporary plays are developed along this motivating principle, dividing plays into French Scenes is one of the best ways of analyzing structure. A detailed breakdown of *The Importance of Being Earnest* into French Scenes can be found at the end of this chapter (See 5.2). In Chapter 6, How to Lay Out a Rehearsal Schedule, you will see how helpful this process can be when you work up a rehearsal schedule.

Unit Objectives

Each French Scene or motivational unit has one or more objectives. Its purpose might be one of the following:

- Establish mood and atmosphere
- Advance the plot
- Reveal character
- Argue a point of view

Some units might emphasize two, three, or even all four objectives equally, but usually, one objective dominates. Before you start rehearsals it is important to note the objectives of each scene in your play. It will help you decide where to place focus in each scene and what moments need to be underscored.

The Shape of the Units

Most plays center around three key moments that need to be clearly identified:

1.   *Disturbance:* An initiating event (first complication) upsets the balance, establishes the conflict, and starts the action (also called *point of attack* or *precipitating incident*).

2.   *Turning point, or crisis:* The protagonist, facing a crisis, makes a decision involving some combination of physical, verbal, emotional, and intellectual action which forces change.

3.   *Climax:* Tension reaches its highest point when the crucial decision is made. The climax is often considered the "beginning of the end."

Identifying these three key moments is a basic procedure for directors. Only when these moments are clear in your mind can you give your production the tension, shape, and focus it deserves.

Exposition and Resolution

Two other writing elements need to be given close and careful attention: the way the playwright integrates exposition into the plot, and the way the playwright resolves the action.

Exposition can be defined as basic information about the characters, the circumstances, and certain prior events. Exposition should be held to a minimum and carefully spread throughout the play; it should not be the center of focus in many units. Be wary of plays that include too much exposition.

The resolution of a play is the last unit of dramatic action. The objective is to restore order to the situation and to relieve the tension. The French called this phase the *dénouement,* which literally means "unraveling." Choose plays that resolve their action quickly.

IN SUMMARY

Meaning is the sum of all the parts of a play. To uncover meaning you need to consider the title, when it was written, the names and functions of the characters, the speeches in the play, the playwright's intent, and the structure of the play itself. We are convinced that all this information will make the play seem less a puzzle and more a vision. It will become more alive and clear in your mind and easier to define or describe as a concept to your designers. The better you understand your script and can clearly communicate your ideas to others, the better chance you have of mounting a play of merit and substance.

SO WHAT IS THIS PLAY ALL ABOUT?

1. What does the title tell me about my play?

2. What does the date of the first performance tell me about my play? Concern yourself with major events in the playwright's world.

3. What can I learn from the *names of the characters*?

4. What is the major character's *function*?

    a. Who is/are the protagonist(s), the central character(s) in my play?

    b. Who is the antagonist? Who is standing in the way of the central character?

    c. Who is a confidant to the central character? (**Note:** Not all plays have one.)

    d. Who is the foil to the central character? (**Note:** Not all plays have one.)

    e. Who is the play's raisonneur, the "voice of reason," the playwright's voice? (**Note:** Not all plays have one.)

    f. Who are the stock characters? (**Note:** Not all plays have them.)

    g. Who are the utility characters in the play? (**Note:** Not all plays have them.)

5. What do the *speeches* in my play tell me about meaning? Look especially at soliloquies, monologues, and asides.

6. What was the *playwright's intent*?

    a. To entertain: Does my play stress plot?

    b. To inform: Does my play stress character as well as plot?

    c. To persuade: Does my play stress the playwright's point of view and try to move me to action?

7. What is the moment of *disturbance* in my play (the initiating event in the play that starts the action)?

8. What is the line or action in my play that can be cited as the *crisis*, or *turning point* (the key moment of decision for the protagonist)?

9. What is the line or action in my play that can be cited as the *climax* (the highest point of tension, the catharsis of the play)?

10. How effectively has the playwright handled *exposition* in the play I am going to direct?

11. How well has the playwright handled the *dénouement* (restoring order to the situation) in the play I am going to direct?

MODIFIED FRENCH SCENES FOR THE PLAY *THE IMPORTANCE OF BEING EARNEST* BY OSCAR WILDE

Act I

1. Algernon, Lane

   From — ALGERNON: Did you hear what I was playing, Lane?

   To — ALGERNON: They seem as a class, to have absolutely no sense of moral responsibility.

2. Algernon, Jack, Lane

   From — LANE: Mr. Ernest Worthing.

   To — ALGERNON: It is so shallow of them.

3. Algernon, Jack, Lady Bracknell, Gwendolen, Lane

   From — LANE: Lady Bracknell and Miss Fairfax.

   To — GWENDOLEN: Certainly, Mamma.

4. Jack, Gwendolen

   From —JACK: Charming day it has been, Miss Fairfax.

   To — GWENDOLEN: I hope you will always look at me just like that, especially when there are other people present.

5. Jack, Gwendolen, Lady Bracknell

   From — LADY B.:   Mr. Worthing!

   To —JACK: How idiotic you are.

6. Jack, Algernon

   From —ALGERNON: Didn't it go off all right, old boy?

   To — ALGERNON: However, I don't mind hard work where there is no definite object of any kind.

7. Jack, Algernon, Gwendolen, Lane

   From — LANE: Miss Fairfax.

   To — ALGERNON: Nobody ever does.

Act II

1. Cecily, Miss Prism

   From — Miss P.:   Cecily, Cecily!

   To — Cecily: But I see dear Dr. Chasuble coming up through the garden.

2. Cecily, Miss Prism, Rev. Chasuble

   From — Miss P.:   Dr. Chasuble! This is indeed a pleasure.

   To — Cecily: Horrid, horrid German.

3. Cecily, Merriman

   From — Merriman: Mr. Ernest Worthing has just driven over from the station.

   To — Cecily: I shouldn't know what to talk to him about.

4. Miss Prism, Rev. Chasuble, Jack

   From — Miss P.:   You are too much alone, dear Dr. Chasuble.

   To — Miss P.:   This seems to me a blessing of an extremely obvious kind.

5. Miss Prism, Rev. Chasuble, Jack, Cecily, Merriman, Algernon

   From — Cecily: Uncle Jack!

   To — Jack: This Bunburying, as you call it, has not been a great success for you.

6. Algernon, Cecily

   From — Algernon: I think it has been a great success.

   To — Cecily: I must enter his proposal in my diary.

7. Cecily, Gwendolen, Merriman

   From — Merriman: A Miss Fairfax just called to see Mr. Worthing.

   To — Cecily: No doubt you have many other calls of a similar character to make in the neighborhood.

8. Cecily, Gwendolen, Jack, Algernon

   From — Gwendolen: Ernest! My own Ernest!

   To — Cecily: No, men are so cowardly, aren't they?

9. Jack, Algernon

   From — Jack: This ghastly state of things is what you call Bunburying, I suppose?

   To — Algernon: I haven't quite finished my tea yet! and there is still one muffin left.

Act III

1. Gwendolen, Cecily, Jack, Algernon

   From — GWENDOLEN: The fact that they did not follow us at once into the house, as any one else would have done, seems to me to show that they have some sense of shame left.

   To — ALGERNON: Darling!

2. Gwendolen, Cecily, Jack, Algernon, Lady Bracknell, Merriman

   From — MERRIMAN: Ahem! Ahem! Lady Bracknell.

   To — LADY B.: To miss any more might expose us to comment on the platform.

3. Gwendolen, Cecily, Jack, Algernon, Lady Bracknell, Rev. Chasuble, Miss Prism

   From — CHASUBLE: Everything is quite ready for the christenings.

   To — JACK: I've now realized for the first time in my life the vital Importance of Being Earnest.

6 How to Lay Out a Rehearsal Schedule

"Putting It Together"

from Sunday in the Park with George.

Music and lyrics by Stephen Sondheim; book by James Lapine.

Opened in New York, May 2, 1984; ran 604 performances. The musical starred Mandy Patinkin and Bernadette Peters and won the 1985 Pulitzer Prize.

Now that you have a clearer understanding of your play, it is time to design a rehearsal schedule. You notice we have used the word *design* to describe the process. That is because we honor the procedure; we don't take it lightly. We realize that the quality of a production depends, in large measure, on our ability to use time effectively. A significant number of people will be making a commitment with the hope that their time and effort will result in an excellent production and a truly positive experience.

Another consideration is the audience. A deadline has been set and a number of paying customers will be looking forward to an evening's worth of entertainment. Their reaction is important. Individually and collectively they will have an impact on the reputation, and consequently the support, your school or community program will have in the future.

For these reasons you want to do everything you can to ensure that your actors are well rehearsed, and that those assigned to designing and mounting the production—set, lighting, sound, costume, makeup, special effects, and properties—have sufficient time to execute their tasks effectively. A well-developed rehearsal schedule, designed with forethought and knowledge, is a strong and practical step you can take to ensure the best possible experience for everyone involved.

GETTING STARTED

Find a quiet place and some quality time to work out the design of your rehearsal schedule. Don't tackle the project until you have read the play several times and have worked through an analysis of its themes and meanings. Make sure you have a calendar, a copy of the script, and several sheets of lined paper at your side.

As you deliberate, you will need to communicate five important pieces of information on your schedule:

- The *date* of each rehearsal;
- The *time* rehearsals will begin;
- The *type* of rehearsal you expect to conduct;
- The *act* or *working units* you plan to be rehearsing; and
- The *call:* which actors need to be present

You also need to indicate the location of each rehearsal if it is going to change during the process.

Write these headings out across the top of a sheet of paper. We have found that a legal pad is best for this exercise. By running the dates down one side of a single sheet, you can get a visual image of the amount of time you actually have between your first rehearsal and opening night.

Length and Number of Rehearsals

A rule-of-thumb is that a full-length production needs approximately thirty rehearsals before opening night. Further, it is good practice to spread rehearsals out over a period of five to six weeks and to schedule each session for two to three hours. Thirty three-hour sessions give you ninety hours of rehearsal. If this time is used efficiently it will be adequate to effectively mount a full-length production.

A one-act play needs approximately twenty sessions and can be rehearsed in three to four weeks. Keep in mind that rehearsals need to be long enough for actors to fully develop their roles, but not so long that they become bored with the play. Timing is everything. You must learn to be both practical and sensitive when making decisions about the length of time you spend in each rehearsal as well as the total block of time you spend rehearsing the play.

PHASES OF THE REHEARSAL PROCESS

You will need to work through nine separate phases of rehearsal before your play is ready for production. Some of these phases overlap; others interlock; some need to be repeated; and some are given more emphasis in one production and considerably less in another. Nevertheless, all the phases are essential and all need to be included in the design of any successful rehearsal schedule.

We have listed the phases below in the order in which they are usually rehearsed. The listings can be altered, but never, we feel, with very satisfying results.

The Nine Phases of the Rehearsal Process

1. Orientation
2. Read-throughs
3. Blocking rehearsals
4. Line rehearsals
5. Working rehearsals
6. Run-throughs
7. Polishing rehearsals
8. Technical rehearsals
9. Dress rehearsals

Orientation

Some directors use the first rehearsal strictly for orientation. They hand out scripts and rehearsal schedules; they introduce the stage manager and assistants; they lay down rehearsal policies; and then they spend considerable time discussing the play. Often they invite the set and costume designers to show plates or renderings of their production concepts. If time allows, some directors end the first session with exercises and games designed to break down inhibitions, build trust, and introduce the period and performance style of the play.

Read-throughs

It is important to have a complete read-through with all members of the cast present before you put the play on its feet. It may be a painful exercise; actors don't always read intelligently, especially early in the process. They can misinterpret meaning, mutilate pronunciation, and stumble over words. It is important, however, to hear the play read aloud. The actors get a clearer sense of the story line, and the director gets a clearer understanding of the problems that need to be worked on.

Directors usually schedule only one read-through. In certain productions, however, much can be gained by spending two or even three rehearsals reading through the play, and discussing the meaning of scenes and the motivation of characters in detail. This is especially true of more complex and sophisticated dramas, such as plays by Shakespeare, Chekhov, and Shaw. Actors respond more intelligently to later phases of the rehearsal process when they have a clear perception of their characters and a deep understanding of the play.

Blocking Rehearsals

How directors prepare and handle where and when actors move on stage has become a controversial subject. Some directors believe that all movement should be worked out before rehearsals begin (preplanned) and others let it evolve during rehearsals (process approach). These two approaches are discussed in detail in Chapter 17.

Working Units

You probably realize that it is impossible to work through the entire play at every rehearsal. It is important, therefore, to break your play down into working units. A working unit is a section of the play that can be realistically dealt with during the length of any one given rehearsal session.

The script itself can be quite helpful in this regard. Most plays are divided into two or more acts, and in many plays, acts are divided into several scenes. Scenes are always quite manageable as "working units"; in fact, you can usually work on several scenes at any given rehearsal.

Acts, too, can be manageable units if your play is divided into three acts of equal length. If not, we strongly recommend that you arbitrarily divide your script into three equal sections. Each section can serve as a working unit.

Calls

Not only is it important that you break a play down into working units, but in some rehearsals you need also to subdivide these units into separate calls. A call is a list of the specific actors who need to be present to rehearse at a given time. Nothing will lower morale faster than to call actors to a rehearsal and then let them sit around and wait, or worse yet, not use them at all. We can't overstress what a chronic problem this is with many directors. You need to be organized and considerate enough that when you announce a rehearsal, the actors called can expect to work. Of course, you can't use everyone on call all the time. Anticipate that fact. Encourage those actors who will have considerable free time to bring homework or a book to read—anything to pass the time. During the early phases of rehearsal, you can encourage them to work on lines or prompt others who need help.

If an act is too long, it is best to break it up into working units. A method we recommend is known as French Scenes. A French Scene can be defined as a working unit of the play bounded by the entrance or exit of a speaking character of some significance. "Walk-ons," such as maids, butlers, and other supernumeraries do not interrupt or change the motivation of a scene. French Scenes were discussed in some detail in Chapter 5.

The first act of *The Importance of Being Earnest* has seven French Scenes. During blocking, line, and working rehearsals these French Scenes could be grouped into two separate calls—scenes 1 and 2 and scenes 3 through 7. If you were planning a three-hour rehearsal, we would suggest that you list your call as follows:

Date	Time	Type	Act/Unit	Call
2/10	7:00–8:00	Line Rehearsal	Act I.	Algernon, Jack & Lane
	8:00–10:00	Line Rehearsal		Add Lady Bracknell & Gwendolen

The advantage of calls in this instance is obvious. The actors playing Lady Bracknell and Gwendolen do not need to arrive at rehearsal until 8:00 P.M. In all fairness we need to note that the actor playing the manservant, Lane, would have considerable offstage time during this rehearsal. In instances like these we encourage you to consider one of two options. Either decide not to call the actor playing Lane until a later rehearsal, or call the actor, explain the reality of the situation, and encourage him to bring something to occupy his free time. Either decision is appropriate as long as you are up front with the actor and advise him of the situation.

Line Rehearsals

Start asking for lines early on in the rehearsal process. Actors are notorious for putting this task off as long as they can. They need to be pushed. They can't really begin working on characterization until they get scripts out of their hands.

It is usually best to call for lines after actors have received some general blocking. Most actors claim that they can memorize lines faster when they can visualize their movement.

When you work with full-length plays that have one, two, four, or five acts, we have found that it is best to divide the play into three equal parts and to call for lines, not by acts but instead, by these three equal sections.

When time permits, we allow up to two full weeks for memorization. Our advice is to push while being realistic and fair. Treat each actor individually. Some actors, you will find, can memorize quickly; others will struggle with the process. As long as you see progress, be sympathetic. On the other hand, when an actor is having major problems with memorization, don't wait too long to offer assistance. Assign your stage manager, your assistant, or even another actor to schedule special sessions outside of rehearsals to work on specific scenes. At the very latest, all actors need to be off book by the beginning of the last full week of rehearsal before you start technical rehearsals (tech week).

Working Rehearsals

All rehearsals are working rehearsals but in this phase of the rehearsal process the director concentrates on meaning, subtext, and relationships—all aspects of character development.

In general, you need to be alert and very sensitive during this phase of the rehearsal process. When you feel actors are making poor choices, you must be very specific in your comments. Avoid using sarcasm. Actors are vulnerable creatures; they need encouragement and positive feedback. Cruel and overly negative comments will stifle actors' creativity, undercut their confidence, and force them to fall back on poor habits. Restrict all comments to the actor's work and be gentle and positive with the actor's ego. It usually needs nurturing.

Run-throughs

This is one phase of the rehearsal process that is best spread out over the entire rehearsal period. For example, we like to end each week of our rehearsal schedule with a run-through. This gives us, and everyone in the company—especially the design staff—an opportunity to assess the progress that has been made and the work that still lies ahead.

When you conduct a run-through rehearsal, it is best not to stop the rehearsal for comments. Take notes and comment at the end of rehearsal. During the note session, it is a good idea to give actors an opportunity to raise questions and offer comments. Their observations can be revealing and often quite useful.

Polishing Rehearsals

Try to schedule at least five days for polishing rehearsals. During these rehearsals concentrate on timing and tempo. Timing is the exact amount of time needed to gain the greatest theatrical effect from a line or piece of business. Tempo is the impression of speed (fast or slow), the rate at which a scene is played. The challenge for directors during this phase of the rehearsal process is to make sure that the tempo of the action is in sync with the rhythm of the language in the play. If you and your actors can find the playwright's rhythm, the pacing of your production should have a great deal of variety and sail with the wind.

We have found that it is best when you polish one act at a time. This gives you the luxury to go back and repeat certain moments at the end of a rehearsal until you get your desired effect.

TECH WEEK

The last full week of rehearsals is often referred to as Tech Week. The week involves the last two phases of the rehearsal process, the technical and dress rehearsals. These two phases take a great deal of time and affect a large number of people. They need to be scheduled in a very specific manner.

If possible, begin production week on the Saturday before opening night. If you plan to open on a Friday, we suggest that you schedule Tech Week in the following manner. Note that we have also listed the amount of time we feel you need to allow for each of these rehearsals.

Day	**Type of Rehearsal**	**Time Allotment**
Saturday	Dry Tech	6 to 8 hours
Monday	Wet Tech	4 to 6 hours
Tuesday	1st Dress	4 to 6 hours
Wednesday	2nd Dress	4 to 5 hours
Thursday	3rd Dress or Preview	4 hours
Friday	Opening Night	

Technical Rehearsal

Directors hold two types of technical rehearsals. One is often referred to as *Dry Tech*; the other is *Wet Tech*. We are not at all sure where the terms *Dry* and *Wet Tech* originated but we do know that they have been used professionally for generations.

Dry Tech. The objective of a Dry Tech is to set and run cues. For obvious reasons the rehearsal must be scheduled in the room or auditorium where the play is to be staged. Actors do not attend this call, only the production staff.

In most plays it takes more people to run a production than appear in it. Like the actors, the individuals assigned to crews need to rehearse. Dry Tech is their only solo rehearsal.

Dry Techs can be long and tedious. We suggest that you schedule them on a Saturday and begin no later than 10 A.M.

The Stage Manager is responsible for recording all the cues in an official prompt book during Dry Tech.

Since actors are not present during Dry Tech, the Production Stage Manager or the director's assistant can "walk" the show, meaning that they move about on the stage indicating the placement and movement of the actors at the moment before a cue.

It is standard to run Dry Tech "cue-to-cue," which means that you deal only with those moments in the play that affect a light, sound, or set change. The rest of the play is omitted. This procedure allows more time to fully integrate and rehearse the efforts of all the designers and their crews.

Depending on the number of cues, the complexity of your lighting and sound equipment, and the experience of your staff, this rehearsal can run from four to eight hours, sometimes even longer. It is important that you communicate this fact to everyone concerned. Take breaks at least every three hours to relieve stress. Do everything you can to keep morale high and concentration focused.

One way to prepare for Dry Tech is to schedule one or more informal sessions with the set, lighting, and sound designers to discuss cues. Your Stage Manager should also be present if possible. It is best if you meet with one designer at a time. During each session (sometimes known as *Paper Techs*) mark and discuss your desired effect for each cue. Especially in highly complicated productions, this procedure can save time, stress, and incident.

Wet Tech.   Actors are integrated into the Wet Tech, although it should be made clear that this rehearsal is primarily for the benefit of the crews, not the actors.

It is best to run Wet Tech as a full rehearsal. This gives the crews an opportunity to get a feel for the entire production. Choose to run a cue-to-cue rehearsal only if the play is long and the effects are complicated.

The director's main objective during Wet Tech is to make sure that all actors can be heard and seen. Don't let sound levels get set too high or light levels get set too low. Take time to reset levels and make adjustments. Better to restage a scene than to leave actors in a poorly lit area.

Start Wet Tech early and plan for this rehearsal to last up to six hours, especially if your production contains cues and set changes. The crews need to totally integrate their efforts by the end of Wet Tech so that Dress Rehearsals can run smoothly.

Dress Rehearsals

First Dress Rehearsal.   Be aware that more often than not Murphy's Law takes effect on first dress, and everything that can go wrong does. It can be quite devastating. Not only do you face technical difficulties, but every nuance you've worked on falls apart. You can spend the entire rehearsal wondering how you will ever have enough time to get the play back into shape. Not to worry. Even though the opening is only three nights away, don't expect First Dress to play as a performance. It never does.

Approach First Dress strictly as a technical rehearsal. Don't concentrate on the actors' pacing and characterization; instead, focus on all the technical aspects of the production. All props should be in place and actors should wear full makeup and costumes for this rehearsal. Base the majority of your comments on how well the actors adjust to these elements.

Stop the show and work out any major technical difficulties on the spot. Simplify if necessary, but make sure that problems are eliminated before you move on.

Second Dress Rehearsal.   This is the night for actors to find the shape of the production again. By Second Dress they will feel more comfortable in their costumes and be more familiar with the technical aspects of the production.

Don't stop this rehearsal unless a major error occurs that you feel needs to be fixed at the moment. Otherwise, take notes and rerun problem spots at the end of an act, or even at the end of the rehearsal.

If the rehearsal really goes poorly, you may need to hold the company and, if time permits, rerun parts or all of the play again. Another option is to schedule an emergency rehearsal before the official Third Dress.

Third Dress Rehearsal.   It is important that you run this final rehearsal as a performance. You may even want to consider inviting residents from a retirement home or a few close friends. Having an audience of any kind gives the company the psychological edge it needs to prepare for opening night. Even if you don't have invited guests, treat this rehearsal as a performance. Don't stop the rehearsal for any reason; let the actors and crews work through any problems.

Some directors allow parents and friends to take pictures during final dress. We do not encourage this practice, but if you offer this option, make sure that you insist that no flash cameras be allowed. Better to offer an open photo call after final dress or one of the performances than to allow too much disruption during a final rehearsal.

You might also receive some pressure to allow video cameras to record a final dress (or performance). We advise you to be very cautious on this issue. Copyright laws regarding the recording of plays or musicals are constantly being challenged and rewritten. It is quite clear that you may not make multiple copies of any performance for sale or profit. Even permanent copies of some properties for private use only are restricted, so make sure you have complete clearance before granting permission.

Preview Performance

The following are pointers you need to consider if you elect to run your Third Dress as a preview.

- Unless you pay royalties, you cannot charge guests at a preview performance.
- Don't expect an invited audience to respond as a paying audience. Invited audiences are usually a small but friendly group. They scatter themselves throughout the auditorium and are often too inhibited or polite to respond as a regular paying audience might.
- If you are working on a comedy, warn your actors that they can't use a preview audience to judge how funny their performance really is.
- Be careful that you don't invite anyone to a Preview who might otherwise pay to see a regular performance. You don't want to cut into your profits.
- If you are looking for small groups of people to invite, consider calling retirement homes. The residents are usually on limited budgets and wouldn't otherwise be able to attend. You may have to provide transportation and start the previews early, but you will be doing a fine public service.

In many productions Tech Week is better remembered as "Hell Week." To ensure that your company doesn't have a negative experience, keep communications open between you and all members of the production staff. Carefully plan together the working procedure for each rehearsal.

LENGTH OF THE REHEARSAL PROCESS

Now that you understand the objectives of each of the nine phases of the rehearsal process, you need to decide how many days need to be assigned to each phase. We offer the following suggestions:

- *Orientation:* One half to one day. In many productions this phase can be combined with the next phase, Read-through.
- *Read-through:* One to three days depending on the length and complexity of the script.

- *Run-throughs:* We recommend that you have a walk-through or run-through at the end of each week. During the last full week of rehearsal before you go into Tech Week, you need to have a minimum of three run-throughs.
- *Polishing Rehearsals:* Five days; at least two of the five rehearsals should be run-throughs.
- *Technical Rehearsals:* Two days; Dry Tech: allow six to eight hours of rehearsal time; Wet Tech: allow four to six hours of rehearsal time.
- *Dress Rehearsals:* Three days; the Third Dress may be considered a Preview.

Double Rehearsals

If you have fewer than five weeks for rehearsal, you might try scheduling two rehearsals on one day each week, say on Sunday afternoon and evening. We don't advocate this practice, but it can work if you are pressed for time.

If you do implement double rehearsals, try not to call the same actors to both sessions, and make sure they are forewarned and prepared for some stress.

"T.B.A."

As a protection, you might want to signal a couple of days as possible rehearsal slots and, in writing, request that the cast hold the time for a possible rehearsal. T.B.A. (to be arranged) rehearsals can be especially helpful if you find yourself running behind schedule near the end of the process just before you go into Tech Week. The most popular days and times for T.B.A. slots are Saturday mornings and Sunday afternoons.

"Subject to Change"

Add the phrase "Subject to Change" in bold type near the top of your rehearsal schedule. The flow of the rehearsal process should not be dictated by a piece of paper. It is essential that you have the freedom to make whatever adjustments you feel are necessary. You never know when an emergency will arise. You are dealing with human beings, not machines. You need to be able to adjust or make changes without comment or repercussions from members of the company.

Other Considerations

It is appropriate and considerate to list that strike will follow final performance and everyone in the company (actors and crews) is expected to participate. Strike is when you tear down the set, clear and sort properties and costumes, and in general, clean up the stage and backstage areas. Some strike sessions can last two to three hours. A responsible Technical Director should organize and supervise the strike.

You can also list the evening of Picture Call, if you decide to have one. Picture Call is usually held after a performance. It is an occasion to take official production shots as well as pictures of individual actors. A well-organized Picture Call should not take longer than one hour unless your production has a number of set and/or costume changes to slow down the process.

A rehearsal schedule, professionally typed and detailed, gives everyone in the company a sense of confidence. Figure 6.2 is an example of a rehearsal schedule for *The Importance of Being Earnest*. It suggests that you have given a great deal of forethought to the production and that you have arrived at a plan that you feel can effectively and realistically achieve your objectives. It sends out a clear signal that you as director are organized and serious in your intent to mount a production of the highest quality. Can you think of a better way of starting the rehearsal process?

A FINAL CHECKLIST

Once you have completed the design of your rehearsal schedule, use the following check-list to ensure that your copy is ready for distribution.

____ Is your schedule specific, with enough detail that all members of the production staff and company can clearly anticipate your day-by-day procedure?

____ Are all phases of the process, especially deadlines, clearly indicated?

____ Is your schedule typed? Does it look neat and professional? First impressions are important!

____ Have you scheduled each day of rehearsals carefully so that actors do not have to sit around and wait too long?

____ Have you included the phrase "Subject to Change" near the top of your schedule?

____ Have you run enough copies for all key members of the production staff as well as your stage managers and assistants?

____ Have you made extra copies to post in strategic places so crew members and other interested parties can refer to the schedule if necessary?

REHEARSAL FOR *THE IMPORTANCE OF BEING EARNEST*

Subject to Change
NOTE: All rehearsals will take place in the auditorium.

Date	Time	Type	Act/Unit	Call
2/1	7:00–10:00	Orientation		Company
2/2	7:00–10:00	Read-thru		Company
2/3	7:00–10:00	Read-thru		Company
2/4	7:00–10:00	Blocking Rehearsal	Act One	All in I.
2/5	7:00–10:00	Blocking Rehearsal	Act One review	
2/8	7:00–10:00	Blocking Rehearsal	Act Two	All in II.
2/9	7:00–10:00	Blocking Rehearsal	Act Two review	
2/10	7:00–10:00	Blocking Rehearsal	Act Three	All in III.
2/11	7:00–10:00	Blocking Rehearsal	Act Three review	
2/12	7:00–10:00	Walk-Thru for blocking		Company
2/15	7:00–10:00	Lines	Act One	All in I.
2/16	7:00–8:00	Working Rehearsal	Act One/Units 1 and 2	
	8:00–10:00		Act One/Units 3, 4, 5, 6, 7	
2/17	7:00–8:00	Working Rehearsal	Act Two/Units 1, 2, 3, 4, 5	
	8:00–9:00		Act Two/Units 7 and 8	
	9:00–10:00		Act Two/Units 6 and 9	
2/18		Repeat 2/17 rehearsal schedule		
2/19	7:00–10:00	Walk-thru Act One and Act Two		
2/22	7:00–10:00	Lines	Act Two	All in II.
2/23	7:00–8:00	Working Rehearsal	Act Two/Units 1, 2, 3, 4, 5	
	8:00–9:00		Act Two/Units 7 and 8	
	9:00–10:00		Act Two/Units 6 and 9	
2/24	7:00–10:00	Working Rehearsal	Act Three	All in III.
2/24	7:00–10:00	Working Rehearsal	Act One	All in I
2/25	7:00–10:00	Run-thru Acts I, II, and III All Lines!		
3/1	7:00–10:00	Polishing Rehearsal	Act One	All in I.
3/2	7:00–10:00	Polishing Rehearsal	Act Two	All in II.
3/3	7:00–10:00	Polishing Rehearsal	Act Three	All in III.
3/4	7:00–10:00	Run-thru	Acts I, II, III	
3/5	7:00–10:00	Run-thru	Acts I, II, III	
3/6	10:00–???	Dry Tech		
3/8	6:00–10:00	Wet Tech		
3/9	6:00 call	7:30 Go	1st Dress	
3/10	6:00 call	7:00 Go	2nd Dress	
3/11	6:30 call	7:30 Go	3rd Dress/Preview	
		(NOTE: Picture Call after 3rd Dress)		
3/12	6:30 call	8:00 Go	Performance	
3/13	6:30 call	8:00 Go	Performance	

(NOTE: Strike after performance. ALL ACTORS MUST ATTEND.)

LAYOUT FOR A TYPICAL REHEARSAL SCHEDULE

Title of Play
Rehearsal Schedule
Subject to Change

Date	Time	Place	Type of Rehearsal	Act/Unit	Call

How to Work With a Set Designer

"Pick-a-little; Talk-a-little"

from The Music Man. *Music, lyrics and book by Meredith Willson.*

Opened in New York, December 19, 1957; ran 1,375 performances. It took eight years to write, including over thirty drafts and forty songs.

At this point you are going to run into your first opportunity. (You notice we have consciously chosen the word *opportunity*. We could have said "challenge" or "snag," but we want to remain as upbeat as possible.) You have read your play over two, three, maybe four times, and you have begun to picture some of the scenes in your head. You realize that it is getting dangerously close to auditions and that after auditions come rehearsals, and, early on in rehearsals you must start blocking your play. So what are you supposed to do about a set, a floor plan? You don't have a clue!

Our advice is take an aspirin and get out the phone book. In point of fact, you cannot tackle this job alone. You need professional advice. When you are sick, you call a doctor; when you need a set, you call a scene designer. It's that simple. Contact someone within an hour's drive—university, community theaters, dance companies, other arts organizations—someone will be able to give you the names of individuals who might be available to assist. If you can't afford to hire a professional, or a trained amateur, then negotiate for the services of a graduate or upperclass student who is majoring in design. You will still need to pay a stipend; however, students will often work for less because they want the experience and need to build up a résumé. Sometimes they can receive academic credit for their work. Suggest this possibility when you are negotiating.

Ideally you need a trained individual who will not only design but will also oversee the construction and rigging of the sets and the hanging and focusing of the lights. If you are fortunate enough to find someone who has the expertise and the time to handle all these tasks, make sure that you line up a number of other people to serve as technical assistants.

DIRECTOR'S INPUT

The title of this chapter is quite apropos. "Pick-a-little; Talk-a-little" is exactly what you need to do when you meet to discuss the design for your production. Theater is a collaborative effort, and this is definitely one instance when the input of two creative minds is better than one. You hold the key to the meaning of the play; your designer holds the key to the principles of design. Together you can develop a creative and functional setting for your production. Time, effort, and (let us not forget) a little money are all you need.

Assume that you have decided to direct *The Importance of Being Earnest*. What kind of information does a designer need from you at this time? The answer: facts and impressions. Work on the facts first. Be prepared to provide the following information:

- The amount of money you have to spend on set construction
- The number, size, and type of flats you have in stock
- The number and size of platforms you have in stock
- The exact dimensions of the stage
- The amount of storage space backstage
- The amount of time you have to build the set
- The number of people you have to help build the set
- The exact times when student and parent help is available
- The equipment (power and hand tools) you have to build with

- The space you have to build in
- The availability of the space
- The complete list of your lighting equipment

Once your designer has a clear picture of your situation and its limitations, move on and share your impressions of the play. We suggest that during the dialogue you discuss the following questions:

What do you think the play is about? Keep your answer simple but don't limit yourself. Throw out a number of different words and phrases.

When you see the play in your head… What images do you see? What music do you hear? What colors do you see? Are you reminded of any particular place? Do certain paintings or photographs come to mind? Be specific; bring in examples. Don't expect designers to copy these ideas, but they might use them for inspiration.

How do you want the audience to feel as they watch the play? Should they feel nostalgic? Should they feel threatened or uncomfortable? Should they feel warm or cool?

What do you feel are the key moments in the play? Many professional designs have been built around a particular scene in the play. Sometimes it is essential. For example, near the end of the second act in *You Can't Take It With You,* twelve people have to sit around a dining room table.

How many different settings are called for? Sometimes you can cut down on the number of sets required. For example, *The Importance of Being Earnest* calls for three complete set changes: Act One takes place in the Morning room of Algernon's flat in Half-Moon Street; Act Two is set in the garden at the Manor House; and Act Three is set in the Morning room at the Manor House. Without a single line change, you can cut the Morning room at the Manor House and play the third act instead, on the second act "Garden" set. Some years ago we staged a production this way and it worked quite effectively. Needless to say, from a technical point of view, it saved us a great deal of time, effort and money.

What items in the design need to be practical? Practical means, "Does it have to work?" Does the sink have to have running water? Do the windows have to open and shut? Does the bookcase have to hold real books? Does the window seat have to have an escape? (It does if you're producing *Arsenic and Old Lace.*)

Do you plan to cut lines or eliminate scenes in the play? Make sure your designer gets a cut script. Also, talk through any other business or lines you are considering cutting. If the cuts are for technical reasons, your designer may have some suggestions.

Have you considered setting your play in a different place or time period? If you and your designer feel that you can make the play more palatable for your audience by placing it in a contemporary time and place, do so. However, do not make this decision for practical considerations, only for artistic ones. Whatever your design concept, make sure that it does not compromise the integrity of the play, the intent of the playwright, or the spirit of the script.

DESIGN OPTIONS FOR A REALISTIC PLAY

The sets for most of the plays you are likely to consider will call for a realistic treatment of some kind. The following illustrations will show you the various options you can consider in the design for your production.

Realism   Realism is photographic replication, an attempt to replicate complete detail on the stage. Slice-of-life realism requires a great deal of attention to detail and can be expensive to execute. If your funds are limited and labor force is small, you may want to consider other options.

The Lion in Winter, by James Goldman; Directed by James W. Rodgers; Scenery Design by Russell Jones; Produced by University of Kentucky

Selective Realism   This style can be one of the most useful and artistic ways of addressing production limitations. Instead of providing total naturalistic detail, only select pieces like door, window, fireplace, and selected wall units are provided. They are set in relief against a black, blue, or neutral background. Audiences love to use their imaginations, and in theater, less can say more. If you elect this option, the detail on the selected pieces must be thoughtfully made and skillfully executed.

To Kill a Mockingbird, by Harper Lee; Directed by James W. Rodgers; Scenery Design by Russell Jones; Produced by University of Kentucky

Stylization   This style of setting is a highly exaggerated and colorful interpretation of reality. It draws attention to itself but can be especially effective for selected forms of comedy, such as farce and fantasy. Like Selective Realism, Stylization also requires highly skilled painting techniques since so much of the detail is painted directly onto the setting.

HAIR, Music by Galt MacDermot, Book and Lyrics by Gerome Ragni & James Rado; Directed by Dominic Missimi; Scenery Design by Russell Jones; Produced by Northwestern University

Symbolism   This style requires the selection of characteristic elements or symbols to represent the whole. It is a highly impressionistic form that can be an effective option, especially for plays that are more presentational in form and require many changes of setting.

The Skin of Our Teeth, by Thornton Wilder; Directed by James W. Rodgers; Scenery Design by Russell Jones; Produced by University of Kentucky

Formalism   This style option is the most simplistic form of design. It merely provides a neutral background for a play. Platforms and sometimes large, self-standing units can be added, but basically, furniture sits in relief in a pool of light. The rest of the stage appears as a void.

The School for Scandal, by Richard Brinsley Sheridan; Directed by James W. Rodgers; Scenery Design by Russell Jones; Produced by University of Kentucky

As you can see, you have many ways of approaching the design concept for your production even when a play calls for a realistic setting. The important principle to remember is not to allow the design for your production to be an unattractive and distracting element. Better to attempt less and execute it well than to try to do more and have the results end up being an embarrassment to you, your actors, and the audience.

GUIDELINES FOR JUDGING FLOOR PLANS

After several meetings, the designer will present you with a floor plan (sometimes called a ground plan), which is a drawing of the stage with the setting in place as seen from above without perspective. You need to check a number of practical considerations before you sign off on this sketch. The following items are some of the most obvious.

Balance The first step is to see how balance has been achieved, symmetrically or asymmetrically. Asymmetrical designs appear more natural and aesthetically are more formal and are best suited to classic plays. *The Importance of Being Earnest* is an excellent play to design symmetrically, because of the way Oscar Wilde structured his plot.

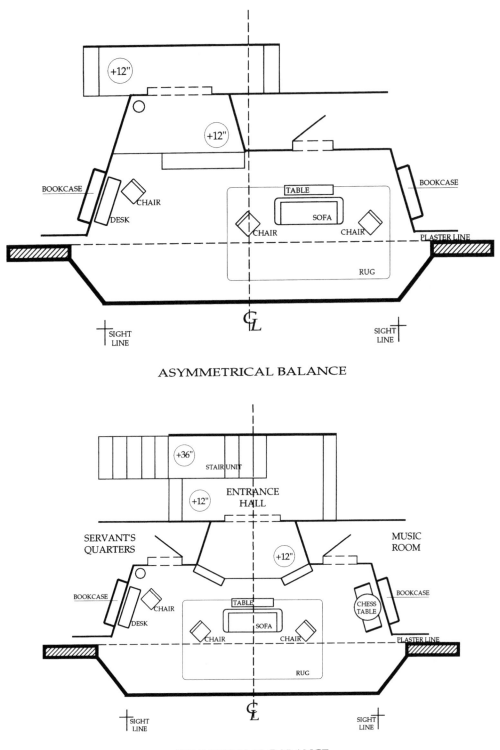

ASYMMETRICAL BALANCE

SYMMETRICAL BALANCE
The Importance of Being Earnest

Architectural Logic A design needs to take some theatrical liberties; however, it must maintain architectural integrity. If your setting is a room of a home, make sure you can visualize the rest of the house. Look to see that a fireplace is placed on an outside wall, that a window is not placed next to a door that leads to another part of the house, or that a staircase leads up to what is obviously an outside wall.

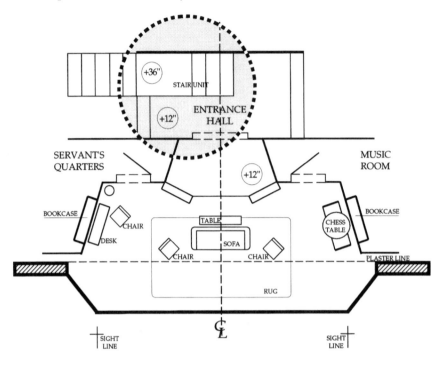

Entrances Check your sketch to make sure that key archways and doors have been placed where actors can make strong entrances. Be advised that upstage center is the strongest position on stage.

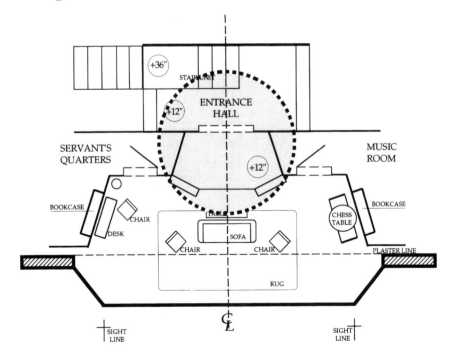

Sight Lines   Check each sketch to make sure that all the playing areas can be seen from every seat in your auditorium.

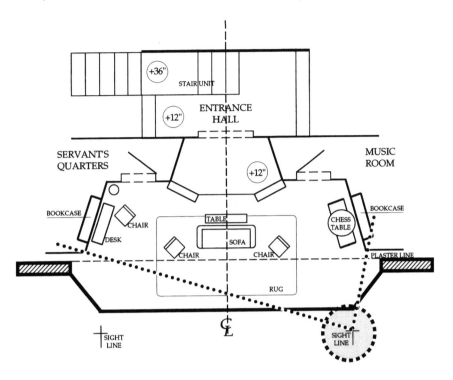

Broken Lines   Make sure the floor plan is interesting to look at. Has the designer avoided long straight lines? Nothing is more boring than a plain box set.

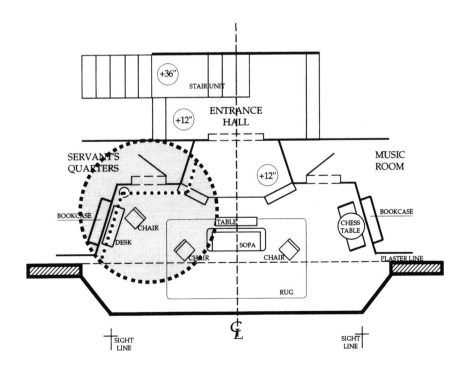

Variety   Has the designer provided various levels for actors to work on? This might be an important consideration especially in plays that call for large numbers of people being on stage at the same time.

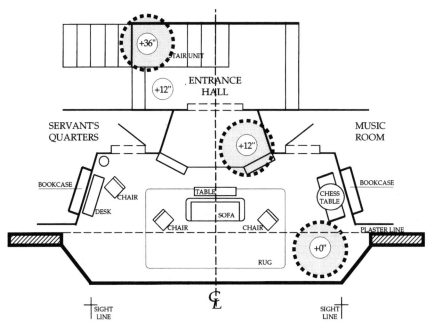

Placement   Has the furniture been grouped into interesting conversational units? Have pieces been placed out away from walls into the playing area? Actors need obstacles to confront and barriers to hide behind.

Focus   If you need a key piece of furniture around which a great deal of action takes place, like the dining room tables in *You Can't Take It With You, Life With Father,* and *I Remember Mama,* make sure that the item has been placed in a dominant acting area and that you have free and open access to and around it.

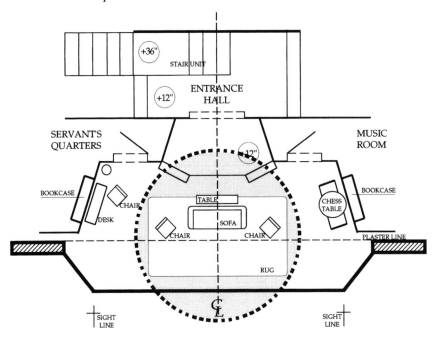

Movement Pattern   Does the composition of the furniture provide a nice flow or traffic pattern? Actors need to be able to move freely in and about the playing space.

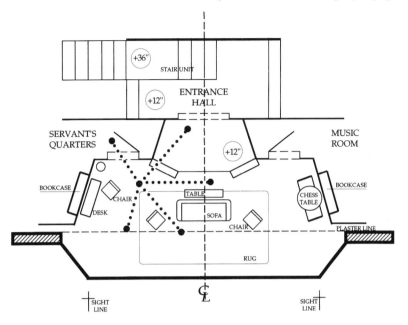

Door Units   If you have key scenes in a doorway, make sure you check the designs to see where the door has been hinged and which way it swings open. If the door opens offstage, make sure that masking is provided.

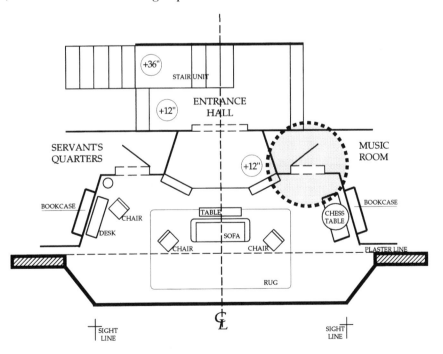

After you have signed off on a floor plan, the designer should provide you with detailed plans (working drawings) and either a vertical rendering or a scaled model of your set.

Renderings: A rendering is a perspective drawing of the set. Even though it will not include all details, it should give an accurate impression of what the finished set will look like.

Scale Models: Some directors prefer looking at a scale model rather than a rendering of a set. Models are three-dimensional; they give you a clearer sense of the acting space available.

It is best if all the design steps discussed above are completed before you start auditions. You should be able to show either renderings or a scale model to your cast at the first rehearsal.

FACTS YOUR SET DESIGNER NEEDS TO KNOW

Be prepared to provide your set designer with the following information at your first production meeting.

1. The amount of money you have to spend on set construction
2. The number, size, and type of flats you have in stock
3. The number and size of platforms you have in stock
4. The exact dimensions of the stage
5. The amount of storage space backstage
6. The amount of time you have to build the set
7. The number of people you have to help build the set
8. The exact time when student and parent help is available
9. The equipment (power and hand tools) you have to build with
10. The size of the space you have to build in
11. The availability of the space you have to build in
12. The complete list of your lighting equipment

YOUR IMPRESSION OF THE PLAY OR MUSICAL YOU ARE DIRECTING

Before you meet with any of your designers, think through the answers to the following questions.

1. **What do you think the play is about?**
   Keep your answer simple but don't limit yourself; throw out a number of different words and phrases.

2. **When you see the play in your head. . .**
   What images do you see? What music do you hear? What colors do you see? Are you reminded of any particular place? Do certain paintings or photographs come to mind? Be specific; bring in examples.

3. **How do you want the audience to feel as they watch the play?**
   Should they feel nostalgic? Should they feel threatened or uncomfortable? Should they feel warm or cool?

4. **What do you feel are the key moments in the play?**

5. **How many different settings are called for?**

6. **What items in the design need to be practical?**
   Practical means it has to work, or be functional.

7. **Do you plan to cut lines or eliminate scenes in the play?**
   Make sure your designer gets a cut script. Also, talk through any other business or lines you are considering cutting.

8. **Have you considered setting your play in a different place or time period?**
   Make sure that it does not compromise the integrity of the play, the intent of the playwright, or the spirit of the script.

8 What You Need to Know About Stage Properties

"Pretty Little Picture"

from A Funny Thing Happened on the Way to the Forum.

Music and lyrics by Stephen Sondheim; book by Burt Shevelove and Larry Gelbart.

Opened in New York, May 8, 1962; ran 964 performances. The original cast included the comic talents of Zero Mostel, Jack Gilford, and David Burns. The vehicle was intended for Phil Silvers, who had a chance to play Pseudolus in the 1972 revival.

Set designers are usually responsible for either the design or the selection of all stage furnishings which, using theater terminology, are called properties. Properties can be defined as all pieces of furniture, set dressing, or handheld objects needed for the look or action of the play. Properties can be subdivided into four categories:

> *Set props:* All large or fixed objects, such as furniture and draperies.
>
> *Hand props:* Small objects used by a single character, such as fans and cigarette cases.
>
> *Personal props:* Items worn as part of a character's apparel, such as wallets, handkerchiefs, and pocket watches.
>
> *Decor or filler props:* Paraphernalia that add color and personality to a room or space, such as pictures, figurines, and magazines.

The set designer is responsible for all but personal props; these items are usually supplied by the costumer.

To save on costs, you will want to borrow as many properties as possible. Locating the right items can be as time consuming as a scavenger hunt. A designer needs the crew to assist in this process. It is important that at least one person on the property crew have a car at ready disposal. Be prepared to pay for gas mileage.

Quite often you will find a property list printed at the back of each script. Even when this is the case, it is important for you or your Stage Manager to go through the script carefully and make your own list of properties. Make sure that someone, preferably your designer, spends some time with the crew describing in detail the size, color, shape, and use of each piece on the list. A great deal of time can be wasted when this communication is not clear.

You can use substitute props, called rehearsal props, in the earlier weeks of rehearsals. It is important, however, to allow actors to work with the real item before first dress rehearsal if the actual prop involves the safety of the actor or is part of an intricate piece of business that must be timed out carefully. This is especially true of breakaway furniture and weapons of all kinds.

Make sure all perishable props stay fresh, including foods. Sometimes you need to substitute a food item if the one called for spoils easily or is difficult to eat. For example, never feed an actor peanut butter on stage, or dry toast. One can stick to the roof of the mouth, the other crumble and get caught in the back of the throat.

As we pointed out in Chapter 2, make sure you take out an insurance policy on all expensive items that you borrow. Also, make sure you have included in your budget the cost of replenishing perishable props not only for performances but also for all final run-throughs and dress rehearsals.

PROPERTY LIST FOR YOUR PRODUCTION

Use the following form to list all the properties needed in your production. Make sure you include all known Set, Hand, Personal, and Decor props.

Item	Act/Scene	Description

Property Inventory List

Use the following form to list all borrowed props.

Item	Owner	Borrowed/ Returned	Instructions

8.3

PROPERTY CHECKLIST

This form can be used by both the Property Head and the Stage Manager to ensure that all properties are in their proper location during the production of the play

ACT:_____

Item	Location			Personal Prop
	On Stage	Right Stage	Left Stage	Actor's name

9 What You Need to Know About Stage Lighting

"Let the Sunshine In"

from Hair.
Music by Galt MacDermot; lyrics and book by Gerome Ragni and James Rado.

Opened in New York, April 29, 1968; ran 1,742 performances. Melba Moore and Diane Keaton were in the original New York production.

Designing and executing stage lighting is a great deal more than just flipping a couple of switches and throwing some light on the stage. In fact, in recent years lighting has become the most powerful stage element. It not only illuminates actors, it also has the capacity to isolate space, set mood, shift attention, suggest time, season and locale, and establish and/or reinforce a play's tempo. When the equipment is sophisticated enough, it can even create the stage magic of special effects.

In many productions lighting needs to be the primary design element. Two examples are *Our Town* by Thornton Wilder, which has no scenic requirements, and Harper Lee's *To Kill a Mockingbird,* which requires a simple unit setting so that many different locales can be suggested at the same time or immediately following one another.

Lighting is the most flexible of the design elements; it can enhance your production greatly, or it can be the most obtrusive element. You need a great deal of technical knowledge as well as artistic sensitivity to handle the requirements of this area effectively. Safety is also of paramount importance when it comes to both the rigging and circuiting of your lighting instruments. For these reasons, you need a skilled technician to collaborate on the artistic concept, design a light plot, and oversee the mounting and circuiting of all electrical equipment.

If your production calls for a sophisticated light plot, you may want to consider borrowing or renting some lighting equipment. Because of the popularity of rock concerts, a wide variety of portable equipment is available on the market, and much of it is very accessible and affordable.

SPECIAL CAPABILITIES OF STAGE LIGHTING

The following are four specific ways that lighting can greatly enhance your production.

Draw focus. Perhaps the greatest asset of sophisticated lighting is its ability to direct our attention *to* a specific place on stage, and *away* from other areas. Controlling focus can hasten scene shifting and reduce the need for large scenic elements.

Establish mood. Lighting is the best method for creating mood and atmosphere. This is especially true in mysteries and serious dramas. Be warned, however: Don't play your light too low; you can lose the expressions on actors' faces. Audiences, remember, are paying to see a play, not watch a light show. Also, psychologically, audiences feel they can hear and understand actors better when they can see their faces clearly.

Designate time. With color, shade, and intensity, lighting can do an excellent job of suggesting the seasons of the year as well as indicating general, if not specific, times of the day and night. This can be especially helpful in plays that require exterior settings like, for example, *Dark of the Moon.*

Bridge scenes. The way stage lighting is manipulated affects the style of your production. Slow fades, gradual cross-fades, stark blackouts—all these shifts need to be choreographed so that the cueing of light complements the tone you have set in the play. These details are worked out during the last phase of the rehearsal process and need to be given careful and thoughtful consideration.

INVENTORY OF LIGHTING EQUIPMENT

Use this form to keep track of all borrowed items in the area of lighting: instruments, cable, auxiliary boards, etc.

Item Borrowed	Owner	Date Borrowed/Returned

LIGHTING CUE SHEET

Use this form to describe all the lighting effects you would like to see incorporated into the design of the production.

Number	Page	Cue Line	Desired Effect Requested

10

What You Need to Know About Sound and Special Effects

"The Sound of Music"

from The Sound of Music.
*Music by Richard Rodgers;
lyrics by Oscar
Hammerstein II;
book by Howard Lindsay
and Russel Crouse.*

Opened in New York, November 16, 1959, and ran 1,443 performances. The original company starred Mary Martin and Theodore Bikel.

SOUND

Sound has become an increasingly important design element. It includes not only the design of offstage music and sound effects; more recently it has also come to include the electronic enhancement of the spoken word. Stage microphones and body mikes have become an integral part of staging musicals, especially in large auditoriums. If you decide to make this a component of your production, you will need to add another expert to your production staff. Controlling both the level and quality of the human voice is a complicated science and requires the expertise of a competent sound technician. Do not be duped into using enthusiastic students without first knowing their abilities. Electronic feedback, static, and other "buzzes" or "hums" can distract attention and even destroy the overall quality of a production.

As far as sound effects are concerned, you can find a large collection of recorded human and mechanical noises on both tape and CD recordings. You can order these through catalogs at your local music stores, or sometimes borrow collections from larger lending libraries, university theaters, radio stations, or television affiliates. Sometimes a local station will even record the cues you need for little or no cost. Today, special software for computers equipped with CD-ROM as well as samplers and synthesizers can create practically every and any sound at the pitch level, rate, and volume you want.

It is best to record each sound or music cue on a separate cassette tape. When you use this method you can add, cut, or adjust the length of one cue without having to resplice an entire reel-to-reel tape.

When you use recorded sound effects, don't run the sound through the auditorium speaker system. Instead, place an auxiliary speaker near the source and adjust the volume to a level that makes the sound effect seem real and natural to the audience.

SPECIAL EFFECTS

The demands of special effects cover a wide range: the crackle and glow of burning logs in a fireplace; a hanging picture that falls on cue and breaks; even Peter, Wendy, Michael, and John flying six feet above the ground in James Barrie's *Peter Pan*. The glow from the fireplace and the falling picture are standard cues and can be easily worked out by your set and/or lighting designer(s). The flying effect is far more complicated and may require the expertise of a specialist. Safety is the major consideration here; don't put yourself or your actors in a compromising situation.

Consider three important factors before you decide to direct a play that requires one or more complicated special effects:

Time: Many effects are worked out during production week and can take considerable time to rig. Make sure your designers have budgeted the extra time into their schedules.

Money: Special effects can add considerable expense to your budget. Make sure you have added this line item to your budget.

Safety: Special effects that involve actors need to be carefully choreographed, one step at a time. Insist that all staging be completed early and that the effect is integrated into the rehearsal process well in advance of your first dress rehearsal.

Don't rush actors when they are learning to work with special effects such as explosions or flying gear. Ultimately you are responsible for their safety. Effects must be fail-safe. Make sure they are thoroughly tested before each rehearsal and performance. The more complicated the effect, the more carefully it needs to be worked out.

SOUND CUE SHEET

Use this form to describe all the sound cues and effects you would like to see incorporated into your production.

Number	Page	Cue Line	Desired Effect Requested

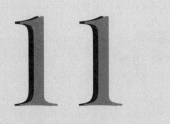

11

What You Need to Know About Costuming

"*Put on Your Sunday Clothes*"

from Hello Dolly!
Music and lyrics by
Jerry Herman;
book by Michael Stewart.

Opened in New York, January 16, 1964; ran 2,844 performances. Carol Channing starred and Gower Champion directed and choreographed.

Real magic exists in the area of costuming, and too many directors may not be fully aware of the subtle but powerful messages this design element transmits to an audience. In theater, costuming embraces everything the actor wears: clothes, accessories, shoes, even undergarments. It is a highly personal design element and one that projects a great deal of information about the character. Care must be taken, therefore, to ensure that the signals are clear and the selections worn are both functional and artistically correct.

SELECTION OR DESIGN

Because costuming is so personal, many beginning directors allow, or even require, actors to supply their own clothes, makeup, and accessories. This has become the standard practice in many high school and community theaters even when period plays are being produced. We do not support this practice. Actors are vain; they want to look their best regardless of the role they are playing. Besides, most actors' wardrobes are restricted and their resources limited. More important, they have no notion of what the overall look of the scene should be. At the very least you need to recruit an individual who has a keen eye for color, line, and texture. It would also help if this individual has strong organizational skills and finds sewing machines user-friendly.

The Costumer

Once you have located someone who will take on the responsibility of coordinating or building costumes, you need to spend considerable time together discussing the play. It is important that you clearly articulate your interpretation of all of the characters in the play and their relationships one to another. Also, be specific in explaining what you expect each costume to be able to do on stage. For example, it is imperative that a costumer know, before the final week of rehearsal, that a certain costume needs two pockets, one large enough to conceal a prayer book, the other, a gun, or that a certain garment needs to be flexible, stain-proofed, and durable because you have directed a scene where the actor crawls around the stage on his hands and knees.

The Objectives of Costume Design

Costumes communicate a wealth of information about the individual wearing them. In everyday life we make snap judgments about people based on the clothes they wear; audiences carry this same perception into the theater. For this reason you must be very selective about the color and cut of the clothes, the style of hair, and the amount of makeup a character wears in a production. The following are five major ways that costumes communicate to an audience.

1. Costumes can define the period, locale, time, and occasion of each scene of the play.
2. Costumes can project each character's psychological profile.

3. Costumes can show relationships between individuals and groups.

4. Costumes can complement the director's concept and design style of a production.

5. Costumes can accommodate the physical requirements of the performers.

Defines period, locale, time and occasion. As soon as an actor walks out on stage in costume, the audience should be able to place that character in an approximate historical period and place, for example, late sixteenth century (Shakespeare's) England, or mid–nineteenth-century (Dickens's) England.

The color and texture of the costumes can often help us to identify the season of the year, particularly the extreme temperatures of winter and summer.

In some instances, a costume can also tell an audience the occasion the character is anticipating; for example, a character could enter dressed for a tennis match, a formal ball, or bedtime. Through color, texture, line, and design a costume can relate all the above information—and more.

Projects a character's psychological profile. In addition to historical period, time, and place, a single garment can also signal more personal information about a character. For example, a costume can signal the character's occupation (police officer, construction worker, prostitute, nurse); the character's social status (upper, middle, or lower class); the degree of the character's conformity to society (independent or regimented); the character's relative personality (flamboyant or modest); and the current state of the character's mind (slovenly or well groomed).

Shows relationship between individuals and groups. A more astute costume designer can help an audience distinguish relationships between characters. For the ball scene in *Romeo and Juliet* (Act I, Scene V), a clever designer can help an audience distinguish the Capulets from the Montagues through the use of color, texture, and a repeated pattern or design in a textile. A careful manipulation of accessories can further help to distinguish certain major characters within each family. For example, a costumer might dress Paris in an elaborate, brilliant garment and give Tybalt a darker, more severe look.

Complements the director's concept and design style of the production. It is essential that the costume designer work closely with the other designers in the production to ensure that all the costumes complement the director's concept as well as the other visual aspects of the production. It would be a mistake, for example, to put actors in muted, realistic clothes when the director's and set and lighting designers' approach is bold and highly theatrical. Design elements should never be confusing to an audience. They may contrast one with the other but never be in conflict. The final product should be perceived by the audience as a seamless, unified production.

Accommodates the physical requirements of the character. One final and very important consideration is to design or adjust each garment in a production to permit actors to perform the actions required freely and without restriction. If a scene calls for a character to engage in hand-to-hand combat, the costume must allow for proper freedom of movement. It also must be reinforced and be made of materials that can withstand the constant wear and stress required in performance.

Anticipating Special Problems

In many plays actors have to make quick changes. Two methods have become quite popular to accommodate this requirement: (1) the breakaway costume; and (2) overdressing.

A breakaway costume stitches all pieces of the ensemble together into one garment, splits the garment up the back, and then bastes in a long piece of velcro or a zipper as a fastener. When the actor exits the stage, he can literally be ripped out of a breakaway costume in seconds.

When the overdressing method is used, the actor puts several layers of costume on, one over the other. When the actor strips down out of one costume, the next costume is already in place and ready for minor adjustments.

These two methods, breakaway and overdress, were used together in a design that proved quite successful in the recent Broadway revival of the musical *Gypsy* starring Tyne Daly. Near the end of the second act, the character Louise is introduced into Burlesque. Between several choruses of the musical number, "Let Me Entertain You," the young star made several complete costume changes in a matter of seconds. The costumer accomplished this feat by carefully designing several breakaway garments that would not look too bulky on the actress who overdressed in all of them before she made her first entrance in the preceding scene. The outcome was both exciting and effective and added greatly to the impact of the scene.

11.1

DIRECTOR'S COSTUME NOTES

You may use this form to keep organized notes about the following:

1. The number of costumes you feel each character in your play needs; and
2. What you feel the actor playing each role needs to be able to do in each costume.

Role	Act/ Scene	Description of Costume	Special Requirements

12

What You Need to Know About Makeup

Applying makeup before a performance used to be an important ritual. Today the practice is not nearly as popular. Perhaps one of the reasons is because so many contemporary plays are seated in realism. Actors feel they appear more natural when they wear little or no makeup. In larger auditoriums and under intensified lighting, wearing makeup is often necessary. Without a foundation, actors look too pale and washed out, and without some highlighting, the features and expressions on actors' faces are difficult for audiences to read.

Ironically, while the popularity of wearing stage makeup has diminished, the popularity of wearing street makeup has increased. Commercially, makeup has become a highly advanced and sophisticated commodity. It is readily available in a wide range of colors, shades, and styles. In fact, almost everything an actor needs can be purchased across the counters of a variety of stores.

When makeup is used, we suggest that you consider the following recommendations:

1.   When applying a foundation, actors should select a shade that either matches their own skin tone or is just one tone darker.

2.   Blend all makeup up, out, and away from the center of the face.

3.   At a minimum, actors should make up their eyes. They are the actors' most expressive facial feature.

4.   As a general rule, use a brown eyeliner, not black.

5.   For health reasons, actors should not share makeup, especially mascara and eyeliners.

6.   Actors should purchase their own powder puffs and powder brushes.

7.   Be careful of lip rouge; use it sparingly. Men should not need to use it at all if they keep the foundation off their lips.

8.   When trying to age a young actor, be selective. Here is an instance when you could choose not to use a foundation and allow the face to appear pale and blotchy. In addition to highlighting, you might add a little light shadow under the eyes and below the cheekbones. If you feel you must line the face, remember to use a brown, not a black, eyeliner. Don't invent age lines; instead, follow the actors' own laugh and frown lines. Again, we plead, be selective; less can say more. Perhaps it would be best if you just grayed the young actor's hair a bit.

9.   After applying any makeup, actors need to powder. Use only loose powder, never cake powder, and make sure that the shade is either translucent or skin tone.

10.   The first time actors apply makeup (First Dress Rehearsal), allow plenty of time to experiment.

11.   All actors should learn to apply their own makeup. Some boys will complain that they can't learn and that it is not manly. This is obviously absurd and, as part of the learning process, they need to learn the craft.

12.   Store any unused makeup in a cool place, even a refrigerator. This will prevent any separations or breakdown in the compound and will slow the buildup of bacteria.

13.   Makeup and costumes do not mix. Make sure the actors wash their hands after applying makeup and before they put on any part of their costume. It is also best when you separate the makeup area from the costume area. Once their costume is on, actors should not return to the makeup area. Makeup causes stains that only dry cleaning can remove.

14.   If your play calls for any special makeup effects, for example, stage blood, scars, black eyes, we suggest you consult Richard Corson's outstanding text, *Stage Makeup* (Prentice Hall, Englewood Cliffs, NJ, 1975). He offers a number of suggestions.

15.   Remember, when it comes to stage makeup, keep it simple and follow the old adage, "less can say more."

HAIR AND WIGS

One of the best ways to help actors capture the look of a character is by providing them with the proper hairstyle. The hairline, the color, the length, the style, and the thickness or body of the hair all contribute to what we have defined as "hairstyle." One of the best ways of doing this—especially for the women in your company—is to have them wear wigs. Wigs used to be more popular than they are now, but even today they are relatively easy to find and many brands are modestly priced. The advantage to using wigs is that they can be properly styled without tying up the actor's time. Hairpieces also have become so well made and accessible that more and more men are using them to alter their looks to better fit the characters they are portraying.

If you are working on a period play, we suggest you secure the services of a hair stylist from your community. You will find that many professionals will be interested in working on a production for program credit and a few complimentary tickets. It is best if you can introduce your hair stylist to your company during the first week of rehearsal. Most probably the actors will be asked to let their hair grow out so it can be shaped into a style that best suits the character they are playing. Regardless of the period of the play, we suggest that you discourage actors from getting their hair cut during the production process without your permission. A newly cut head of hair can draw attention to itself and never reads well from onstage.

12.1

DIRECTOR'S NOTES ON MAKEUP

Use this form to give specific directions regarding the makeup, hairstyle, and/or wigs all actors will wear in the production.

Actor/Character Name	List of Makeup Needed	Application

13 What Your Stage Manager Needs to Know

"A Little Brains, A Little Talent"

from Damn Yankees.
Music and lyrics by Richard Adler and Jerry Ross;
book by George Abbott and Douglass Wallop.

Opened in New York, May 5, 1955; ran 1,019 performances. A very successful revival opened on Broadway, May 3, 1994.

If you haven't done so already, you need to start looking for a unique individual to serve as Stage Manager of your production. Actors Equity, the professional union that represents both actors and stage managers, defines the stage manager's duties and obligations in part as assuming active responsibility for the form and discipline of rehearsal and performance, and being the executive instrument in the technical running in each performance.

That, in a nutshell, says it all. You are looking for an individual who shows real leadership capabilities: who can be firm but tactful; can remain calm during a crisis; can complete tasks in an efficient and orderly fashion; can anticipate problems and resolve them before they happen; and can remain friends with peers and still demand their respect and trust when the time comes to take charge.

Sound like a tall order? It is, so take your time in recruiting. Look for "people persons" with leadership capabilities. It also doesn't hurt if they have "a little brains, a little talent."

STAGE MANAGER'S SPECIFIC RESPONSIBILITIES DURING REHEARSALS

During rehearsals, stage managers have certain specific responsibilities. Directors may add to these but the following five are basic:

Preparing Rehearsal Space

Stage managers should arrive at least fifteen minutes before rehearsals to prepare the space. The ventilation should be checked, the floor swept, and the acting area prepared for the first scene scheduled to be rehearsed.

Prior to the first blocking rehearsal, stage managers need to tape the floor plan out on the stage or rehearsal hall so the actors and director will have a clear and accurate indication of the amount of space they have to play on.

Keeping Rehearsals Running Smoothly

If actors miss a call, stage managers are responsible for trying to locate their whereabouts.

Stage managers should also be the first to speak to actors who are late or actors who cause any discipline problems during the rehearsals. If they are going to "run" performances, stage managers need to be in an authoritative position early in the process. They also need to keep rehearsals running smoothly and on schedule.

Preparing and Maintaining the Prompt Book

The prompt book is the production's bible. It contains all the cuts and added lines made during rehearsals, the director's blocking (actors' movement), and, most important, all the cues for lights, sound, scene shifts, and special effects. The stage manager is responsible for both setting the book up and maintaining it. During dress rehearsals and performances, the prompt book becomes the single most important piece of property in the theater.

Prompting the Actors

The stage manager really has two responsibilities in this area. The commonly accepted expectation is throwing actors cues while they are still struggling with their lines. The other equally important part of this process is making sure actors are delivering their lines as they are written in the script.

Cueing actors is a relatively simple and straightforward job. Without exception, the stage manager should wait until actors ask for "line" before calling out a cue. This is less frustrating on the actors who may be pausing "in character," and not hesitating because they have forgotten their next lines.

Knowing how to handle instances when actors change line readings presents a more delicate situation. We have found it works best when stage managers take notes and talk to actors privately after rehearsals. If the situation is not corrected, however, we feel that it is perfectly acceptable for stage managers to stop rehearsals and correct line readings on the spot. Whatever method is used, it needs to be worked out carefully with the director.

Selecting and Maintaining Rehearsal Props

Stage managers are responsible for selecting suitable substitute furniture and props so rehearsals can simulate real performances. It is important that the substitute props and the blocks or benches used for furniture during rehearsals be approximately the same size as the pieces that will be used during performances.

STAGE MANAGER'S SPECIFIC RESPONSIBILITIES DURING DRESS REHEARSALS AND PERFORMANCES

During dress rehearsals and performances, stage managers have complete charge of the backstage area. Their responsibilities are many. The following step-by-step checklist should help new recruits through this challenging but rewarding experience.

1. Be the first to arrive, approximately ninety minutes before curtain.

2. Post sign-in sheet on the call board (a form that actors and crews check when they arrive).

3. Check in with the house manager and the head of wardrobe for messages.

4. Dry mop stage floor.

5. At one hour before curtain, check sign-in sheet to make sure all backstage personnel have signed in.

6. Run light and sound checks with the board operators to make sure all equipment is in working condition.

7. Check all props to make sure they are where they belong and in good working condition.

8. Set the stage. Check all furniture and set pieces to make sure they are on their proper "spike" marks. (Spike marks are tape or chalk marks that position scenery, furniture, and other set pieces.)

9. Before half-hour call, clear the stage, lower the curtain and call the pre-set cue for lights and the pre-curtain call for sound.

10. Call and inform the house manager that the house is ready to open.

11. At half-hour give actors and crews their first call. Check the sign-in sheet on the call board; all cast members should be in the theater by this time. (Many theaters require actors to sign in one hour before curtain. A great deal rests on the amount of preparation that is necessary and the size of the backstage space.)

12. Collect valuables from actors and secure them in a safe place.

13. Give "fifteen minutes to curtain" call.

14. Check in with all crews backstage and make sure everything is ready to go.

15. Give "five minutes to curtain" call.

16. Give "places" call two to three minutes before curtain.

17. Inform house manager that you are ready backstage.

18. When you get the "Go" from the House Manager, start the play.

19. During performance, call all cues for lights, sound, fly and scene shifts, and actors.

20. Continue to give calls (warning and "places please") during intermissions.

21. After performance, personally return all valuables to actors.

22. Check with crews to make sure everything has been cleared and put away.

23. Check and lock all doors and windows.

24. Unless other arrangements have been made, be the last to leave the theater.

STAGE MANAGER'S CHECKLIST DURING REHEARSALS

Make a copy of this form for your Stage Manager.

Before Each Rehearsal Begins

1. Arrive at least fifteen (15) minutes before rehearsal begins.

2. Check the ventilation (heat/air-conditioning). Know who to call if you need to report a problem.

3. Sweep the floor.

4. Set up the space in readiness for the first scene to be rehearsed.

5. Check in all rehearsal props.

6. Check mailbox or bulletin board for messages.

7. Start rehearsal on time.

During Rehearsals

8. Call or try to locate late actors.

9. Keep rehearsal running smoothly and on schedule.

10. During rehearsal, prompt actors (unless otherwise informed by the director).

11. In your prompt book, mark obvious light, sound, and special effect cues.

After Rehearsals

12. Collect and store all rehearsal props.

13. Turn off lights and other equipment used during rehearsal.

14. Secure rehearsal space: check all windows and lock doors.

STAGE MANAGER'S CHECKLIST DURING DRESS REHEARSALS AND PERFORMANCES

Make a copy of this form for your Stage Manager.

Before Curtain

1. Arrive ninety minutes before curtain.
2. Post sign-in sheet on the call board.
3. Check for messages with House Manager and head of wardrobe.
4. Dry mop stage floor.

One Hour Before Curtain

5. Check sign-in sheet for latecomers.
6. Run light and sound checks with the board operators.
7. Check all props for readiness and proper working condition.
8. Set the stage.
9. Place all furniture and set pieces on proper spike marks.
10. Lower house curtain (if one is used).
11. Give lights pre-set cue and sound pre-curtain cue.
12. Call and inform the House Manager that the house is ready to open.

Half Hour Before Curtain

13. Give half-hour call to actors and crew.
14. Check sign-in sheet for latecomers.
15. Collect valuables from actors and secure them in a safe place.

Fifteen Minutes Before Curtain

16. Give "fifteen minutes" call to actors and crew.
17. Check in with all crews backstage and make sure everything is ready to go.

Five Minutes Before Curtain

18. Give "five minutes" call to actors and crew.

Two Minutes to Curtain

19. Give "Places" call to actors and crew.

20. Inform House Manager that you are ready backstage.

21. When you get the "Go" from the House Manager, start the play.

During Performance

22. Call all cues for lights, sound, fly and scene shifts, and actors.

During Intermission

23. Give "two-minute warning" and "Places" calls.

After Performance

24. Personally return all valuables to actors.

25. Check with crews to make sure everything has been cleared and put away.

26. Check and lock all doors and windows.

27. Unless other arrangements have been made, be the last to leave the theater.

14 How to Conduct Auditions

"I Hope I Get It"

from A Chorus Line.
Music by Marvin Hamlisch;
lyrics by Edward Kleban;
conception by Michael Bennett;
book by James Kirkwood and Nicholas Dante (Neil Simon uncredited).

Opened in New York, April 15, 1975; ran 6,137 performances. Holds the record as the longest-running production on Broadway. Won the 1975 Pulitzer Prize for drama. The first touring company traveled for seven years; the second for five years, eight months.

We're going to make a bold statement: the most important phase in the entire production is the auditioning and casting process. That may sound like a broad generalization, but it is not. It is a fact. In countless productions, even on Broadway, strong casts have overcome weak scripts, or strong scripts have been ruined by miscast actors. Most professional directors agree that more than fifty (some claim as high as seventy to eighty) percent of their job is over when they complete the audition process and post their cast. Learning how to prepare for and run this process effectively is essential to the success of any production.

PREPARATION

Character Descriptions

Before casting, it is essential that you not only analyze the structure of the play but that you also become familiar with the unique qualities of each of the characters. To aid in this process, we strongly suggest that you write your own brief descriptions for each role. Start by taking note of what we refer to as the "three given circumstances":

1.   *Comments by the playwright.* A brief description of all key characters is usually given before their first entrances. While this description can be the most objective and precise, it is not always infallible. For example, a playwright might describe a character as being tall and blond, yet no reference to either the character's height or hair color is found in the dialogue itself.

2.   *Comments by other characters.* These comments can be most illuminating, but be careful. Characters are not always truthful about each other. Evaluate the validity of each remark from the audience's point of view.

3.   *Comments by the character.* Again, these comments may be quite revealing; however, you must be careful that characters are being truthful about themselves. Consider who they are speaking to and under what circumstances they are making a confession about themselves. Quite often they have something to gain by giving a distorted view of themselves.

After you have taken notes on each character's "three given circumstances," study the citations carefully, then write a brief description based on their "unchangeable" traits. "Unchangeables" are characteristics, both physical and emotional, that cannot be altered. For example, if you were going to produce the Pulitzer Prize winning play, *Abe Lincoln in Illinois* by Robert E. Sherwood, you might describe the title character as, "a tall, gangling, and pensive young man with a quiet, but resonant voice."

It is helpful if you post a list of character descriptions with audition notices. They can be an excellent guide for actors as well as an invaluable tool for directors. For an example, see Figure 14.1, Sample Audition Notice, at the end of this chapter.

Cuttings

A major decision directors need to make before the audition process begins is what scripted material they are going to use. Some directors ask actors to memorize monologues or bring in their own material, others provide cuttings but not from the play itself, and still others do not use scripted material at all but instead do exercises. We feel strongly that these methods can be intimidating and are never as effective as using selected cuttings from the play itself. You need to hear how actors are going to handle the material you are going to produce. To this end, we can offer some helpful advice:

Keep most cuttings relatively short. Scenes should not run more than two or three minutes in length—about two or three pages in an acting edition. Longer cuttings can be used during callbacks.

Pick key scenes for each of the characters. Choose scenes that display their emotional range. You may need to select more than one scene for major characters.

Pick scenes with only two and never more than three characters. Two-character scenes are best. If you find that you must include a scene with a number of characters, have an assistant read all but the two or three major roles.

Make sure you have enough copies of the script on hand to keep auditions running smoothly. If the cast is relatively small and you have only ordered a limited number of scripts, you might consider making copies of the cutting for audition purposes only.

Consider posting your list of scene cuttings with the character descriptions. We have found that actors give a better reading when they know in advance the scenes that will be read. (See Figure 14.2, Sample of Audition Scenes from *The Importance of Being Earnest,* at the end of this chapter.)

Announcements

Announcements for auditions should be made at least a week before tryouts. The copy should include the name of the play, the author, the director, the dates of the production, the date of the first rehearsal (especially if it does not follow immediately after the play is cast), the place and times auditions will be held, plus a brief description of the play and a note describing where scripts can be found. It is always important to stress that the play should be read before auditions. (See Figure 14.3, Sample Audition Announcement, at the end of this chapter.)

Tryout Form

Before the day of auditions you need to prepare sufficient copies of a tryout form. The form should be clear, straightforward, and designed to fit your specific needs.

General Information Most Often Requested on Audition Forms
- Name, Address, Phone Number
- (For Schools Only:)
  — Year: Fr. Soph. Jr. Sr.
  — Class schedule and Room numbers
- Age, Sex, Height, Weight, Hair Color, Complexion
  — This is a highly controversial list of questions, requested on most audition forms; but quite frankly, the information is unnecessary. Actors could be insulted if

asked to list their complexion and embarrassed to reveal their weight. It is strongly recommended that none of these questions be included. If you are concerned about remembering names and faces, you can request that actors attach a photo to their audition form, or you can arrange to have an assistant take instant photographs on-site.

- Special Talents (singing, dancing, playing musical instruments, fencing, etc.)
  — This request should be specific to the needs of the production itself unless you are planning to start a file on talent for future reference.

- Known Conflicts
  — This is a very important question and needs to be spelled out as specifically as possible. For example, you might write:

Rehearsals and performances for this production will cover a five-week period beginning Monday, January 4 through Saturday, February 16. Most rehearsals will be held Monday through Friday between 7:00 P.M. and 10:00 P.M. Please list all known conflicts.

- A casting policy statement:
  — This is a very important question and can avoid actors dropping out after they have been cast. Your statement might read:

Please sign and date your signature on the space provided after you have carefully read the following statement:

I am interested in being in this production and will accept any role offered to me.

Name: _____

Date _____

Additional information.   Some forms allow actors to list roles for which they would like to be considered. This is not always a good idea, especially if you have a large turnout. Individuals may feel that they were not fairly considered if they list roles that they did not read for. We recommend that you do not include this item on your form.

Some forms solicit the names of people who are interested in working on the production in some related capacity. A statement might read as follows:

Please indicate below if you would like to be considered for one of the following:

__set construction	__properties	__costumes
__lighting crew	__sound crew	__stage crew
__makeup	__publicity	__ushers

We have included a sample of an audition form (see 14.4) at the end of this chapter.

Time

It is usually best to hold auditions at different times over a two-day period (Monday, 7:00 P.M. to 9:30 P.M.; Tuesday, 3:00 P.M. to 5:30 P.M.). You might also want to post "other times by arrangement" to ensure that everyone who wants to read knows that you will make time to hear them. Each announced audition should be at least two but never more than three hours in length. You will discover that you begin to lose focus and your sense of concentration after three consecutive hours. You need, at that point, to take an extended break.

Place

Choosing the right space for auditions is an important decision. A large auditorium can be intimidating especially for inexperienced actors auditioning for the first time. Classrooms and studios are better options. The important considerations are that the room have good acoustical properties, that the location be in an area that is quiet and free from outside distractions, and that the room be large enough to provide sufficient distance between the director and those auditioning.

PROCEDURE

Now comes another critical decision: what tryout system should be used. Keep three objectives in mind as you deliberate this question:

Be fair and impartial.   First and foremost, actors must come away from auditions feeling that they were given a fair and impartial reading. Nothing will dampen support and enthusiasm more than a number of disgruntled people who feel that the audition process was a sham, a setup for certain favorites. Their attitudes can have a negative effect, not only on the current production but on future projects as well.

Announced casting. On some occasions you may decide, or even need, to precast one or more roles in a production. You may elect to bring in a more seasoned actor as a Guest Artist to help inspire and even coach other members in your company. You may be working with an all-female situation and decide to recruit a few males; or you may choose to feature one of your own actors. Whatever the reason, it is important, no, imperative, that you clearly announce and state this fact in writing before you begin the audition process.

Silent casting. Avoid silent casting at all costs. It is only natural to have certain actors in mind for specific roles, and it is perfectly acceptable to encourage them to audition. However, never—we repeat, *never*—promise anyone a role. In the first place, someone may show up who is better suited to the part. In the second place, actors who have been promised a role quite often develop an attitude and expect special attention. They often assume a "star" complex and destroy any possibility for *esprit de corps*. In the third place, actors you are tempted to pre-cast will probably turn out for auditions anyway so you have nothing to gain, and a great deal to lose, by promising them a role.

Be organized. It is also important that people feel that the audition process was organized and that their time was used efficiently. Actors develop a strong first impression of directors at this time. Directors who appear unprepared and disorganized often find that their cast is cautious and less than enthusiastic during the early stages of rehearsal. A poorly run audition can also have a long-range negative effect. It can discourage people from trying out for future productions. It is far better on the morale for the entire drama program when everyone comes away from auditions saying, "That was fun. Even if I don't get cast, I had a good time and I learned a lot."

Be effective. While actors are mainly concerned that auditions are fair and organized, directors must be concerned that the system they choose is the most effective in uncovering talent and predicting potential. No one correct system exists, and systems can be mixed. Your own personality and circumstances will determine what system is best for you. We have tried to point out the advantages and disadvantages of each.

Open Auditions

As the name suggests, the doors are wide open in open auditions and anyone can watch as long as everyone remains quiet. Many actors and directors prefer this method: actors, because they can see and hear their competition, and directors, because they can mix readers and partner them in several different ways. Actors are usually supportive of each other's work, so watching others audition can build confidence and self-esteem. Further, open auditions can take on a life of their own. They can become very stimulating and generate a lot of enthusiasm, not only for the production, but for the process as well.

On the down side, open auditions can take a long time. You have to be sensitive to the fairness issue and make sure that everyone has an equal opportunity. That means that everyone reading the same cutting should be able to read it for the same length of time, even when after thirty seconds you know that they are not right for the role. Also, if someone gives an especially strong reading, others competing for the role will either try to copy it or become discouraged and drop out. Young actors, especially, can be reluctant to take risks during an open call; it is more important that they look good in front of their peers.

We do have a suggestion on how you can keep momentum going during an open call. Set up three or four scenes in advance and let the readers prepare in the hall while you continue to watch others audition. This method can create a very stimulating and competitive atmosphere. You will need at least two assistants: one to collect audition forms and answer general questions, the other to hand out scripts or cuttings and to call couples when they are needed.

Closed Auditions

In a closed audition, actors sign up for a specific time. They can be called individually or in small groups. If they are seen individually, they read either monologues extracted from the play or scenes with the stage manager. Directors have more control over the process in a closed audition. They can take time to talk and even work with actors in a quiet and more personal manner. They have a better opportunity to break down inhibitions and see how well an individual can follow direction. Actors do not have to give up as much time when they sign up for a closed audition. They make an appointment, and although they may have to wait, they know when they are finished, they can leave.

At least two disadvantages can be found with this system. From the director's point of view, closed auditions take even longer than open auditions. Because actors are shut out from the process, they find closed auditions analogous to attending an interview and not nearly as much fun as open auditions. Like open auditions, you need at least two assistants to make closed auditions run smoothly.

Callbacks

After you have listened to everyone read at least once in either an open or closed call, you may find that you need to hear certain actors read again before you can make a final casting decision. Post callbacks. A callback notice is a list of actors being seriously considered for one or more roles in a production. The notice usually includes just a list of names; some directors list the specific roles each actor is being considered for as well. Unless you are holding callbacks for all roles in the production, you need to state that you are only recalling a select number of individuals, and that if their name does not appear on the list, it does not necessarily mean that they are not being considered for a role.

The announcement should also clearly state the time and place of the final call and request that people initial their names after they have read the notice. To save time, it is also advisable to give specific instructions on what you want those being called back to prepare. Sometimes, especially in productions that call for a large cast, you may not need to call back everyone you are considering for a role. If this is the case, make sure you make this clear on your notice. An example of this kind of notice is given on the layout form for callbacks (14.5) at the end of this chapter.

Callbacks are usually closed to the public. At this vital stage of the audition process directors need the full concentration and cooperation from actors without outside comment or distraction.

The advantages of callbacks are obvious. They give the director the opportunity to match and compare, and ultimately, eliminate actors from the list. The disadvantage, of course, is that competition becomes more keen and the atmosphere more stressful. It is imperative, therefore, that this phase of the audition be handled as efficiently as possible.

SPECIAL AUDITION TECHNIQUES

Several special techniques can be used to screen, compare, and evaluate actors' creativity. Some techniques work better during the initial stages of the audition; while others are especially effective during callbacks.

The Number Game. This is an effective way to evaluate vocal, physical, and creative skills. Actors are asked to count from one to ten. On each count they are asked to accomplish a specific task. For example, if the play you were directing was a farce, you might ask an actor, on each count, to make a broad switch from one caricature to another. In response, a male student might be a crying child on one, a sinister old curmudgeon on two, a hoodlum on three, a gentleman's gentleman on four, a nerd on five, and so on.

Movement Exercise. Most actors stand still when they are reading from a script. When movement is an important consideration for a role, it might be helpful to request selected actors to pantomime a specific task in character. For example, if one of the characters in your play is a butler or maid, you might ask those auditioning for the role to move about the stage offering drinks to a large number of guests at a cocktail party. You should instruct actors that they may speak if they choose, but the emphasis should be placed on movement, not words.

Improvisation. Some directors like to break away from the script altogether and instead ask actors to improvise a scene either from the play itself or one closely related to it. This technique might be helpful for actors who are poor readers; however, it is our opinion that improvisations require a very specialized technique and are not always a fair or effective means of evaluating acting potential. It is our recommendation that improvisations should be used sparingly and under highly controlled circumstances.

Round Robin. This is a great technique for screening actors. The director lines up a number of actors who are being considered for a specific role. They are asked to read the same short passage one after the other. The director has the opportunity to compare voices and physical differences as well as differences in interpretation.

IN SUMMARY

As we have pointed out, auditions are the most important phase in the production process and directors must develop their own style and approach if the process is going to be successful. The important criteria to keep in mind are: be open and friendly, work to create a trusting environment, keep noise down and traffic moving, articulate clearly what you are looking for, and encourage actors to take risks. Your casting pool is going to be limited, so you must go into auditions knowing that you are not going to find your ideal image for each role. It is important that you remain open and receptive to interpretations, and that you be willing to compromise and deal with limitations creatively.

Sample Audition Notice for
The Importance of Being Earnest

AUDITIONS
THE IMPORTANCE OF BEING EARNEST
Oscar Wilde
A Trivial Comedy for Serious People

Directed by Miss Doe

A Brilliant Comedy of wit and satire set in London
during the late 1890s.

CAST REQUIRES NINE ACTORS

Jack, Algernon, Gwendolen, Cecily
All young, sophisticated, attractive, blasé

Lady Bracknell
Highly sophisticated, a forbidding Grande Dame

Rev. Canon Chasuble & Miss Prism
Very respectable and proper; somewhat timid

Lane & Merriman
Highly sophisticated Gentlemen's Gentlemen

AUDITIONS ARE OPEN TO ALL—EVERYONE WELCOME

January 15th—January 16th

WCHS AUDITORIUM

3:30 P.M.–5:30 P.M. — 7:00 P.M.–9:00 P.M.

Come prepared to read from the play.

Selected scenes are posted.

Scripts are available in the library.
You may check them out overnight.

Rehearsal will begin next Monday, January 20, at 7:00 P.M.
* * * * * * * * * *
Production Dates
March 15, 16, 17, 1995

SAMPLE OF AUDITION SCENES FROM *THE IMPORTANCE OF BEING EARNEST*

The following scenes will be used for auditions.

Please Note
It is strongly recommended that you read the entire play before auditioning.

AUDITION SCENES

LANE and ALGERNON: Act I. (opening) p. 66–67
    from ALGERNON: Did you hear what I was playing, Lane?

    to LANE: Thank you, Sir.

JACK and GWENDOLEN: Act I. p. 80–82.
    from JACK: Miss Fairfax, ever since I met you…

    to GWENDOLEN   …especially when there are other people present.

LADY BRACKNELL and JACK: Act I. p. 86–88.
    from LADY B.:   Are your parents living?

    to JACK: Good morning.

CHASUBLE and MISS PRISM: Act II. p. 97–98.
    from CHASUBLE: And how are we this morning?

    to MISS PRISM: Even these metallic problems have their melodramatic side.

JACK, ALGERNON and MERRIMAN: Act II. p. 109–110.
    from MERRIMAN: I have put Mr. Earnest's thing's…

    to ALGERNON: I make up for it by being immensely over-educated.

ALGERNON and CECILY: Act II. p. 112–114.
    from ALGERNON: Oh, I don't care about Jack.

    to CECILY: You dear romantic boy.

GWENDOLEN and CECILY: Act II. p. 118–119.
    from CECILY: Dearest Gwendolen, there is no reason I should make a secret of it to you.

    to GWENDOLEN: It is obvious our social spheres have been widely different.

MISS PRISM, LADY BRACKNELL and JACK: Act III. p. 141–144.
    from CECILY: I was told you expected me in the vestry, dear Canon.

    to JACK: Gwendolen, wait here for me.

(then skip to…)

    JACK: Is this the handbag, Miss Prism?

    to JACK: Cecily, how could you have ever doubted that I had a brother?

Auditions for a Musical !

A Winnie - the - Pooh Christmas Tail
By James W. Rodgers
(In Which Winnie - the - Pooh and His Friends Help Eeyore
Have a Very Merry Christmas)

Oct. 10 - 11 3:15p.m.
Chorus Room

Cast:

Christopher Robin:	A Very Special Friend
Eeyore:	A Gloomy Donkey
Piglet:	A Pig Of Very Little Courage
Winnie - the - Pooh:	A Bear of Very Little Brain
Rabbit:	A Efficient Friend
Tigger:	A Very Energetic tiger
Kanga (and Roo):	A Very Proud Mommy
Owl:	A Very Wise Bird

Performance Dates: Dec. 2,3,7,9,& 10

Scripts and Music for auditions may be checked out overnight from Room 156

14.4

SAMPLE AUDITION FORM

AUDITION FORM

_____
Name of Play

_____
Production Dates

NAME:_____

ADDRESS: _____   PHONE: _____

YEAR (circle one):   Fr. Soph. Jr. Sr.   HOMEROOM NUMBER: _____

CLASS SCHEDULE
Include subject and room number

1ST PERIOD   4TH PERIOD

2ND PERIOD   5TH PERIOD

3RD PERIOD   6TH PERIOD

PLEASE INDICATE BELOW IF YOU HAVE HAD TRAINING IN THE FOLLOWING:

DANCE: folk _____ ballroom _____ ballet or modern _____

FENCING: _____ GYMNASTICS: _____ SINGING: _____

PLEASE NOTE
Rehearsals and performances for this production will cover a five-week period from Monday, January 17, through Saturday, March 3. Most rehearsals will be held Mondays through Fridays between 7:00 P.M. and 10:00 P.M. Please list all known conflicts below:

_____

_____

If you are not cast, indicate if you would like to work on the production:

set ___ props ___ costumes ___ lights ___ sound ___ tickets ___ program sales ___ publicity ___

CASTING POLICY
Read carefully

Please sign and date your signature on the space provided after you have carefully read the following statement:

I am interested in being in this production and will accept any role offered to me.

Name: _____   Date: _____

LAYOUT FORM FOR CALLBACKS

CALLBACKS

_____

(Title of Play)
Please initial your name below

CALLBACKS WILL BE HELD

_____

Date   Place   Time

INSTRUCTIONS
Please read carefully

PLEASE NOTE

It does not necessarily mean that you are not being considered for a role if your name does not appear on the list above. At this point, I only need to hear certain people read again. I hope to be able to cast the play by tomorrow. Thank you for your patience.

15 How to Make Intelligent Casting Decisions

"Matchmaker, Matchmaker"

from Fiddler on the Roof.
Music by Jerry Bock;
lyrics by Sheldon Harnick;
book by Joseph Stein.

Opened in New York, September 22, 1964; ran 3,242 performances. Zero Mostel, Beatrice Arthur, and Bette Midler were in the original production.

It's 1:00 A.M. You have all your casting notes and audition forms spread out in front of you. You can't sleep because you are desperately trying to figure out who is best suited to play each of the roles in your production. At this point you could be feeling anxious because you have many talented actors to choose from but not the right roles to cast them in, or you could be feeling desperate because your turnout was poor and you don't see how you can cast the production at all. Take heart. In this chapter we are going to address these and other related problems. We may not be able to totally eliminate the stress, but it is our hope to provide enough guidelines and options so that you can walk confidently up to the call-board the morning after your final auditions and post a solid, balanced, and potentially proficient cast list.

WHOM TO CAST

We'll start with the obvious. If you had an unlimited pool of actors, you would want to cast those who looked, talked, and performed exactly like images you carry around in your head—images, probably, of a combination of Broadway, film, or television stars. Dream on. The possibility of finding even one actor who comes close to your ideal perception is rare. So, practically speaking, who should you cast from your pool of second choices? What traits are the most important to consider? The following are criteria we have always found useful. They have been incorporated into a checklist included at the end of this chapter for you to reproduce at your convenience (Figure 15.1).

Who best captures the spirit of the play?   One suggestion is to give strong consideration to those actors who seem to understand the play and read the script with some ease. Even though these individuals may not exactly have the looks, the voice, or the personality you had in mind, if they are able to capture the spirit of the play, we have found that they at least have a fighting chance of making an audience believe in them.

Whom will the audience most readily accept in the role?   This may sound like a contradiction to the first suggestion, and to a certain extent it is. At least, it's a warning. A large majority of high school and community theater audiences know the true personalities of the performers you are considering. Therefore, if you are thinking of casting the class or neighborhood clown in a serious romantic role, or a shy, retiring girl as the brazen hussy because they read best for the roles, you need to consider potential audience reaction. You don't want to embarrass actors in front of their peers or jeopardize the success of the production. While it is honorable to cultivate talent, it is more important that each person cast has every opportunity to succeed. Your objective should be to build confidence and provide a positive learning experience so that your actors will want to audition again. For these reasons, don't give in to, but be sensitive to, the audience factor.

Who complements and offers variety and contrast?   You don't want to cast a Romeo without thinking about his Juliet. The two actors need to complement each other, physically and vocally. Further, the rest of the players around them need to provide physical and vocal variety. It is important to consider a wide range of types, especially in large-cast productions.

Who will fit in best with the rest of the cast? Here comes another contradiction. At the same time that you are looking for actors who complement each other and offer variety, you need to be aware of potential personality conflicts and the dynamics offstage relationships could have on the rehearsal process. For example, it probably isn't a good idea to cast a couple that has just broken up as George and Emily in *Our Town*. Actors must be able to work effectively with each other. If they don't, it is obvious that their offstage conflicts can greatly interfere with your ability to mount a quality production.

Whom would I most like to work with on this role? If all else is equal, nothing is wrong with casting actors you feel you would enjoy working with. In fact, you are more likely to have success directing an actor you have a friendly and trusting relationship with over another who reads well but has an attitude problem. Further, we need to pass on a warning about actors who read exceptionally well but have a reputation for being difficult. Often "what you see is what you get." In other words, because of their egos and their "you-can't-tell-me, I-know-it-all" attitudes, they don't develop during the rehearsal process. Consequently, by performance, they're not part of the ensemble and they stand out for all the wrong reasons. Our advice is to cast a slow developer with a positive attitude, an individual who is enthusiastic and appears open and willing to accept direction.

Educationally, who would gain most from this experience? Sometimes you need to consider other factors when casting a school production. Perhaps you have a senior who has been cast in other productions but has never had a major role, or maybe a freshman who shows great potential and might blossom if given an opportunity. These can be valid reasons for casting a less secure student over a more skilled one who has had a number of major roles. You don't want to get the reputation for running a closed shop. One of your objectives should be to identify new talent and another, to provide a creative outlet for as many people as possible.

Remember, casting represents a long-range commitment. You and the rest of your company will be working together over a five- to eight-week period. You will want to surround yourself with individuals who are dedicated to the project, committed to their work, and fun to be around. Therefore, our advice is to cast from the heart. Let your instincts guide your decisions. Nine times out of ten the results will be rewarding.

Double Casting

We still have not addressed the problem of what to do when you have a large number of talented actors and not enough roles. Quite frankly, the options are limited. Some sympathetic directors have tried double casting one or more roles, sometimes even the entire play. Except on rare occasions, we have found that this effort creates more problems than it solves. For the actors, double casting can cause undue friction. Too often actors cast in the same role copy each other's work or spend much of the rehearsal process competing against each other. Rarely is it a healthy or productive learning experience.

As a director, you have to be prepared to spend almost twice the time and energy rehearsing the play. You must be careful that you give each of the two actors double cast equal time or one will feel slighted and become disinterested or disgruntled.

Still other problems arise. You must be sure that each double-cast actor has an opportunity to perform and, unless some other arrangement has been clearly stated, that each actor has an equal number of public performances. Dress rehearsals don't count. Costumes are also a consideration. Unless the two actors are close to the same size, two costumes must be provided. In our opinion, a better option over double casting is offering another production opportunity.

Poor Turnout

Now we come to the more frustrating but realistic problem. What do you do when you find, for whatever reasons, that you don't have enough talent to cast a production? Quite often this can be the scenario: You announce the play and set auditions. You generate a lot of enthusiasm. When the day arrives, scores of females turn out but only a handful of males, and, worst yet, some of the males—the better ones, of course—have conflicts that you can't work around. What do you do? Well, relax, we can offer some possibilities.

First, you can *consider cutting some of the minor roles.* This is risky and can go against copyright laws, so read the arrangement page in the acting edition carefully. If you are within rights, make sure that in cutting, you do nothing to compromise the author's intent. A far better option is to combine the lines of two or more characters into one role. Another option is to cast one actor in several roles.

Cutting characters or combining roles may not solve your problem. You may still have major holes in your casting. Some directors have tried to *recruit* at this point. They have made personal contacts with actors and flattered them into playing a role. This is not a good option. A recruited actor rarely has the same attitude or commitment as those who show up at auditions. Also, actors who have been recruited are not always easy to direct. They know they are doing you a favor and their egos often get in the way, causing friction not only with you, the director, but with other members of the cast as well.

In some plays you can *change the gender of a character* and not destroy the intent of the play. Neil Simon rewrote *The Odd Couple* for two women; some seasons past, during the Broadway run, the leading male role in the drama, *Whose Life Is It Anyway,* was rewritten for Mary Tyler Moore; and an all-female acting edition of the popular courtroom drama *Twelve Angry Men* has been published under the title *Twelve Angry Women.* After careful and sensitive analysis, you might discover that some male roles in your play can easily be renamed and played with the same effect by women. This must be done judiciously and with great care. Remember, the director's first and legal obligation is to the playwright.

One final option, which might be the best and fairest alternative, is to seriously *consider changing plays.* You can weigh and analyze the abilities of the actors you want to cast from your audition pool and then search for a play that best suits their talents. This option can present image problems for community theaters and other organizations where a season is announced and presold to the public in the form of a season ticket. This is rarely the case in high schools. Most high schools do not start publicizing the play until rehearsals are in progress. Therefore, any changes in the bill-of-fare will probably go unnoticed by a large majority of the potential audience.

SPECIAL WARNINGS

You need to be alerted to a few other areas of concern before you even enter into the casting phase of the production process.

Never Cast by Committee

It is perfectly acceptable to get input during the casting process from whomever you choose—students, faculty, even parents. However, you need to make it clear to these individuals that they are consultants only and that the final decision in all casting matters is your responsibility. After all, you are the individual who must work with the cast; it is your artistic energy that needs to guide all design decisions, and ultimately, the success or failure of the production rests squarely on your shoulders. If you assume these responsibilities—in addition to all your others—you don't need anyone else casting your play for you.

Never Cast Understudies

Professional actors will tell you the most frustrating and often disheartening job in their profession is playing understudy or stand-in. In large companies, understudies are usually members of the company cast in minor roles, but stand-ins are never in the production. Rather, they are required to check into the theater each night and stay on call throughout the performance. They must rehearse, usually only with the stage manager or other stand-ins and understudies, once a week to keep up in the role, but they never go on unless the actor they are covering gets sick. Even when a leading player takes a scheduled vacation, no one has any guarantee that the stand-in will go on. In many productions, the producers will use this occasion to bring in another "name" (star), perhaps someone being groomed for a touring company. Why then do actors accept understudy and stand-in offers? The answer is simple—money. The pay is respectable, and, of course, they always have a wild chance that they will get to go on. The sad fact is that many fine actors have spent their careers being lost as stand-ins for stars who never missed a performance.

High school, community, and university theaters rarely cast understudies. Acting pools are limited, rehearsal periods are short, and the number of performances is fixed and rarely extended. When directors do decide to cover roles, it should be for a definite purpose and their motives should be made clear to the individuals being assigned the responsibility. On rare occasions a director might want to groom a young performer for an upcoming production, or a director might decide to cast an individual who has a known conflict and needs an understudy to cover the role for key rehearsals or even a performance. Whatever the situation, the director should make it clear to the actor the limitations of the assignment. If possible, understudies should be given another assignment in the production, such as assistant stage manager or assistant to the director, so they feel part of the ensemble. If you do decide to use understudies, recognize that it is a thankless and frustrating job and the actors cast in this position can easily feel like second-class citizens.

Be Sensitive to Social Issues When Casting

All communities deal with prejudice on some level and directors need to be sensitive to issues that are prevalent. This is especially true in high schools. Parents or school administrators may not be ready to accept ethnically or racially mixed casting, especially in romantic roles. Other communities may expect, or even demand, a cast that is balanced by race or religion. These kinds of issues can be awkward and should be addressed before casting begins. A misjudgment or defiance on the part of a director might ruin morale, cause humiliation, and even jeopardize not only the production but an entire theater program for years. Even more important, actors need to be protected from embarrassment. Our suggestion is to draw up a policy in collaboration with your school administrators or with your community theater board. This policy should specify requirements for special needs plays. For example:

> *Raisin in the Sun:* seeking seven males, three females, and one child who are African-American, and one male who is white.

> *Winnie-the-Pooh Christmas Tail:* seeking eight actors of any gender or any ethnic background.

Be Prepared for a Casting Backlash

Regardless of how fair and sensitive you might be in casting, a director is bound to bruise someone's ego. The more exciting and competitive the audition, the more vulnerable and emotional the reaction. Be prepared to deal, for a day or even up to a week, with extreme displays of emotion. The actors who have been cast, especially the leads, will be on a high, the like of which you'll probably not see again. However, those who did not get cast, or, worse yet, got cast but not in a major role, will likely display in public and especially in front of you, all seven stages of the grief process. Even when reactions seem extreme and out of proportion, it is important that you take time to be with those individuals, especially the ones who are extremely angry, hurt, or depressed. We have found that the best way to counsel is to be open and sincere. Acknowledge feelings ("I can see that you are very angry"), and when possible, identify with the moment ("I remember how depressed I felt when I didn't get the role I thought I was born to play"). Regardless of your personal reaction, don't belittle the actors. Try, instead, to put the situation into perspective. Tell them honestly, but tactfully, the real reasons they were not cast. The most important thing you must do before you end a session is to affirm an individual as a person. If possible, also try to preserve their enthusiasm for theater. If you feel that they are not talented, try to guide them to other areas of the production process, areas not just where they might be of service to you, but more important, where they might excel. If, on the other hand, they did display talent but were not quite suited for the current play, assure them of this fact and encourage them to try again.

ANNOUNCING THE CAST

Before we bring this chapter to a close, we wanted to discuss the items you need to include on a casting notice. Obviously the centerpiece of the announcement will be a cast list. We have found it is best to announce the cast using the order that appears in the acting edition, which is usually the order of appearance, or alphabetically by name. In addition, we suggest that you include the time, date, and place of the first rehearsal. Also request that the actors initial their names to assure that they have read the notice. It is important to include a short, sincere acknowledgment to everyone who auditioned. The note needs to be addressed primarily to those who were not cast. It should be personal and not perfunctory. Its main purpose is to smooth the waters and to generate continued interest in the program. A sample cast announcement can be found at the end of this chapter (Figure 15.2).

It is important that you don't delay posting your cast notice. Holding up the announcement, for whatever reasons, can cut into your rehearsal time, add undue stress on those who auditioned, or worse yet, dissipate the enthusiasm for the production. If you find that you are unable to cast all the roles, simply list "To Be Announced" after a character's name. You might even include a footnote stating that you are still reading for certain roles and anyone interested should contact you immediately.

As we noted at the beginning of the previous chapter, the whole audition process, which of course includes casting, is the most important phase of the production. The rest of your journey is shaped by the decisions you make over a brief two- or three-day period. You have to hope that your preparation and instincts have served you well. Only time will tell, so on with the journey!

CASTING DECISIONS CHECKLIST

Consider the following questions carefully before making your final casting decisions:

1. Who best captures the spirit of the play?
2. Whom will the audience most readily accept in the role?
3. Who will complement the other actors I am considering, and who offers variety and contrast, both physically and vocally, to the cast?
4. Who will fit in best with the rest of the cast?
5. Whom would I most like to work with on this role?
6. Educationally, who would gain most from this experience?

NOTES

_____

_____

_____

_____

_____

_____

_____

_____

_____

_____

_____

_____

SAMPLE CAST ANNOUNCEMENT

Final Casting
for

THE IMPORTANCE OF BEING EARNEST

Algernon Moncrieff	Eric Johnson
Lane	To be announced*
Jack Worthing	Roger Leaser
Lady Bracknell	Georgia Farrell
Gwendolen Fairfax	Martha Brenier
Miss Prism	Shelley Scott
Cecily Cardew	Lisa Jones
Rev. Canon Chasuble	Paul Jones
Merriman	To be announced*

Stage Manager: Todd Lacy

NOTE: PLEASE INITIAL YOUR NAME AFTER YOU HAVE READ THIS NOTICE

*I am still reading for the roles of Lane and Merriman. Anyone interested in being considered for these roles should contact me immediately in room 106. Thank you.

FIRST REHEARSAL: WEDNESDAY EVENING, SEPTEMBER 15 7:00 P.M.

You may pick up your script in the Secretary's Office.

Please bring a pencil to the first rehearsal.

TO ALL WHO AUDITIONED

Over twenty-five (25) people auditioned for this production. You all gave fine readings, and I had many options to consider. I sincerely appreciate your interest and wish I could have used more of you. Perhaps some of you would be interested in working on one of the crews. If you didn't get cast, please don't be discouraged. We will be auditioning the spring musical late in January.

Act Three

REHEARSALS
AND PERFORMANCES

How to Get the Most Out of Rehearsals

"It's a Simple Little System"

from Bells Are Ringing. *Music by Jule Styne; lyrics and book by Betty Comden and Aldolf Green.*

Opened in New York, November 29, 1956; ran 924 performances. Directed by Jerome Robbins, choreographed by Robbins and Bob Fosse; the musical starred Judy Holliday.

In Chapter 6 we discussed in detail the nine sections of a rehearsal schedule: Orientation, Read-through, Blocking, Line, Working, Run-through, Polishing, Technical, and Dress Rehearsals. These sections can be divided into three stages:

- *Study and Analysis.* This stage includes the Orientation and Read-through rehearsals.
- *Development.* The second stage includes Blocking rehearsals, Line rehearsals, Working rehearsals, Run-throughs, and Polishing rehearsals.
- *Mounting.* The final stage includes Technical rehearsals, Dress rehearsals, and Previews.

Morale and discipline are important throughout all phases of the rehearsal process and can be most volatile during the Development stage. This is the longest and most decisive phase, and particularly during these sections, maintaining a positive atmosphere in rehearsals requires a delicate balance.

- The energy should be focused but relaxed.
- The cast should be loose but never lazy, excited but never fearful.
- Suggestions should be offered by everyone, but decisions made only by the director.

How is this possible? In this chapter we are going to offer a number of suggestions and some guidelines, "a simple little system," that can help make the Development phase of the rehearsal process a positive and enriching experience.

GUIDELINES FOR EFFECTIVE LEADERSHIP

Enthusiasm, energy, efficiency, and effective communication are the four cornerstones of successful direction. If you possess these qualities, you are well on your way to winning respect from your performers and providing the kind of atmosphere that is most conducive for creative growth and development. In addition, we can offer six specific suggestions that can make the Development phase of the rehearsal process more enjoyable and fulfilling.

1. *State your agenda.*   Set specific goals for each rehearsal and state them clearly to the company at the beginning of each rehearsal.

2. *Be flexible.*   Be sensitive to the individual needs of each cast member; know when to push and when to let go.

3. *Encourage and praise.*   The best way for actors to improve is to know when they are doing something right. Don't dwell on what doesn't work unless you have a specific suggestion on how to fix it.

4. *Give attention to all members of the group.*   Actors get nervous if they don't receive any feedback.

5. *Be human.*   Be open and honest; don't be afraid to admit that you don't have all the answers.

6. *Listen well.*   Seek to create an ensemble. Theater is a collaborative art, not a one-person show.

REHEARSAL ETIQUETTE

Another way of ensuring that rehearsals run smoothly is to establish a standard list of rehearsal rules. All directors expect certain things from their casts, but few take the time to clearly articulate these expectations. We strongly recommend that you print your standard list of rehearsal rules and hand out a copy with the rehearsal schedule at your first company meeting. The list should be simple and short and written in direct but positive language. The rehearsal etiquette list that follows is a sample that you can use as a guideline. A reproducible form can be found at the end of this chapter (Figure 16.1).

1. *Rehearsals will start promptly.*   It is recommended that you arrive at least five minutes before rehearsal begins. Use this time to clear your mind and focus on the work ahead.

2. *Dress appropriately.*   Wear loose clothing and comfortable shoes—an ensemble that will not restrict movement in any way.

3. *Bring a pencil and a small journal to each rehearsal.*   Use your journal to record director's comments, summary of any research, observations about your character, as well as your character's relationship to other characters in the play.

4. *Don't chew gum during rehearsals.*

5. *Hair should be kept out of the face.*   The face is the most *expressive* part of your body; it needs to be seen.

6. *Smoking and eating are not permitted in the rehearsal hall.*

7. *Visitors are permitted to observe most rehearsals.*   Permission needs to be cleared by the director at least one day before the request.

8. *Casual and excessive talking is not allowed in the rehearsal hall.*

9. *Stay in the rehearsal room.*   If you need to leave the rehearsal room for any reason, make sure you inform the stage manager as to your whereabouts.

10. *Actors waiting to work are strongly urged to use their time productively.*   Memorize lines, review blocking, or read materials related to the production.

REHEARSAL FORMAT

Our final suggestion is to establish a standard format for each rehearsal during the Development stage. A set agenda will not only keep you on track but will give your actors a sense of security.

Suggested Format for Development Rehearsals

Warm-ups	10 to 30 minutes in length
Work period	not to exceed three hours
Break	10 minutes in length
Wrap-up	5 to 10 minutes in length

Warm-ups.   We recommend that the first twenty to thirty minutes of all rehearsals during the Development phase of the rehearsal process be set aside for group warm-ups. Relaxing and then preparing both the body and the voice for a vigorous workout should be an integral part of the rehearsal process. Each session should include three types of activity:

- physical exercises to limber up the body
- vocal exercises to open and strengthen the voice
- group exercises or games to engender team spirit

The first two exercises, physical and vocal warm-ups, protect actors against damage to their instrument, while group exercises are a valuable step in building esprit de corps, a true sense of ensemble. A standard set of warm-up exercises has been provided at the end of this chapter (Figure 16.2). Other suggestions can be found in *Theater Games for Rehearsal: A Director's Handbook* by Viola Spolin.

Work Period.   The work period of each rehearsal should be planned very carefully. Set a specific agenda for the two to three hours available to you and try to stick to it. Don't call actors unless you plan to really work with them; let the stage manager read in the lines of characters that only make a brief entrance.

Breaks.   If you are working the same people during the entire work period, it is probably best if you take a ten-minute break after about ninety minutes of rehearsal. Be aware, however, that a break can dissipate both energy and concentration. For this reason, we recommend that you include breaks only when they are absolutely necessary. We would rather complete the rehearsal early rather than extend it with one or two breaks.

Wrap-up.   Conclude each rehearsal with a wrap-up session. Give your assessment of the rehearsal; comment on each actor's work and development, when appropriate, and announce what you plan to cover at the next rehearsal session. Always allow time for the actors to ask questions or offer observations. Encourage their input and listen carefully to their comments. Follow up immediately on any frustrations or problems that might surface.

In summary, if you can remain open to your cast and have a well thought-out agenda for each rehearsal, Development should be the most enriching and rewarding phase of the rehearsal process.

16.1

A STANDARD LIST OF REHEARSAL EXPECTATIONS

1. *Rehearsals will start promptly.* It is recommended that you arrive at least five minutes before rehearsal begins. Use this time to clear your mind and focus on the work ahead.

2. *Dress appropriately.* Wear loose clothing and comfortable shoes—an ensemble that will not restrict movement in any way.

3. *Bring a pencil and a small journal to each rehearsal.* Use your journal to record director's comments, summary of any research, observations about your character, as well as your character's relationship to other characters in the play.

4. *Don't chew gum during rehearsals.*

5. *Hair should be kept out of the face.* The face is the most *expressive* part of your body; it needs to be seen.

6. *Smoking and eating are not permitted in the rehearsal hall.*

7. *Visitors are permitted to observe most rehearsals.* Permission needs to be cleared by the director at least one day before the request.

8. *Casual and excessive talking is not allowed in the rehearsal hall.*

9. *Stay in the rehearsal room.* If you need to leave the rehearsal room for any reason, make sure you inform the stage manager as to your whereabouts.

10. *Actors waiting to work are strongly urged to use their time productively.* Memorize lines, review blocking, or read materials related to the production.

11. *Additional expectations:*

_____

_____

_____

_____

_____

_____

_____

_____

_____

_____

_____

_____

A STANDARD SET OF WARM-UP EXERCISES

Step 1: Stretching and Relaxing

Tense and then relax each section of the body: the neck, arms, wrists, torso, legs, ankles, and feet. Identify each section of the body by first tensing it; then use slow, circular movements to relax the area. At the end of this step, involve the entire body in a free-flowing, dancelike motion that takes you around and about the room. Music can enhance this part of the exercise.

Step 2: Vocal Relaxation and Flexibility

First, yawn and work out all the tension in your jaw. Relax the lips by pushing air through them and making a motorboat sound. Relax the tongue by opening your mouth wide, sticking it out and working it around the opening of your mouth. Don't adjust the size of your mouth to accommodate your tongue; make your tongue do the work. Work the tongue both clockwise and counter clockwise.

Next, engage your vocal cords by singing on a comfortable, neutral tone, "ma, me, my, mo, mu." Really flex the placement of your lips during this exercise.

Now involve your entire vocal mechanism in a tongue-twisting exercise. The objective is to speak the piece in one breath and to pronounce all the words correctly. Start slowly and then gradually work up to a rapid rate.

> Betty Botta bought some butter
> But she said, "This butter's bitter.
> If I put it in my batter,
> it will make my batter bitter.
> But if I buy a bit of butter
> better than my bitter butter,
> and I put it in my batter,
> it will make my batter better."
> So Betty Botta bought a bit of
> better butter.
> And she put it in her batter.
> And her batter was not bitter.
> So 'twas better Betty Botta
> bought a bit of better butter.

Step 3: Group Exercises to Build Ensemble

Partner with someone you have a scene with in the play. Face your partner and leave at least two feet of space between you. Now imagine that you are standing in front of a mirror. One partner leads, the other follows. Go slowly at first and then, as you find each other's rhythm and begin to communicate on a subliminal level, speed up the movements until you are making gestures and facial expressions naturally. Communicate with your eyes and switch leadership often. The objective is to mirror so well, that someone watching the two of you could not tell who is initiating the movement.

17 How to Stage, or Block, Your Play

"Every Little Movement"

from Madame Sherry. *Music by Karl Hoschana; book and lyrics by Otto Hauerbach (Harbach).*

Opened in New York, August 30, 1910; ran 231 performances. Billed as a "musical vaudeville" in three acts.

Many directors would agree that the most stressful rehearsal is the first day of blocking when they are scheduled to get actors up on their feet and start moving them about on the stage for the first time. Regardless of how long you have been practicing your craft, the beginning of this stage of the rehearsal process is like learning to walk all over again; you feel anxious and more than a little intimidated. However, we have learned that you don't have to be overwhelmed. If you have thoroughly familiarized yourself with your play and the motivations of the characters, the initial blocking rehearsals can be a stimulating and satisfying time.

OBJECTIVE

Traditionally, blocking rehearsals have been scheduled early in the rehearsal process to help actors. Most actors will tell you that it is much easier to memorize lines when they can visualize them with actions or business. For directors, early blocking can also surface any design problems that have not been addressed in preproduction meetings.

Stage Movement and Stage Business

Before we get too involved in the main issues of this chapter, it is important for you to understand the difference between stage movement and stage business. Stage movement is the process of shifting actors from one place to another on stage. Stage business is all visual activity performed by actors that does not require movement (e.g., fixing drinks, lighting and smoking a cigarette, embracing and kissing.).

Warning: Many scripts include specific directions for both stage movement and stage business. In most instances these directions were not written by the playwright but rather by the stage manager from the first professional production. Your concept of scene, or the arrangement of your stage space (the ground plan) may differ from the original production. Therefore, we recommend that you consider these directions but don't be limited by them. If they seem to work for you, follow them; if they don't, discard them and follow the actors' and your own instincts instead.

A THREE-PHASE PROCESS

Over the years we have discovered that there are three phases to the blocking process: preparation, layout, and fine-tuning. To succeed in each phase, you need to focus your attention, clear your mind, and free your imagination. Throughout the entire process play the magic "if" game: "If I were this character (not "if I were playing this character," but "if I *were* this character") where would I go and/or what would I do at this given moment?" In order for you to respond within the context of the play, it is imperative that you have a thorough knowledge of the script and its structure, as well as a complete understanding of each of the characters: their goals, motivations, and their function in each scene. (If you are confused or totally lost at this point, we suggest that you review Chapter 5, How to Unravel a Play's Meaning.)

Phase 1: Preparation

To be fully prepared for your first blocking rehearsal, you need to devote several long sessions to pre-blocking certain aspects of the action. We suggest that you set aside three to six one-and-one-half-hour to three-hour sessions depending on the length and complexity of your play. Sequester yourself away from the maddening crowds in a cozy cottage with a copy of the ground plan, your script, several pencils, and a pot of strong coffee. If you can't afford the cottage, at least get away from the phone, the TV, and human distractions. (Some cats and dogs are exceptions.)

Before you start blocking, divide your script into workable segments: acts, scenes, or working units. Never try to pre-block more than one act per session. If your play is divided into one or two long acts and each act is highly involved, or if your attention span is short, you may need to separate these acts into several sections or working units.

In Chapter 5 we explained that the best breakdown of working units is French Scenes. Remember, a French Scene is a division of an act or scene framed by the entrance or exit of a major character in the play. If the same characters remain on stage during the entire act or scene you are going to work on, divide your material into motivational units. Motivational units are short intervals marked by a change in subject matter or motivation.

Time to get down to work. First, use your imagination and place yourself squarely on your stage in the middle of the world of your play. Envision your set complete with all furniture and props in their proper places. Stay in this virtual reality state throughout this phase of the process.

Second, determine all the entrances and exits of all the characters in the scene. This should be a rather obvious and easy process, especially in a realistic play. In a script calling for a unit or open setting, follow your intuition and try to incorporate as much variety as possible into your decisions. To make it easier to record blocking when an open or unit set is designated, we recommend that you mark all the possible entrances with a number and all the platforms and other acting areas with a letter. When you get on stage, you can chalk all these numbers and letters on the floor of your rehearsal space. Then it becomes easy to give general directions; you simply tell an actor, for instance, to "enter *four* and cross to platform *C.*"

Third, read through the section you are working on and underline and record all the movement and business given by the playwright in the actual lines of the play, and consider if you want to incorporate any of the movement and business suggested in parentheses. At this point you may have to make some decisions. For example, if in one of the lines of the scene, a character invites another character to sit, your job will be to determine where. Look closely at your ground plan, get into the head of your characters and make a decision. Follow your instincts. Don't worry if it's right or wrong; you can always change it later. The important thing is to get inside the world of your play; once you do, the characters will start taking over and tell you where they should move, sit, and stand. It's the creative process at work.

Fourth, determine the purpose of the scene. Why has it been written? Is it there to

- advance the plot;
- further our understanding of the characters;
- debate a point-of-view;
- create atmosphere;

- provide a diversion or distraction; or
- more than one of the above?

Fifth, find the key moment in the scene. If you understand the purpose of the scene, the key moment should become obvious. Look to see who has the focus at this moment. Decide the best, the most interesting, or the most logical place for this character to be standing or sitting at the key moment. Then, place the other characters in what you consider the best relationship to the focal character. Here, again, is where it is important to get inside the head of the characters and let them tell you where they want to be in relationship to each other. What item on the stage (a particular chair, a window, a liquor counter, etc.) would they most likely be near? So much of this method is common sense and a thorough understanding of the play. Use the given circumstances in the script and your own intuition as a guide. Trust your instincts and don't step out of the situation too often to analyze or judge your decisions; you will only stifle your creative juices.

Don't worry about blocking every moment in your scene. At this point, you need only set entrances and exits, underline and record all business and movement given by the playwright in the dialogue of the play, consider the selected suggestions given by the original stage manager in parentheses, and decide on the stage compositions for the key moment in each French Scene. The rest of the blocking can be worked out in collaboration with your actors when you get into rehearsal.

Phase 2: Layout

Before you start blocking rehearsals, you must make sure that the ground plan has been marked out to scale with tape on the floor of the stage or on the floor of your rehearsal space. Find substitute crates, chairs, cubes, benches, whatever, to simulate the furniture that will be used on the set. These substitutions do not need to look like the actual object but they do need to be the approximate size.

Begin your first blocking rehearsal by going over the ground plan in detail with your actors. Make sure that they understand the height of all platforms as well as the shape, size, and stability of each object in the acting space. Spell out precisely how each item will work and what they can sit, stand, and/or lean on. Also make sure that you explain in detail where each entrance leads and what they can see out of each window.

When you start to dictate your blocking, make sure that each actor has a pencil. Never allow an actor to record blocking in ink. Go slowly so actors can record your exact directions to them. As you talk through what you have pre-blocked, make sure that you take time to explain the motivation behind the direction. For example, you might say, "You cross to the window at this point because you need to pull away; you would like to leave but can't. By going to the window, you can at least look out beyond the boundaries of the room."

We have found that it is best for the actors and you if you talk through the blocking for two or more pages at a time, before you ask the actors to execute it. In this way, you can let them run an entire sequence without constant interruption. When you use this technique, you can watch the scene instead of your script. Getting your nose out of your script is an important prerequisite to good blocking. You need to work off the instincts of the actors. More often than not, they will give you the inspiration you need to make sound decisions for those moments that you have left open. You can only play off the actors' instincts when you watch and listen closely to the scene.

As you watch, your actors may start to improvise their own blocking. Don't discourage them. Quite often, the actors' instincts are far more exciting and interesting than your own because while you have been working on the play as a whole, each of your actors has been concentrating on just his or her own character. If your actors are at all bright and intuitive, they will have some strong instincts and will want to follow them. Encourage them; the more they can contribute to the effort, the more ownership they have in the production.

Phase 3: Fine-tuning

The final phase of blocking will take place over the remaining course of the rehearsal process. Each time you return to a scene, you may need to reshape or retune it slightly. This is part of its natural development. When it occurs, it is a clear indication that both you and your actors are becoming more and more familiar with the script, the character's motivations, and the meaning behind the lines. To give clear focus and shape to each scene, you need to constantly fine-tune it. Plays, like many other forms of art, need a gestation period. Be open and receptive to this fact. Continue to ask questions that encourage actors to use their creative instincts and to respond in character.

SPECIAL AND IMPORTANT TECHNIQUES

You can do several things to move the blocking process forward in a positive and creative way. The following are just three suggestions that we have found are positive reinforcements to this process:

Complement: When an actor makes a bold choice and the move looks good to you, say so. You don't need to interrupt the scene. Just call out, "Good," or "Yes." After the first couple of times, the actors will know that you are not stopping the scene, only indicating your approval.

Challenge: When an actor freezes and cannot find a motivation to move, prod a little. Try asking questions: "You have just been insulted. Does your next line suggest that you hold your ground or move away?" or "You told me your character is nervous in this scene but you haven't moved yet. What do you think your character would do if he felt trapped in this space?"

Comment: Sometimes actors will move based on their own instincts rather than on the instincts of their characters. When this happens, it is important to stop the scene and comment on the movement: "It weakens your character to sit on that line," or "Try delivering that line with more anger and see how it feels."

SPECIFIC GUIDELINES

When you start blocking actors, we can offer a number of specific pointers. Use these guidelines when they seem appropriate but do not be restricted by them. Like so many aspects of the art of directing, there are exceptions. However, we believe that it is best to learn the basic rules of the craft before you break them. More often than not they do apply and will serve you and your production well.

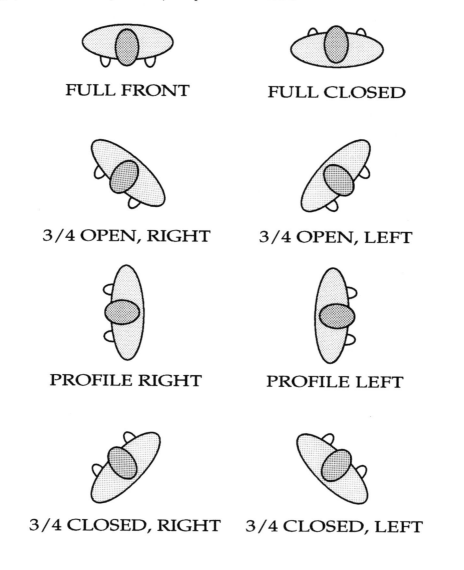

FULL FRONT   FULL CLOSED

3/4 OPEN, RIGHT   3/4 OPEN, LEFT

PROFILE RIGHT   PROFILE LEFT

3/4 CLOSED, RIGHT   3/4 CLOSED, LEFT

Body Positions: It is best when an actor's face can be seen by the audience. This does not mean that actors need to face the audience; in fact, only on rare occasions is this appropriate. We do suggest, however, that actors keep their bodies in an open position and when they are sharing a scene, that the two actors play three-quarters front rather than full profile.

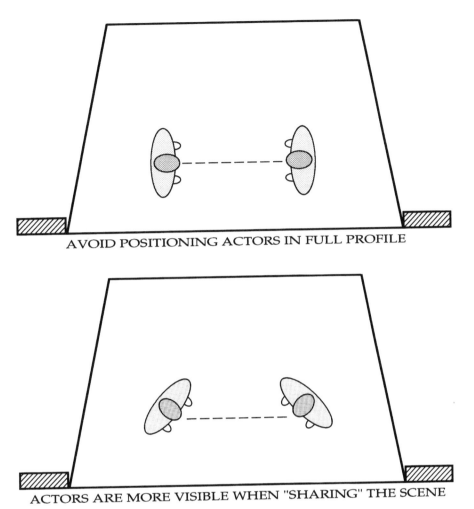

AVOID POSITIONING ACTORS IN FULL PROFILE

ACTORS ARE MORE VISIBLE WHEN "SHARING" THE SCENE

Arrangements: When three or more actors are sharing a scene, it is best when they arrange themselves in a triangle. Triangles appear more natural than semicircles. In fact, it is usually necessary to break up actors standing in straight lines and semicircles into smaller, more interesting triangular groupings.

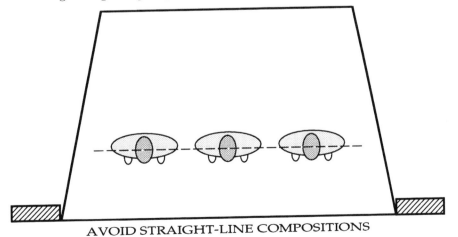

AVOID STRAIGHT-LINE COMPOSITIONS

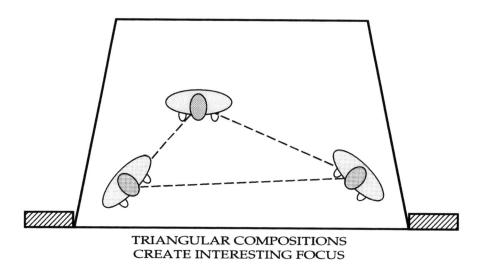

**TRIANGULAR COMPOSITIONS
CREATE INTERESTING FOCUS**

Placement: It is important that you know the strength of various playing areas on a proscenium stage. The stage, itself, can be divided into fifteen areas:

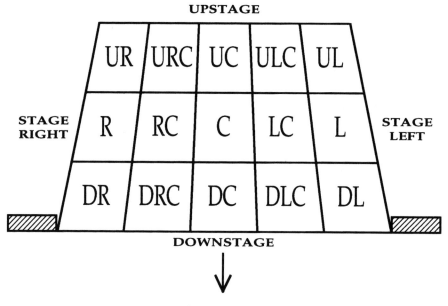

The terminology in this figure has been reduced to symbols to help actors and stage managers record blocking quickly. *R, C,* and *L* stand for right, center, and left. *U* and *D* stand for up and down. Also take note that the nomenclature is based on the actors' right and left as they face the audience, and that upstage is away from the audience and toward the back of the stage.

The prominence of the area is dictated by the sight lines of the auditorium. The strongest areas are downstage center, center, and upstage center. Downstage right is considered by some directors to be more prominent than downstage left because our eyes are more accustomed to read from left to right.

Turns: Since it is important that the audience be able to see the actor's face as much as possible, we recommend that actors position themselves so that they can make an open rather than a closed turn. An open turn is made toward the audience, while a closed turn is away from the audience. However, the guiding principle should be that all turns appear natural. If a closed turn is the only natural option, use it.

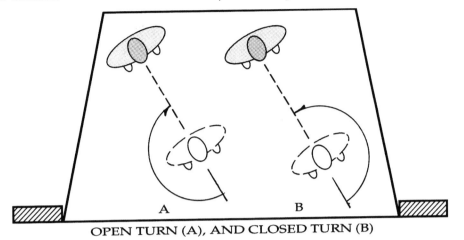

OPEN TURN (A), AND CLOSED TURN (B)

Crosses: When actors move on one of their speeches, in most instances, they should cross downstage or in front of other actors.

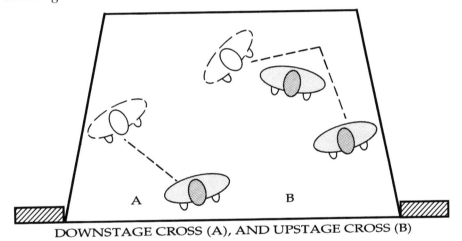

DOWNSTAGE CROSS (A), AND UPSTAGE CROSS (B)

Dressing Stage: When one actor moves away from a grouping of three or more, it is important for the remaining actors to counter or adjust their positions in order to better balance or "dress" the stage.

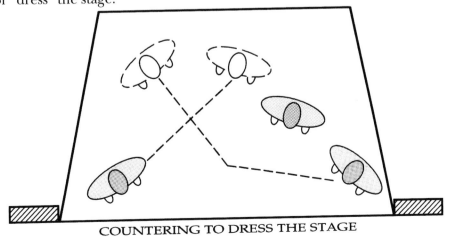

COUNTERING TO DRESS THE STAGE

Exit Lines: Actors need to time their last lines to avoid a meaningless pause as they exit. One of the best ways to do this is to break the last speech into sections. *The Importance of Being Earnest* is full of challenging exit lines. Let's look at an example from Act Two. The Rev. Canon Chasuble asks Miss Prism if she would like to go on a walk "as far as the school and back." She replies,

> That would be delightful. Cecily, you will read your Political Economy in my absence. The chapter on the fall of the Rupee you may omit. It is somewhat too sensational. Even these metallic problems have their melodramatic side.

We would suggest the following movement and business to make the exit smooth and more fun for the audience:

> (*Speaking to Rev. Canon Chasuble:*) That would be delightful. (*Crossing to Cecily and handing her the book:*) Cecily, you will read your Political Economy in my absence. (*Crossing to Rev. Canon Chasuble who is standing near the exit:*) The chapter on the fall of the Rupee you may omit. It is somewhat too sensational. (*Taking Rev. Canon Chasuble's arm and speaking to him directly:*) Even these metallic problems have their melodramatic side. (*Turns and exits on Rev. Canon Chasuble's arm.*)

Combative Scenes: It is best to approach all stage fights and stage falls as a choreographer rather than as a director. Break down every sequence into movements and rehearse each movement slowly, step by step. Timing is everything. Do not pick up the pace until the actor or actors involved have memorized every movement and are totally comfortable with the sequence.

Eating and Drinking: Don't wait until too long into the rehearsal process to introduce food and drink. Pantomiming these activities does not take the place of actually having to drink liquid or to bite, chew, and swallow food during a speech.

Intimate Scenes: Again, don't put off having actors deal with kissing scenes. They will be awkward for the actors at first; however, if they are going to look natural and comfortable with each other by opening night, they need to deal very specifically with these moments early in the rehearsal process.

IN CONCLUSION

You are bound to encounter some frustrating moments during the blocking process. Nevertheless, if you are open and receptive to both your actors and your own creative instincts, blocking rehearsals can be among the most stimulating and inspiring times during the entire rehearsal process. If you are prepared, and handle these rehearsals with a balance of authority and openness, we can promise you that they will be among the most satisfying hours you spend.

CHECKLIST FOR BLOCKING YOUR PLAY

Follow the checklist below when you work out blocking for your next production.

I. PREPARATION

_____ 1. Read your play several times.

_____ 2. Reread Chapter 5, How to Unravel a Play's Meaning.

_____ 3. Schedule three to six one-and-one-half-hour to three-hour sessions to pre-block your play.

_____ 4. Divide your play into workable segments: acts/scenes/working units.

_____ 5. Break down each segment into French Scenes or motivational units.

_____ 6. Place yourself in the middle of the world of your play, in a virtual reality state of mind.

_____ 7. Determine all entrances and exits throughout the play.

_____ 8. Underline and record all movement and business dictated by the playwright in the dialogue of the play itself.

_____ 9. Consider the adoption of movement and business suggested by the stage manager of the original production and found in parentheses throughout the script.

_____ 10. Determine the purpose of each French Scene or motivational unit:
   — To advance the plot
   — To further our understanding of the characters
   — To debate a "point-of-view"
   — To create atmosphere
   — To provide a diversion or distraction
   — A combination of one or more of the above

_____ 11. Find the key moment in each French Scene or motivational unit.

II. LAY OUT

_____ 12. Tape out the ground plan on the floor of your rehearsal space.

_____ 13. Explain, in detail, all aspects of the ground plan to the cast: entrances, practical furniture, levels, etc.

_____ 14. Lay out the blocking two or three pages at a time rather than constantly interrupting the action.

_____ 15. Collaborate with the actors in deciding on the movement and business that falls between entrances, given circumstances, suggestions made in the text, and key moments in each French Scene or motivational unit.

III. FINE-TUNING

_____ 16. Throughout the rehearsal, fine-tune and reshape as needed.

18 How to Help Actors Develop Characters

"*Happy to Make Your Acquaintance*"

from The Most Happy Fella.

Music, lyrics, and book by Frank Loesser.

Opened in New York, May 3, 1956; ran 676 performances. In 1993, there were two revivals of this musical running simultaneously on Broadway.

Know the needs of your actors. This is one of the most important maxims to remember. The best directors are those who are sensitive to the concerns of actors and consider meeting these needs their primary responsibility Many directors believe that the audience and the critics are their major concern. They feel justified in using any means within reason to ensure that the product, the production, is successful. Our argument against this practice is that you cannot predict or control how audiences and critics are going to respond. This is clearly brought out when you read Broadway reviews. You will find that they will run the gamut from raves to pans. The musical *Camelot* by Frederick Loewe and Alan Jay Lerner is an excellent case in point. The original Broadway production opened December 3, 1960, and received seven notices: one rave, one favorable, two mixed, and three unfavorable.

We argue that since directors have little or no control over audiences or critics, they should concentrate their efforts instead on making all phases of the rehearsal process as creative and positive an experience as possible. Since the majority of the director's time is spent with actors, it seems obvious that their needs should be the focus of attention.

We are not suggesting that actors should be pampered or given special privileges. Rather, we firmly believe that actors should be team players and work as an ensemble, not only with the other actors, but with all members of the company: the designers, crews, and front-of-house personnel. Directors do need, however, to be sensitive to the actor's plight. Over a relatively short period of time the cast needs to become so familiar with their roles that they can convince an audience of the characters' reality. This is not an easy task. Directors can make the actors' job less intimidating if they assume the role of acting coach as well as director. In addition to reviewing scenes over and over again during the rehearsal process, directors can provide a number of specific exercises to help actors uncover various facets of their characters. This chapter will concentrate on those activities.

Character Profile

We suggest that early in the rehearsal process, even as early as orientation, you request that all actors begin collecting information that can round out and build a total life for their characters. They can go about this task in many ways. We have found one of the best ways is to work up a "Who Am I?" questionnaire and have all the actors complete it as their characters would. Explain that their answers must be based on facts and clues given by the playwright.

In *The Importance of Being Earnest*, for example, Jack responds to Lady Bracknell's inquiries that he is twenty-nine years old, that he knows nothing, that his income is between seven and eight thousand a year, "in investments, chiefly," that he owns both a country house and a home at 149 Belgrave Square, that he is a Liberal Unionist, that both of his parents are lost, and that he was found in a handbag. All of these facts are called "given circumstances" and cannot be debated or altered by the actor. Some of the other questions can be answered based on deduction from actions or from lines in the script. Again, from *The Importance of Being Earnest*, we can make the assumption that both Jack and Algernon are well read and have probably had an advanced education based on their knowledge and their wit. The following exchange from Act One can serve as an example:

> JACK: That, my dear young friend, is the theory that the corrupt French Drama has been propounding for the last fifty years.
>
> ALGERNON: Yes! and that the happy English home has proved in half the time.

The rest of the questionnaire should be based on information regarding the time period and the setting of the play. All other unanswered questions can be based on the actor's own intuition. When you make this assignment, stress that there are no right or wrong answers except for specific information given by the playwright. A sample "Who Am I?" character profile has been included at the end of this chapter (Figure 18.1).

Understanding the Milieu of the Time

When actors uncover facts, it is important that they totally understand the impact of these facts on their characters. For example, the actor cast as Jack needs to research what it meant to live in London in the late nineteenth century (the play was written in 1895) with an income of seven to eight thousand pounds a year.

Encourage actors to look at photographs and paintings and to read books and watch films that depict the period and locale of the play. It is imperative that the entire cast become totally immersed in the milieu of the time. A worksheet for this purpose has been provided at the end of the chapter (Figure 18.2).

Character Journal

Another excellent way for actors to get more in touch with their characters is to keep a journal. During and after rehearsals, encourage actors to write entries as their characters commenting on what they have learned about themselves, and what they think and feel about other characters in the play. Writing in first person helps actors get deep inside their characters and can be quite a revealing and useful resource. A sample page for a character journal can be found at the end of the chapter (Figure 18.3).

Collective Creation

Actors can learn a great deal about the times that their characters lived in if they are required to make a "collective creation." Ask actors to paste pictures and objects on a poster board that they feel reveal the interests and attitudes of their characters. This exercise is best suited to plays that are set in this country between the years 1930 and 1970.

CHARACTER RELATIONSHIPS

We suggest that during the middle of the rehearsal period, preferably after actors have memorized their lines, you schedule time during selected rehearsals to conduct a number of exercises that explore character relationships and deeper levels of character motivations. Actors should be relaxed and never feel the need to perform during these exercises. We suggest, therefore, that you approach them as games. We have found that it is best to allow twenty to thirty minutes for each exercise, and to schedule them right after warm-ups.

Coffee Klatsch: Match actors who share scenes and have them talk together in character. We have found that this exercise works best when it is done privately and no one, not even the director, observes. After the exercise is completed, the actors can gather together and share their discoveries.

Around the Clock: You need a large rehearsal area for this exercise. Ask actors to find a space and to imagine that it is their character's bedroom. Tell them to take time to really see their space; decorate it: decide what kind of bed they sleep on, how the walls are painted or papered, what kind of curtains hang on the windows. Ask them to look in their closet and see the clothes that are hanging there. Next, have them look out the window and see the yard and the neighborhood. When they are completely familiar with their immediate environment, tell them that you are going to call out the hours for one complete day, starting with four o'clock in the morning. The actors' objective is to go through the activities they think their characters would experience in a typical day. Instruct the actors to lie down as if they were in bed asleep. Then, slowly call out the hours. When each hour is announced, the actors should respond by going through the routines and activities their characters might experience on a typical day. Actors should relate to each other in character as appropriate. Make sure you allow enough time to discuss what each actor discovered after this and every exercise.

Hot Seat: This is a very popular exercise. Actors are called on, one at time, to sit in front of their colleagues and respond to questions. They, of course, must answer in character and should respond as if the person asking the question was a confidant.

A Two-minute, Ten-line Walk-through: This is an excellent exercise to do late in the rehearsal process. It can help actors step back and see their characters in perspective. Ask each actor to go through the script and find the ten lines that are the most important or revealing about their character. They are to prepare and perform for you and their colleagues a two-minute performance that strings these lines together. They may approach the transitions as creatively as they choose. The rules are that they may speak only ten lines; they must incorporate some movement, and they should complete the exercise in approximately two minutes.

The Moment Before: This exercise works best when it is incorporated into the rehearsal process. Before actors make an entrance in selected scenes, ask them to explore, in detail, everything they did in the two minutes immediately preceding it.

These are just a sampling of the exercises we have used to help actors get more in tune with their characters and to better understand their relationships with each other. We suggest you devise your own exercises to best serve your cast and the play that you are presenting. Don't lose sight of the fact that the objective of introducing exercises is to find a variety of ways to help actors appear more natural and feel more comfortable.

CHARACTER PROFILE

Who Am I?
Rounding Out Your Character Exercise

Answer all the questions from your character's point of view. Base all of your answers on the Given Circumstances.

What is your full name?

What else are you called? (nicknames)

Where do you live? (city, state, country)

Where were you born?

Date of birth (Day, Month, and Year)

Do you have any brothers and sisters? How many older and younger?

What do you remember about the house you grew up in?

What do you remember about the neighborhood you grew up in?

What were some of the special occasions in your family? (holidays, reunions, picnics, vacations, etc.)

Name some of the special homemade foods you ate as a child.

Name and describe some of the games you played as a child.

What is your favorite childhood memory?

What is your worst childhood memory?

18.1 continued

What was/is your relationship with your family?

What year in college are you?

What subjects do you excel in?

What was your overall grade point average?

What do you like best about this college?

Are you now a member of any clubs, organizations, or religious congregations?

Did you ever smoke? (when, why, and how much?)

What is your favorite drink, alcoholic and nonalcoholic?

What kind of limits do you put on your alcoholic drinking?

What section of the newspaper do you read?

What do you enjoy doing most in your free time?

What kind of music do you enjoy listening to?

What have you read recently? (book, magazine)

How do you feel about your age?

What do you do for exercise?

What is your best feature?

If you could change one thing about yourself, what would it be?

What is your favorite meal?

What are your favorite foods?

List three of your favorite films.

Who are your favorite movie stars?

In what other forms of entertainment/recreation do you enjoy and/or take part?

What is your favorite sport? Do you follow it professionally?

What time do you usually get up in the mornings?

What time do you usually retire?

What is your favorite time of day? Why?

What is your favorite season? Why?

18.1 continued

Which do you prefer: city or county living? Why?

Do you like intimate parties or large gatherings? Why?

What is your favorite color and why?

What is your greatest fear?

Who is your closest friend?

How would you like to spend your next vacation?

What type of clothing do you most like to wear?

What are your favorite TV programs?

What would you enjoy doing on an evening out?

What would you like to be when you grow up?

What is your favorite animal?

What are your prejudices?

Do you consider yourself an indoor or outdoor person?

What are your feelings or opinions about:

    sex?

    politics?

    war?

    old age?

What role does religion play in your everyday life?

Are you happy with your lot?

What do you feel the future holds?

How do you feel about each of the other people you meet in this play?

UNDERSTANDING THE PERIOD OF YOUR PLAY

Have actors use this worksheet to better understand how their character lived and functioned in a time and place different from their own.

Make a list of the books your character might have read. (What were the popular books of the period?)

_____

_____

_____

_____

Make a list of the music your character might have listened to. (What was the popular music of the period?)

_____

_____

_____

_____

Make a list of the films that are placed in the same time and place as the play you are working on.

_____

_____

_____

_____

Make a list of paintings and/or photographs that depict the same time and place as the play you are working on.

_____

_____

_____

_____

Look at history of fashion books and make a specific list of the clothes and accessories your character would have used.

_____

_____

_____

_____

_____

Make a list of the major events that were happening in the world during the time when your play takes place.

_____

_____

_____

_____

How would your character have passed the time of day? Make a list of the pastimes and popular forms of entertainment during the period in which your play takes place.

_____

_____

_____

_____

When possible, read a newspaper or magazine from the period your play takes place. Make a list of interesting observations that might help you better understand your character.

_____

_____

_____

_____

CHARACTER JOURNAL

Encourage your actors to keep a daily journal to get in closer touch and in better tune with their character. The following is a list of basic questions they can use for this exercise.

What new information have I learned about my character today?

What questions do I still have about my character?

How does my character feel about the other characters in the play? (Let your character's voice respond to this question.)

What one or two things do I plan to accomplish during the next rehearsal?

19

How to Work with Actors

"You've Got to Have Heart"

from Damn Yankees.
Music and lyrics by
Richard Adler
and Jerry Ross;
book by George Abbott
and Douglas Wallop.

Opened in New York, May 5, 1955; ran 1,019 performances. Gwen Verdon and Ray Walston were featured in the original production.

We stressed in the last chapter that actors are unique human beings. Many directors forget this fact when they start giving direction. Instead of approaching actors as individuals, they attempt to manipulate them like puppets and expect them to follow orders like soldiers. They forget that, in actuality, actors have only one gift in common—the desire to perform. The level of their ability and their technical skills differ greatly. Truly effective directors are sensitive to this. They realize that actors progress at different times and in various ways. They know when to give suggestions and when to back off. They are quick to recognize that all actors are more proficient in some areas and less confident in others. They respond to this challenge by finding ways to highlight actors' strengths and disguise their weaknesses. They know, that above all else, "You've Got to Have Heart."

We have developed thirteen guidelines for directors to solve specific problems you may encounter with actors during the course of rehearsals. Our intent has not been to comment on all possible problems that may arise; instead, we offer a baker's dozen of suggestions that we feel cover the most common ones.

GUIDELINES FOR DIRECTORS: A BAKER'S DOZEN

How to Offer Direction

Knowing how to offer feedback and constructive criticism to actors is among the most difficult tasks a director faces. Each actor is unique, and your relationship with each of them is so precarious that one word too harsh can close down trust and communication. It is a highly delicate process and you must learn to trust your instincts. Your objective is to put actors at ease; you can't accomplish this if you yourself are on guard and uncomfortable. The following are some specific pointers that can assist you in being more effective in this area.

Attack the acting problem, never the actor. Say, "Your character would look stronger if he didn't have so many extraneous movements." Avoid saying, "Don't mince around so much; you look weak."

Never draw attention to a problem unless you have a solution to offer. "It doesn't seem to be working when you yell at him for such a long period of time. Why don't you try a quieter, more deliberate approach and see how that feels?"

Always precede negative comments with something positive. "I was pleased to see that you had the lines down for this scene. Now you need to stop worrying about the lines and start listening."

Remember to follow up on negative comments. If you have told an actor that you have not been able to hear her, that she needs to project, make sure that you follow up on that comment at the next rehearsal. "You were getting the words out here tonight, Jane. I was able to hear over fifty percent of what you had to say, but continue to work on supporting your sounds and throwing your voice."

Make light of actor's serious mistakes. It is our opinion that in most instances it is best to comment on mistakes and put them in perspective. Saying nothing can often be frustrating and intimidating to the actor. "Don't worry about forgetting your line, Mike. It could have happened to anyone. That's why we have rehearsals."

Don't give too much criticism. Don't give actors more criticism than they can handle at one time. Correct one or two areas before you address others. "Don't worry about holding for laughs yet. Let's work on your timing and clean up the business first."

Don't neglect actors. Sometimes actors develop their characters quickly and are living up to your expectations. From your perspective, others need your attention more. Still, actors can get frustrated if they don't get any attention from you. Take time to comment on their work, even if you do it in private and in passing. All actors are sensitive and need feedback. It doesn't take long to say, "Really good job tonight, Nancy."

Challenge, but always remain upbeat. It is important to continually prod and ask for more; excellence is an honorable goal. However, don't let your actors feel that the odds for success are against them. Even when everything seems to be going wrong, it is important for you to be upbeat and optimistic. In theater, magic does happen. "Look, I know everything that could go wrong did. But as the old tradition tells us, bad dress rehearsal, good performance."

When to Give Criticism

Knowing when to give criticism is another delicate issue directors need to master. We have discovered no hard or fast rules. In our own practice we have let our intuition guide the best approach for each rehearsal. Among those methods which have worked best for us are the five listed below.

End of rehearsal note giving. The most common method is for directors to take notes during rehearsal and to give them orally to the entire cast before you dismiss them. This approach works best during final run-throughs and dress rehearsals. By this time the company is comfortable with each other and the type of notes you are most likely to give at this time are in the area of fine-tuning: "John, if you take a step closer to the window on your monologue, you will be in a better light." "Julie, don't forget to take your purse with you when you exit in Act Two." These types of comments will not embarrass or intimidate actors in front of their colleagues. Early in the rehearsal process, however, this is not the best method of giving direction.

On-the-spot direction. During early rehearsals, the best way to give feedback to actors is to let them know immediately what is working and what needs to be changed or adjusted. This is why we have advocated throughout this book that you break down the play into small working units or French Scenes. Actors get distracted when they are interrupted too often, yet they need to know soon after they try something if they are on the right track. It has been our observation that actors are more receptive to negative comments when they are delivered on-the-spot and in-the-moment. When you do this, you are perceived as a partner with the actor trying to solve problems. Your comments are not written down; they have not been processed. For most actors this approach seems less intimidating than comments read publicly at the end of rehearsals.

Private comments. In most instances, the best way to deal with a serious problem is to discuss it privately outside of rehearsal. You may need time to talk at length and even coach the scene. You don't want to hold up the rehearsal, and actors are more open to experimentation when other actors are not watching.

Casual comments. Sometimes comments, especially compliments, given away from rehearsal, in a different setting, can have a very positive effect. If you happen to see an actor in the hallway, or even while you are out shopping, and can say something specific and positive, it can build morale and give added incentive: "By the way, Billy, I've been meaning to tell you, I really like the way your scene with Nancy is coming along. You seem to have your lines down cold now and are beginning to have fun with it." We suggest that you go out of your way to make comments like this when you see members of your acting company outside of rehearsal.

Written comments. We have found written notes either handed to the actors or posted on the call board are the least satisfactory way of communicating. Some directors use them in order to save time. In our opinion, written notes are very impersonal and accomplish little more than to distance directors from their actors. They serve well for specialists, like vocal coaches and fight directors, who are brought in to assist. In these instances, written comments on specific problems can help. Actors can take them home and review them away from rehearsal.

How to Help Actors Memorize Lines

Learning lines can be very difficult for some actors and quite easy for others. A lot depends on the number of lines an actor has to memorize. Strangely enough, we have found that quite often, actors with the greatest number of lines will be the first to have them memorized. Those with smaller roles tend to put off the task, thinking that they have plenty of time. They need to be prodded so they don't hold up the process. Encourage actors who have difficulty with this task to divide their scripts into sections and learn a few pages every day.

How to Help Actors Deal with Monologues

Breaking down long, involved speeches into small units called "beats" is a good way of helping actors deal with monologues and soliloquies. A beat is a word, phrase, sentence, or combination of sentences that expresses one idea. Whenever an idea changes, the beat changes. Once actors understand their characters' logic and can understand the structure of the speech, we have found that it is easier for them to memorize. In essence, they start memorizing ideas first and words afterwards.

How to Help Actors Who Have Lost Their Confidence

Many actors go through a phase during rehearsals when they feel overwhelmed and discouraged. They don't feel good about what they are doing; they sense that you are not pleased with their work; the progress of the other actors begins to intimidate them; and in every way they become overwhelmed and frightened. Address the problem immediately. Our suggestion is to talk with them privately first. Assure them that this is not unusual, even among professionals, and that you have every confidence in them or you wouldn't have cast them. Then work on a key scene, either alone or with the other actors in the scene. Work slowly and easily until they have a breakthrough. This is what they need, a moment when they feel good about what they are doing. Build that moment into a short scene and then encourage the actors to use that scene as an anchor. Return to it every time another scene doesn't work. Transfer the good qualities from the first scene to the second. We have seen some remarkable results. Your role, however, is the key. You must sincerely believe in your actors and be willing to partner with them until they work themselves out of their depression. Keep the faith and have heart.

How to Help Actors Project

Many actors have problems with projection, especially young high school actors. We have found the best way to deal with this problem is by first showing them how to support their voices ("Breathe from the diaphragm, John."), and then showing them how to throw the voice without yelling or raising its pitch. We have had success in this area by using the following exercise.

Have actors find a one-page scene with a partner. Place the two actors fairly close to each other and tell them to start the scene and speak conversationally. Repeat the short scene several times. Each time move the two actors further apart and don't allow either of them to change their pitch. Just have them throw their voices, keeping a conversational tone. Eventually move the two actors to opposite ends of the auditorium. If you do this gradually enough, they should be able to project naturally and comfortably. Once actors have experienced the sensation of supporting their voices and sending them out as if the receiver were some distance away, they rarely have serious problems in this area again. You must keep at them, however, or they will fall back into old habits.

How to Help Actors Slow Down

Another problem that is prevalent, especially with young actors, is the tendency to rush lines once they have been memorized. Actors get excited or become so comfortable in their roles that they start racing through their scenes without even realizing it. One method to help them slow down is to tell them to visualize a line and see all the vowels in it. Explain that, quite practically, the only way to slow down is to elongate each vowel sound. Have them try it. Like everything tried the first time, it will seem very awkward and highly artificial. Once they get the hang of it, however, it can have satisfying results.

Another method is to have actors play a scene in slow motion, as if they were under water. Once they allow the scene to slow down and they can sense the beats that they were rushing through, they will return to a regular speed that is much slower and more natural than the way they were playing it previously.

How to Help Actors Find Variety

Some actors, during the middle phases of rehearsal, will begin to read every line alike. They lack variety of any kind; their voices go flat or they speak in a sing-song manner. We have come to the conclusion that these actors are not thinking about what they are saying; instead they are thinking about the lines themselves. Their inner voice is saying, "My next line is blah, blah, blah," and that's about the way it comes out. We suggest that you have actors with this problem paraphrase their lines; have them put each line in their own words and say them aloud. We have found that once they begin thinking about what they are trying to communicate and for what purpose, they forget about the lines themselves, and instead, find the variety that is necessary to get their ideas across.

How to Help Actors Stay in Character

Actors who are on stage for long periods of time but have little to say, often have problems staying in character. Concentration is the key word here. You've got to help them really listen to the scene, in character, as if for the first time. You must convince them that their subtle, but honest, reactions are very telling to an audience. They communicate a great deal and help the audience to better understand, not only their characters, but, more important, the play itself. Remind them that when they "drop out," they draw attention away from the scene and break the illusion of reality. For actors who continue to have problems listening, have them write out a subtext of what they are thinking throughout the scene. Nothing is worse than "dead eyes."

How to Help Actors Find the Correct Line Reading

Many directing texts will tell you to "never give an actor a line reading." While we do agree that directors should not demonstrate an emotional interpretation of a line, we do feel that it is proper to give a literal reading of a line when an actor is misreading it. Often actors need to hear the line said aloud to understand it. Right or wrong, we have found that our method saves time and a great deal of frustration.

How to Help Actors Be More Natural

Often players get carried away and want to "act" rather than "be." They force reactions and telegraph them to an audience. Our advice is to temporarily change environments; move into another space. Pick a key scene and ask the actors to improvise it using their own words rather than the words in the script. Don't allow anyone else to watch but you and the Stage Manager. Explain that you want both of the actors to narrow their circle of attention to the immediate surroundings. Their challenge should be to really focus in and try to connect with each other. They must listen carefully to what the other actor is saying and react out of the moment. After they have completed the improvisation, discuss the differences. Focus on specific moments when the work seemed very honest and real and explain that this is the type of work you would like to see when they return to their rehearsal space and to the script. When we have used this approach, we have been pleased with the results.

How to Help Actors Take Stage

Sometimes young actors get cast in large roles and have a difficult time opening up and taking stage. When this is the case, you need to do everything in your control to help the actor. Teach them to use pauses to their full advantage. Silence can be very powerful. When the actor enters a room and takes a few moments to draw focus before speaking, that individual commands a great deal of attention. Have the actor work on posture, eliminate all extraneous gestures, move with purpose, and speak with authority. In addition, do everything at your disposal to enhance the performance: check body positions and make sure the actor remains open as much as possible. Block strong entrances, and, when possible, place the actor in a dominant position during key scenes. Use lighting to help add focus, and costume the actor in dominant colors. When appropriate, place the actor on higher levels and in positions that are slightly separated from other actors.

How to Help Actors with Special Problems

When actors have speech problems, difficulties with dialects, or have to execute a dance or a fight during the play, don't hesitate to call in a specialist to assist. Unless you are trained in these areas, don't try to help; you could do more harm than good. The safety of actors should be the major consideration whenever fights are staged. Don't expect immediate results. In the early stages of the process, schedule special sessions outside of rehearsals. Give the specialists plenty of time to work with the actors; if they are good at what they do, they will need both time and a great deal of concentration from the actors.

Remember, throughout the process, actors are sensitive and need encouragement if they are going to excel. Compliment often. Although you are the director, they are the ones who have to stand out on stage and give the performance. Have heart and treat them with respect.

20 How to Direct Period Plays

"Agony"

from Into the Woods.
Music and lyrics by
Stephen Sondheim;
book by James Lapine.

Opened in New York, November 5, 1987; ran 764 performances and 43 previews. Winner of three 1988 Tony Awards including Best Book and Best Score. Bernadette Peters played the witch in the original production.

In all the previous chapters, we have made the assumption that the script you would elect to direct, especially if you are working on your first production, would be a modern, realistic play with a moderate to large cast. In this chapter we acknowledge that this may not be the case. You may have been assigned, coerced, or have risked on your own, to direct a period play.

Unlike "costume plays," those that are set in earlier times but written by modern playwrights for a contemporary audience, period plays were written before 1900, and for an audience with somewhat different needs and expectations from our own. The scripts are obviously worthy—they have stood the test of time—but today, they often "read" better than they "play." This is true, in part, because, while many of the themes of these plays are universal, the situations often seem remote and the language stilted and foreign to our ears. This is true even when the plays were originally written in English. Some of Shakespeare's works are a good case in point.

While plays in this category may be difficult at first to comprehend, once you overcome the language barrier, they can prove to be a very rich and rewarding experience. This can be true not only for you and your company, but for your audience as well. You must select wisely, however, commit early, and remain involved and focused during the entire rehearsal process. It also helps to have a number of bright and talented people around to assist.

If, after serious consideration, you are willing to take the gamble, and go "into the woods" a bit, we are sure the extra effort will be worth the slight "agony" you might encounter along the way. To assist you, we have prepared a number of guidelines, suggestions you need to consider in addition to the ones we have already shared. They are not meant to overwhelm, but rather, to make your job easier.

GUIDELINES

Spend more time in your rehearsal schedule on read-throughs. Make sure that everyone in the cast understands the meaning of every word and scene in the play. Discuss, in depth, the universal themes, the characters' motivations, and the play's modern implications.

Period plays take longer to rehearse than most contemporary plays. You should allow for at least two more weeks of rehearsal.

Recruit the services of a specialist. A dramaturg can bring deeper insight into the language of the play, the history of the period, and the background of the playwright. In addition, a dramaturg can clarify meanings to words and phrases, and research answers to questions that are not obvious.

Allow time to learn the style of movement and manners of the period. Again, you might consider bringing in a specialist, if one is available, to assist in this area. If not, watch selected films of the period for the way characters move and deal with specific personal props like fans, canes, and snuff boxes. *Acting with Style* by John Harrop and Sabin R. Epstein (Prentice-Hall, Inc., 1982) is an excellent resource.

Put your actors in rehearsal costumes early in the process. It is unfair to wait until dress rehearsals to introduce your women to the restrictions of corsets and long skirts and men to tights and shoes with heels. Find substitutes early in the process so your actors will look natural and feel comfortable during performances.

Emphasize correct pronunciation and clear articulation. It is paramount that the audience understand every word of the play. Again, if you can find one, a vocal coach can be very helpful in this regard.

It may be important to do some judicious cutting in the script. Many period plays are too long for modern audiences, and even advanced companies do some trimming. The rule of thumb is that the play should not run longer than two to two-and-one-half hours.

Period plays can be expensive. Be prepared to increase the budget, especially for costumes and furniture.

Simplify all scenic elements. Most period plays are divided into numerous scenes, many of them very short. To maintain unity and pace, it is best to stage them on a unit set—variety of platforms and vertical pieces that can easily be rearranged to represent several different settings.

Let lighting, sound, and music help you. Light, sound effects, and especially music, can help bridge scenes and establish period, place, and mood.

Select music with care. Don't choose anything that is too familiar or it will draw attention to itself. Also time your selections carefully. If you use a number of cues, it is best to incorporate the sound board operator into the rehearsal process during final run-throughs. We have found that this has saved time during dress rehearsals, when your attention needs to focus on other problems.

Memorizing lines can present special problems in period plays. The lines are seldom distributed equally. Often a few characters carry the majority of lines. They may also have long soliloquies to commit to memory.

Actors must learn their lines word-for-word. Call for lines early in the process and make sure your stage manager is persistent in insisting on accuracy.

Don't neglect pacing and stage business. If you should elect to do a period farce, like *Charley's Aunt* (see details on this play at the end of this chapter, Figure 20.1), you will want to pay special attention to stage business and pacing. Unlike domestic comedies, which are realistic and more sentimental in form and content, farces are broader and much more basic. They depend on sight gags and exaggerated characterizations for their laughs. The humor is in the situations and the action of the play, rather than in the language.

Never allow actors to merely play for laughs. While the characters in farces may be stereotypical, they nevertheless need to be played "straight" and with great sincerity.

It is essential that actors not drop or "break" character.

The stakes in farces are always high, often higher than they are in tragedies. Actors should be working to win their characters' objectives, not just to generate laughs from an audience.

When playing farce, don't hold back. Tilt is a word we often use when we are trying to encourage actors to "go further" and telegraph more.

"Fast" is another key word for directors of farce. Actors must never be out of control, but they need to rehearse long enough that they can execute both their lines and their business at breakneck speed. As long as they have control and a sense of rhythm, the old adage holds: The faster the pace, the louder the laughs.

Old-fashioned melodramas can be lots of fun to work on. Like farce, the actors need to play their characters full out, but never obviously for laughs. Even today, audiences can get very involved with the plots of melodramas.

Melodramas require a special acting style. If you attempt one of these plays, we suggest that you study old posters, early photographs, and silent films for examples of style.

If you attempt a melodrama, consider incorporating "olio" acts between scenes. Adding period songs and dances to the evening's entertainment is not only historically correct, but another way of working more talent into your production.

One of the most challenging tasks in playing period plays is knowing how to handle asides. An aside is a comment directed to the audience that the other characters do not hear. The actor must turn out and deliver the line quickly or the laugh is lost and the audience is confused.

A SELECTED LIST OF STANDARD PERIOD PLAYS

The Birds, by Aristophanes. Acting Arrangement by Walter Kerr. Ancient Greek comedy; unit set; flexible cast. Satire against Greek society; opportunity for flamboyant costumes.

Midsummer Night's Dream, by William Shakespeare. Elizabethan comedy; flexible set; multiple leading roles; good comedy for many ages, many talents.

A Servant of Two Masters, by Carlo Goldoni. Italian Farce; unit set; roles: nine males, four females. A clever servant pulls many tricks and gathers much acclaim to help two sets of lovers who are being kept apart by many complications.

She Stoops to Conquer, by Oliver Goldsmith. Eighteenth-century English comedy; multiple settings; leading roles: four males, four females; many smaller male roles, some that may be played by women. A down-to-earth comedy of manners that centers on five young people.

Charley's Aunt, by Brandon Thomas. English farce; one exterior, two interiors; roles: six male, four female; comments on a more innocent time when young ladies and gentlemen had to have a chaperone. A young man impersonates a female dowager, which leads to much laughter.

The Drunkard or The Fallen Saved, by William H. Smith. Melodrama; various interiors and exteriors; roles: thirteen male, five female; a very popular, long-running, temperance play with all the stock characters and situations.

21 How to Direct Your First Musical

"With a Little bit of Luck"

from My Fair Lady.
Music by Frederick Loewe;
lyrics and book
by Alan Jay Lerner.

Opened in New York, March 15, 1956; ran 2,717 performances. The most influential musical of the fifties and one of the most distinguished productions of all time; starred Rex Harrison, Julie Andrews, and Stanley Holloway.

Most schools and many community theaters want to produce musicals. They can generate excitement and anticipation and incorporate the special talents of a number of students or community players. Nevertheless, musicals are very expensive to mount and they require the collaboration of a number of specialists. If you select cautiously, prepare carefully, and recruit wisely, however, you have an excellent chance of mounting a fine production, one that can bring a lot of pride to your school or organization, and draw attention to your program. Here are a few guidelines that, "with a little bit of luck," will help to make your experience more satisfying.

SELECTION CONSIDERATIONS

Avoid musicals dominated by one or two "stars." Annie Get Your Gun (music and lyrics by Irving Berlin) is a good case-in-point. The leading character, Annie, sings nine of the thirteen songs in the score. It is much more rewarding to select a musical that has a number of featured players. *Bye, Bye, Birdie* (music by Charles Strouse, lyrics by Lee Adams, book by Michael Stewart) is an excellent example because it has at least six leads, an involved chorus, and a number of featured roles. We have listed several other musicals of this type at the end of the chapter (Figure 21.1).

Match available talent to the vocal and dancing demands in the musical. For example, don't consider *West Side Story* (music by Leonard Bernstein, lyrics by Stephen Sondheim, book by Arthur Laurents) unless you have a number of male and female performers who are advanced singers and dancers. If your talent pool is untrained, you might better consider *Grease* (music and lyrics by Jim Jacobs and Warren Casey).

Musicals are expensive to produce. Royalties are considerably higher than for straight plays, and you have to rent orchestrations as well as scripts. In addition, most musicals require considerable technical support: multiple sets, extensive costuming, additional lighting, and other special effects. We strongly suggest that you carefully work out a detailed budget before you make a final selection.

Be aware of the limitations of your stage space. Do you have enough backstage area to store scenery, props, the crews, and all your actors who are waiting to get on stage? Is your stage covered with a hardwood floor? Dancers can permanently damage their bones and muscles dancing on cement. Do you have adequate space for an orchestra? Is your auditorium wired to support additional lighting and sound equipment? The considerations go on and on. Check the space out thoroughly before you commit to anything.

ADDITIONAL STAFF CONSIDERATIONS

You need to add a number of specialists to your staff. The most important individual, of course, is a Music Director, someone who can coach the singers, play the piano, and conduct the orchestra or combo, if you use one. If your Music Director does not play the piano well, you may have to hire a Rehearsal Pianist. If you don't use an orchestra, your pianist will also be needed to play during performances. If you do use a large orchestra, you may decide that it is best to have an Orchestra Director in addition to your Music Director. If your musical requires a number of dance sequences, you will also need to recruit or hire a dance specialist known as a Choreographer.

DESIGN CONSIDERATIONS

Pacing is paramount in musicals. As you work out the details of your set and costume designs, make sure you and your designers keep this fact in mind. Nothing can ruin a show faster than having to pause for long scene shifts or costume changes. Avoid them at all costs.

Scale is important. Broadway audiences love spectacle and producers raise enough money to mount lush and lavish productions. However, if the musical succeeds, it is usually because of the strength of the book, the music, and the lyrics. Worry about emulating these elements, not the set, lighting, and costumes of the original Broadway production. Instead, be creative and imaginative in the way you and your designers approach the concept. Simplify, combine, adjust, even change the locale of scenes if necessary, but keep the show moving. We saw a fine production of Rodgers and Hammerstein's *Oklahoma!* that was staged on one highly realistic set. Jud's shed was downstage right, and the back porch of Aunt Eller's home was upstage, just left of center. The production had excellent pace, and the audience was delighted.

Keep it simple. Selected pieces, well executed, in front of a cleverly conceived unit set can be very effective and satisfying. Remember, less can say more, especially in theater.

Schedule rehearsals for your running crews and wardrobe personnel. Assign specific jobs to individuals, and don't use more people than is necessary. Repeat the shifts and changes several times until all crew members can handle their assignments with ease and precision. Crews can execute changes at least twice as fast once they get the routine down pat. Keep this fact in mind as you are struggling through your first dress rehearsal.

AUDITION CONSIDERATIONS

Establish staff responsibilities. Decide before auditions begin which director—Music Director, Dance Director (Choreographer), or Stage Director (you)—is going to have the final say on who is cast in each of the leading roles. Consensus, of course, is best; however, certain roles require advanced abilities in one of the three performance areas: acting, singing, or dancing. When a decision cannot be reached by consensus, the director who must bring out the most important quality in the role should have the final word. For example, if you were producing Rodgers and Hammerstein's *The King and I*, we would argue that if consensus was not possible, the Music Director should have the final word on which actors play Tuptim, Lun Tha, and Lady Thang and the Stage Director should have the final word on who are cast as Anna and the King.

Allow at least three days for auditions. On the first two days schedule "open calls." Give your Music Director and Choreographer plenty of time to ascertain the technical skills of everyone trying out. If you are expecting a large turnout, you might consider reserving three different spaces: one for music, one for dance, and one for reading. Auditionees can move from room to room and not waste a great deal of time.

Callbacks need to be well-organized. All directors should be present. We have found it is best to hold dance and singing chorus eliminations first. In that way you can dismiss a large number of people before you have to concentrate on those individuals contending for feature and leading roles.

SCHEDULING CONSIDERATIONS

Musicals take longer to mount. Be prepared to commit to between eight to ten weeks to the project.

Allow two to three weeks at the beginning of rehearsal for the Music Director and the Choreographer. Performers need to learn the music and begin the dance routines first.

Schedule rehearsals carefully. Try staggering calls so large numbers of performers do not have to wait around with nothing to do. If you know that you are not going to get to a musical number until late in the rehearsal, don't call the performers in that number until ten or fifteen minutes before. Also, don't hold performers; once they have completed their work for the day, dismiss them. To keep morale up and frustration down, stay organized.

Expect musical rehearsals to run longer than rehearsals for plays. We have always scheduled a minimum of three hours per rehearsal, and have warned performers (and parents, when we were directing high school productions) that final run-throughs and dress rehearsals can run longer.

Once full rehearsals begin, it is possible to schedule two, even three rehearsals at the same time. The Music Director could be working with two or three leads on a song, the Choreographer could be working with a chorus on a dance routine, and you could be working with another group of featured performers on a scene. Since musicals are broken down into many short units, this is relatively easy to work out. We have found that it is the best use of time and talent.

Schedule people but don't try to schedule specific work too far in advance. You may not know for sure which musical numbers, dance routines, or "book" scenes will need more rehearsal time. In many of the musicals we have produced, students knew from the beginning of the process what days they would be rehearsing but did not know specifically what they would be working on until a day or two before, or even the day of rehearsal. We would schedule a brief meeting with the other two directors, the Music Director and the Choreographer, after each rehearsal and determine what needed to be rehearsed the following day. The Stage Manager would post the specific schedule on the call board the following morning.

Be prepared to deal with schedule conflicts. When you work with a large cast over a long period of time, it is inevitable that you will go through a number of rehearsals when one or more performers will be absent. Collectively we have produced a number of musicals and have never been able to get through an entire rehearsal period without dealing with performers who were absent either because of illness or an emergency. Our advice is to keep rehearsing; let someone else stand in and work around the missing individuals.

Don't forget warm-ups. Before you start rehearsals, run-throughs, dress rehearsals, and especially before performances, allow at least a full twenty minutes for warm-ups. It is important that performers' bodies be fully relaxed and their voices open and free of tension before performances or long and strenuous rehearsals.

CASTING CONSIDERATIONS

Most musicals were tailored to the special talents of star performers in the original production. You may find that your pool of actors/singers/dancers, while talented, does not have the same advanced technical skills. We do not feel that it is wrong, therefore, to streamline musical numbers to match the talents of your performers. Do two choruses instead of three, or cut a dance sequence in half. Better that your people handle a cut-down version well, than the full version poorly.

Be open and creative in the way you cast your musical. Some roles that were originally written to be played by either a man or a woman might easily be altered to the opposite sex without changing the meaning of the script or the intent of the writers. You might also consider dividing the requirements of certain roles. We saw an imaginative production of *The Pajama Game* (music and lyrics by Richard Adler and Jerry Ross; book by George Abbott and Richard Bisell) where the actress playing Gladys was a gifted comedienne but obviously, not a very skilled dancer. The director decided to feature someone else in the famous "Steam Heat" number. Only one line in the book was altered, and, unless you had seen the film or another production, you would not have been aware of the substitution. We considered it a very clever way of "having your cake and eating it too."

SCRIPT CONSIDERATIONS

Many musicals run long by today's standards. Doing some judicious cutting in the book or in musical selections might be a very wise decision. Some recent Broadway revivals of standard "hit" musicals have been criticized for their length. We have always advocated that it is best to "leave the audience wanting more."

When you rent script materials, you often receive "sides" for actors. "Sides" are partial scripts that include only the lines and cues for one character. These can be difficult to work with so we suggest that you have two or three read-throughs before you begin full rehearsals to help everyone become totally familiar with their roles and the musical itself.

REVUES

If you have a limited budget, and not enough people to mount a full-scale musical, you might consider staging a more intimate revue. In recent years, this type of presentation has become a very popular form of entertainment both on and off Broadway. All the major publishing houses list a number of fine revues in their catalogues, many of them scored for just one or two pianos and between three and eight performers.

While revues don't exactly take the place of a musical, they are a viable substitute. They can provide excellent opportunities for a smaller, more select group of performers. They are relatively inexpensive to mount, but they can require a great deal of imagination to stage successfully. Variety is the key word to keep in mind if you direct one. Don't stage each number the same way, and keep the entertainment as visually interesting as possible.

A Suggested List of Musicals to Cut Your Teeth On

Annie—Music by Charles Strouse; lyrics by Marin Charmin; book by Thomas Meekan. (Music Theatre International.) Three female; two male leads plus chorus and several featured roles. Needs a dog; several young girl roles, including the lead.

Bye, Bye, Birdie—Music by Charles Strouse; lyrics by Lee Adams; book by Michael Stewart. (Tams-Witmark Music Library.) Three female; three male leads plus chorus; set in 1950s, so relatively easy to costume; lots of roles for teenagers.

The Fantasticks!—Music by Harvey Schmidt; lyrics and book by Tom Jones. (Music Theatre International.) One woman; seven men; the two father roles could be played as mothers; simple staging with few props; can be done with piano only; longest running musical; still running in its original New York theater.

Godspell—Music and lyrics by Stephen Schwartz; book by John-Michael Tebelak. (Theatre Maximus.) Mixed cast of ten; rock musical; set and costumes of found objects; high energy; religious content could be controversial.

Grease—Music, lyrics, and book by Jim Jacobs and Warren Casey. (Samuel French.) Eight female; nine male featured roles plus chorus. 1950s rock musical; easy to costume; lots of young adult roles; may have to use a "high school" version as lyrics can be very "adult."

The Music Man—Music, lyrics, and book by Meredith Willson. (Music Theatre International.) Three female; three male leads plus large chorus and many featured roles. Popular show set in 1912; requires a band, which most schools can supply; period costumes; needs a powerful Harold Hill.

Once Upon a Mattress—Music by Mary Rodgers; lyrics by Marshall Barer; book by Jay Thompson, Marshall Barer and Dean Fuller. (Rodgers and Hammerstein Theatre Library.) Three female; six male leads plus chorus; early fairytale costumes; a crowd pleaser.

The Pajama Game—Music and lyrics by Richard Adler and Terry Ross; book by George Abbott and Richard Bissell. (Music Theatre International.) Three female; two male leads plus large chorus and several featured roles. Set in 1950s; two big dance numbers: "Steam Heat" and "Once-a-Year Day."

You're a Good Man, Charlie Brown—Music, lyrics, and book by Clark Gesner. (Tams-Witmark Theatre Library.) Two female; four male leads; good small-cast musical; appeals to children and adults; the role of Snoopy could be played by female; more a review than a "book musical."

Revues

Perfectly Frank—Music and lyrics by Frank Loesser. (Music Theatre International.) Three women; five men; includes fifty-five songs by Loesser.

Some Enchanted Evening: The Songs of Rodgers and Hammerstein—(Rodgers and Hammerstein Theatre Library.) Flexible cast; includes over thirty-five R&H songs.

The Mad Show—Music by Mary Rodgers; lyrics by Marshall Barer, Larry Siegel and Steven Vinaver; book by Larry Siegel and Stan Hart (Samuel French.) Two women; three men (flexible); inspired by *Mad Magazine*, a spoof on everything.

WHERE TO OBTAIN THE RIGHTS FOR MUSICALS

The following six agencies hold the rights for most Broadway musicals:

Dramatic Publishing Company
311 Washington Street
P.O. Box 129
Woodstock, Illinois 60098

Music Theatre International
545 Eighth Avenue
New York, New York 10018

The Rodgers and Hammerstein Theatre Library
598 Madison Avenue
New York, New York 10022

Samuel French, Inc.
25 West 45th Street
New York, New York 10036

Tams-Witmark Music Library, Inc.
757 Third Avenue
New York, New York 10017

Theatre Maximus
1650 Broadway
New York, New York 10019

22 How to Run a Smooth Production

"Sit Down, You're Rocking the Boat"

from Guys and Dolls.
Music and lyrics by
Frank Loesser;
book by Abe Burrows
and Jo Swelling.

Opened in New York, November 24, 1950; ran 1,200 performances. The original Broadway cast featured Robert Alda, Vivian Blaine, Sam Levene, and Isabel Bigley.

How do you run a smooth production? The answer is, *you* don't. Although it may be difficult to realize, when opening night finally arrives your job is done. You are no longer needed. Your place is with the audience watching the show—if that doesn't make you too nervous. If it does, stand at the back of the auditorium, or pace in the lobby. For better or for worse, the show is in the hands of the Stage Manager. Once the fifteen-minute warning is given, leave the backstage area and don't return until the performance is over. If you stay backstage, you will only get in the way and "rock the boat," so "sit down!"

A DIRECTOR'S FINAL DUTIES

Your final responsibilities must be completed before official performances begin. We haven't had an opportunity to comment on all of them, so we will claim this time and space to do so.

Backstage Policies

Before you move into the final phase of the rehearsal process, dress rehearsals, it is best to gather the company and go over the backstage policies that you, the administration, the set and costume designers, and the stage manager have worked out together. Most of the policies or rules will be safety considerations; the others will deal with proper backstage etiquette. Below we have offered a list of the most general policies—rules that apply to most situations. You may have others to add that are unique to your theater. After you have discussed each item with the actors, post a list on the call board. A one-page reproducible form can be found at the end of this chapter for your convenience (Figure 22.1).

- No smoking backstage, in dressing or makeup rooms, or in the green room.
- No one is allowed to leave the building in costume.
- All actors and crew members must sign in at the call board when they arrive.
- Do not return to the makeup room after you put on your costume.
- Do not eat or drink anything but water in your costume.
- Do not leave the backstage or green room area during performances.
- The Stage Manager will hold all personal valuables in a safety box; however, it is best to leave all jewelry at home.
- No talking backstage during performance.
- No visitors backstage during performance or after half-hour call.
- Immediately after performances, take off your costume before you greet guests!
- Report any damage to your costume immediately to the costume crew before you leave the theater.
- Return all props to the prop table.
- Report any missing or damaged prop to the Stage Manager before you leave the theater.

Check-in Times

Confer with the stage manager and the costumer and set the exact times you want actors to report backstage for dress rehearsals and performances. If you have limited space for applying makeup, you may have to stagger the actors' calls. The usual call before final dress rehearsal and performances is one hour prior to curtain. We set the call earlier for first dress as it usually takes actors longer to apply makeup and costumes the first time.

Curtain Calls

The best time to stage your curtain call is during the final run-through, although some directors wait as late as Second Dress Rehearsal. Stage the call carefully. If the style of your production warrants it, your call can be clever and complicated; it is, after all, the "cap" of the production. The most important aspect of any curtain call, however, is to keep it fast and for it to look professional.

Don't rush the rehearsal of curtain calls. It is the audience's last impression of your company's work and should be a positive one. Make sure that every actor bows correctly and looks comfortable. The actors should take their calls as themselves, not in character. The play is over. The audience is acknowledging the actors, not the characters. Don't worry about maintaining a mood. The audience breaks it the moment the applause begins.

Keep the call moving but make sure that every actor has a full moment in front of the audience. This is, after all, an opportunity for audiences to show their appreciation. They feel frustrated and cheated if it is taken away from them, so we believe firmly that you should always include a curtain call. In large-cast productions, it is best to group actors together. In musicals, for example, you might first acknowledge all the members of the chorus, in one or two groupings. Next, bring out all the featured performers in small groups of twos or threes. We have always grouped actors by the size of their roles, leaving the leads for last. Occasionally, we have grouped husbands and wives or lovers together, even when the sizes of the roles were not equal.

Most important, actors should smile during bows. Regardless of how they feel about their work during the performance, or how the audience reacts, actors should acknowledge the applause with a smile and, in effect, show their appreciation for all the people who purchased a ticket and took the time to watch them perform.

One final reminder, if you are staging bows for a musical, don't forget to have the company acknowledge the orchestra.

Opening Night

It is important for the director to be a cheerleader on opening night. Some directors even call the company together and give a brief pep talk before the fifteen-minute call. Others move around quietly from actor to actor and wish them well personally. Some directors do both. The important thing to remember is that, although you shouldn't stay backstage during a performance, it is important to the actors that you show your support before they make their first entrance.

Prompter or No Prompter

We strongly recommend that you not use a prompter. In fact, you should announce to your cast, prior to final runs-throughs, that they can no longer call for lines. Actors need the discipline of working through line problems before they get into dress rehearsals. They should not feel that if they go "up" during a performance, a prompter will call the line out to them. This is not professional and, of course, breaks any illusion of reality. We have attended many performances when actors have admitted afterwards that they have gone up on their lines. In most instances, the situation was handled so well that no one in the audience was aware that the script had been "altered" and the lines "rewritten." On the other hand, it is embarrassing to an audience when a prompt is obviously given.

Illness and Accidents

If an emergency should occur and an actor cannot go on, think through the situation as calmly as possible. The company will take its cue from your behavior, so be a worthy master of your ship.

 We have found that if you have any time at all, you can put another company member in the role and keep from canceling the performance. The actor can read from a script and not disturb the performance. In fact we have found that audiences will be really supportive of actors in this situation. They want to see them succeed.

 It is really amazing how quickly someone in the company can pick up a role late in the rehearsal process if they really need to. It is more difficult when you have to bring someone in from the outside, but we have had to face two or three occasions during our careers when even this has worked on less than twenty-four hours' notice. The important thing is not to panic. Confer with your cast, your stage manager, and your costume designer. They may have suggestions that you have not considered. Do not cancel a performance unless you absolutely have to.

Continuing Performances

A play doesn't really spring to life until it is performed before an audience. Moments that you struggled with during rehearsal suddenly become clear when you hear an audience's reaction. Other moments you should have stressed slip by without the emphasis they needed. What do you do? If we feel we can handle the situation quickly by giving a few notes, we do it. That's the advantage of giving more than one performance. On the other hand, most actors do not want to receive formal notes from a director after each performance. They consider the roles their own now and want the opportunity to let their characters grow without too much interference from you. You had your opportunity during the weeks of rehearsal.

 That does not mean that actors have the right to change their interpretations or any set blocking. These changes should not be tolerated. However, in subtle ways, actors grow in their roles when they have an opportunity to play several performances over two or more weekends. Directors should not interfere in this maturing process unless they feel that changes are affecting the play adversely.

 Actors should also be warned that audience reaction will differ, night to night, especially in a comedy. During one performance the audience will seem to get in tune with the play early and respond to every laugh, including some you didn't realize were there. On other nights it will seem like you have to hold up prompt cards to get a reaction. Warn actors that they must play the moments and not anticipate the laughs. Audiences may be enjoying themselves even when they are not vocal. It takes two or three people to spark an audience; their openness gives permission to the rest of them to "let go."

Another danger to warn actors against is second-night letdown. It does occur, more often than not, so warn actors not to party too hard, and to literally pump up their energy before curtain. Sometimes a pep talk is more important before the second performance. Rallying the company together is especially appropriate if the production received a poor review, or if the first night's performance has not gone as well as expected.

Picture Call

Most organizations want to keep a permanent document of the production for publicity and future reference, many designers want pictures for their portfolios, and all actors want a picture of themselves in character as a memento. Try to limit the number of shots, but make sure that every actor is included in at least one picture. It is best to coordinate the call with the designers so they get all the set, lighting, and costume shots they need. Designers can also help you organize the call so the session runs more smoothly. Plan carefully; remember, you are holding many members of the crew as well as actors. In this regard, it is nice to include one shot where everyone who worked on the production, including you, the director, has a picture taken with the cast.

We have found it saves considerable time if you type up the call and give copies to the Stage Manager and all the designers. A well-organized picture call should never take more than one hour unless you are slowed down by numerous set and costume changes. Picture calls usually take place after a performance. The date should be clearly indicated on the rehearsal schedule and posted on the call board. It is also a good idea to remind actors of the date during dress rehearsal week.

Strike

All actors should be present during strike. It is best when this fact is clearly stated on the rehearsal schedule. The Technical Director, Set Designer, or Stage Manager should coordinate the activity. Again, it is best when you just observe. For safety reasons, it is important that this event is organized carefully. Strikes work best when the company is divided into teams, with each team assigned a specific task. When that task is completed, the team reports back to the supervisor and receives its next assignment. It is difficult to estimate how long a strike will last; you have too many variables. At our institutions, the usual strike averages two hours.

Acknowledgments

The Monday after strike is a good time to start writing thank-you notes to individuals, businesses, and other organizations who made outstanding contributions. The notes do not need to be long or formal, but they should be written soon after the production closes. When you have quite a few acknowledgments, you might have selected actors assist you. They can comment on how much the experience meant to them.

Postmortem

Although seldom done, we feel that a postmortem scheduled one to two weeks after closing is an appropriate way to bring closure to a production. Everyone in the company could be invited, but it is essential that all directors and designers be present. The time should not be used to make criticisms about things that have already happened but rather to discuss ways that procedures and working relationships could be improved when many of the same people get together again for the next project.

BACKSTAGE ETIQUETTE

Copy and post on the call board next to your sign-in list.

BACKSTAGE ETIQUETTE

1. No smoking backstage, in dressing or makeup rooms, or in the green room.
2. No one is allowed to leave the building in costume.
3. All actors and crew members must sign in at the call board when they arrive.
4. Do not return to the makeup room after you put on your costume.
5. Do not eat or drink anything but water in your costume.
6. Do not leave the backstage or green room area during performance.
7. The Stage Manager will hold all personal valuables in a safety box; however, it is best to leave all jewelry at home.
8. No talking backstage during performance.
9. No visitors backstage during performance or after half-hour call.
10. Immediately after performances, take off your costume before you greet guests.
11. Report any damage to your costume immediately to the costume crew before you leave the theater.
12. Return all props to the prop table.
13. Report any missing or damaged prop to the Stage Manager before you leave the theater.

Act Four

AUDIENCE
DEVELOPMENT

23

What You Need to Know About Tickets

"Who Will Buy?" is a fitting title for a chapter on tickets. As you get closer to your opening, everyone starts worrying about how many people will show up for performances. In this chapter we will discuss how to price tickets; where to print them; what needs to be said on them; and most important, how to get rid of them.

HOW TO PRICE TICKETS

At the time you start working out your budget you need to determine the price or prices you will charge for tickets. Our advice is to be competitive with other similar groups or organizations in your area. Don't under- or over-price yourself. If you undersell your product, the public could think that the production will be very amateurish and may choose not to attend. On the other hand, if you overcharge, you may set the public's expectations too high. Also keep in mind that some families and individuals are on tight budgets and do not have much to spend for entertainment. You have a number of options to consider:

- Are you going to sell all seats for the same price, or are you going to give a discount to select groups, say students, senior citizens, or children under twelve?

- Are you going to have reserved or general seating? If you have reserved seating, are you going to scale the house and sell various sections for different prices; for example, the balcony, or back rows and extreme sides of the orchestra for less than the rest of the main floor?

- Are you going to put your tickets on sale early and offer special reductions to patrons who buy ahead, or to groups that purchase ten or more tickets at the same time?

WHERE SHOULD YOU PRINT TICKETS

Even though you may not have direct responsibility for the sales of tickets, you will ultimately be held responsible if there are losses or any discrepancies. Our advice, therefore, is to have your tickets printed and numbered professionally. You can set up a fail-safe bookkeeping system only with professionally numbered tickets. Also, a professionally printed ticket makes a better impression on the public. It is a tangible item that reflects the quality of your organization. Make sure this first impression is a positive one.

WHAT TO PRINT ON TICKETS

Tickets are small; don't try to print too much information on them. Only the following items are essential:

- Name of presenting school or organization
- Name of production
- Place of performance
- Date of performance
- Time of performance
- Seating location or comment, "General Admission"
- Price of the ticket
- The words "Admit One"
- The ticket number

This information is given for you in a checklist at the end of the chapter (Figure 23.1).

We recommend that you use a different color for each performance. This will help to keep the tickets from getting mixed up; it will make bookkeeping easier, and will assist your ushers. They will be able to spot individuals who have arrived with seats for the wrong performance. This is especially critical if you are going to use reserved seating.

WHEN AND HOW TO SELL TICKETS

We recommend that you start ticket sales soon after you begin your publicity campaign, which is discussed in the following chapter. In some situations, the cast is made responsible for selling a given number of tickets. If you don't agree with this policy, you may, at least, want your cast to promote individual and, especially, group sales.

Starting ticket sales early provides two other advantages. It gives you some ready money for petty cash items, and an indication of the size of your audience. To encourage early sales, you may want to establish a discount for people who purchase tickets in advance. Most organizations start selling tickets four to six weeks before an event.

The box office is the heartbeat of your organization. It is imperative that you clearly establish policies and procedures, and that your personnel know how to be pleasant to the public. Being pleasant is paramount.

Before you open your box office, consider the following questions and determine the answers to those that will apply to your situation. See the end of this chapter for a box office checklist (Figure 23.2).

- What hours will your box office be open?
- Are you going to accept phone reservations?
- Can patrons charge tickets to credit cards?
- Will your box office hold reservations on unpaid tickets, and, if so, for how long?
- Will you accept mail reservations?
- How will you handle group-rate sales?
- What will be your exchange policy?

One final recommendation: Have as few people as possible handle money. Make sure that those who do are responsible and that the accounting system you use is simple but sound. If you are in a school situation, it is always wise to have an adult supervise and hold all monies collected.

COMPLIMENTARY TICKETS

In every production you will need to give out some complimentary tickets. Just be careful that you don't give out too many; you need to meet your budget. We recommend that you do not give out free tickets to the cast and crew. Parents and friends are the most likely people to buy tickets. However, it is appropriate to exchange free tickets for other services rendered or for goods donated or loaned.

When you promise someone free admission, we recommend that you don't hand tickets out directly. Instead, write a letter that expresses your appreciation for their contribution and spells out how they can call in to reserve two tickets and then show the letter at the box office in exchange for their free admission. In this way you are not out the two tickets, and, if the recipient decides not to accept the offer (and quite often they do not), you are not out two tickets that could have been sold.

We have found that in school productions, it fosters good will to give comps to teachers and staff. You want their support in the future, the students appreciate having them in the audience, and sometimes it is only the cost of a ticket that keeps them from attending.

In order to control the number of comps given, all requests should go through you. Make sure you show the box office how to mark the ticket, so it doesn't throw off your tally.

Not only is the box office the heartbeat of any production, it is the one area where you are held the most accountable. Make sure you take time to ensure that all aspects of the area function in a highly organized and professional manner.

CHECKLIST FOR WHAT TO PRINT ON TICKETS

Use this form to help you decide how you want your ticket to look. Use it when you negotiate with your printer.

Name of presenting school or organization:

_____

Name of production:

_____

Place of performance:

_____

Check one: Reserved Seating: _____ General Admission: _____

Reserved Seating:

Price of tickets: _____; Area: _____; Rows: _____

Price of tickets: _____; Area: _____; Rows: _____

Price of tickets: _____; Area: _____; Rows: _____

Date and Day of Performance and Color of Ticket:

1st performance: Date: _____; Day: _____; Color: _____

2nd performance: Date: _____; Day: _____; Color: _____

3rd performance: Date: _____; Day: _____; Color: _____

4th performance: Date: _____; Day: _____; Color: _____

5th performance: Date: _____; Day: _____; Color: _____

6th performance: Date: _____; Day: _____; Color: _____

7th performance: Date: _____; Day: _____; Color: _____

8th performance: Date: _____; Day: _____; Color: _____

A Box Office Checklist

Use the following worksheet to help you set the policies and the organizational procedures for your box office.

1. What hours will your box office be open?

2. Are you going to accept phone reservations? What procedures will you use?

3. Can patrons charge tickets to credit cards? What arrangements have you made? What cards will be acceptable?

4. Will your box office hold reservations on unpaid tickets, and, if so, for how long? Write out your policies.

5. Will you accept mail reservations? Write out your procedures.

6. How will you handle group-rate sales? Write out your procedures.

7. What will be your exchange policy? Write out your procedures.

24

What You Need to Know to Sell Your Production

"You've Got to Have a Gimmick"

from Gypsy.
Music by Jule Styne;
lyrics by Stephen Sondheim;
book by Arthur Laurents.

Opened in New York, May 21, 1959; ran 702 performances. Ethel Merman starred, and Jack Klugman and Sandra Church were featured in the first Broadway production.

In Chapter 2 we suggested that you recruit a volunteer to serve as Director of Audience Development and Services. We pointed out that it is essential to have a dedicated and organized individual you can train to assist you with the myriad of things that need to be done to let the public know that you are doing a play, and that you want them, no!, that you desperately need them, to attend.

In the very first chapter we told you that theater is a collaborative process. We didn't go into detail and explain then that it takes equal parts of four ingredients to make theater happen: "the four A's," we call them: actors, action (the play), area (your auditorium), and audience. The point we want to emphasize here is that the audience is an equal part of the mix. All your work on a production is for nothing if you don't have an attentive group of people—perhaps a full house. Nothing is more exciting than playing to a full house.

It doesn't make any difference what play you are doing—as we kid around in the theater and say, "It could be the second coming, itself!"—if you don't get the word out, if you "keep the secret to yourself," only families will show up to watch.

Advertising is so important in theater—especially in amateur groups like schools and community theaters—because you don't do it everyday. Films have a much better chance of finding an audience because the theaters they play in are open every day of the year. The films themselves change but the theaters they play in are constant. Yet, have you noticed all the advertisement a distributor will lavish on some of its releases? Full-page, four-color ads even, and especially for films that distributors feel will be their sure hits, their biggest money makers. Why? They want to protect their investment and reap even larger profits. To establish new box-office records, distributors are willing to expend huge sums of money on a variety of advertising media—billboards, radio, TV, magazine, window displays, and, of course, newspapers. They want to ensure that the public not only knows about their top property, but is willing to stand in long lines waiting for hours to get a ticket for one of its first performances.

As a rule-of-thumb, film and Broadway producers spend from fifteen to twenty percent of their budgets on advertising. Unfortunately, the total budget for most amateur theater organizations is so small that even a full twenty percent wouldn't buy one decent-sized ad in the local newspaper. So, the smaller theater organizations often get discouraged, pull back, and elect to budget little or no funding at all to advertising. They rely totally on word-of-mouth. This is a mistake.

Now, don't get the wrong impression; we feel that personal contacts are one of the best ways of selling products. If your household is anything like ours, you get at least two long distance calls each week trying to sell magazine subscriptions, books, trips, property—you name it. But telephone soliciting is not one of the best ways of selling theater. It is too time-consuming and the return on the effort is too small. You can reach the public in far better ways. These options do require time, effort, legwork, and a great deal of imagination, but little to no out-of-pocket expenses. If you have some talented volunteers and an organized and committed Director of Audience Development and Services to coordinate efforts, you can get great mileage from very limited funds. Read on.

A PUBLICITY CAMPAIGN

The message in the heading for this chapter is literally true. "You've got to have a gimmick" if you want the public to be aware of what you are doing. Once you find it, it needs to be incorporated into every piece of advertising that you release. It should be the centerpiece of your campaign. Let us give you an example. A local, struggling theater organization began its publicity campaign by plastering the community with posters and handbills which read, "Tuna Is Coming." That's all; just three little words in bright red ink, "Tuna Is Coming." The posters were displayed in nearly every store of this community and the handbills were stuck in the windshields of standing cars in shopping centers. Everyone began asking questions: "What's coming and who is Tuna?" Disk jockeys started commenting about it on local radio stations. Next, the group printed a second set of posters and flyers and added a few words, "Our Tuna Is Greater." They replaced all the posters and repeated their distribution of handbills. A week later, a third set of posters and handbills read, "Our Greater Tuna Is Coming June 12." By this time people began to see through the gimmick and realized that the local theater group was advertising their up-coming production of *Greater Tuna*. For those who didn't catch on, there was a fourth set of posters and handbills that spelled out all the details. The group didn't stop with this one gimmick. They got all three of the local banks to insert a flyer in their monthly statements that advertised the production. They also convinced the local supermarkets to have their "carry out" employees stuff a handbill with all details about the play in each order that they bagged, and finally, they got the floral shop on Main Street to do a window display that featured the play. What were the results of these efforts? The group sold out every one of their scheduled performances and added several more. The campaign cost very little money. The card stock was donated by a local printer; the printing on the poster was hand stenciled; handbills were duplicated free on various photo copiers around town; and the bank flyer was designed on a computer by the husband of one of the members of the group.

As this example shows, advertising does work and it doesn't have to be overly expensive. It does take a great deal of imagination. It is also a fact that some plays are much more difficult to sell than others. Dramas, for example, never sell as well as comedies, and plays seldom sell as well as musicals. It is also true that timing is everything. For example, if you have scheduled your play during a major sporting event, you will definitely have your work cut out for you. But, when everything is equal, when the play has general audience appeal, and when not too many other events are scheduled at the same time, you have an excellent chance of turning a less-than-half-sold house into S.R.O. (standing room only).

PUBLICITY CAMPAIGN STRATEGY

To set up a campaign, call together some of your most creative thinkers and have a brainstorming session. Have everyone read the play before they arrive, and at the beginning of the meeting take a few minutes to explain your concept. Show or describe how the set and costumes are going to look. Give the committee as much information about the production as possible. Then, spend the rest of the meeting selecting specific ways to promote it. Decide on a gimmick, and carefully think through a timetable for deadlines. A flyer arriving too late is money wasted. Public announcements given air time before you start selling tickets are fruitless. We can't stress it enough: timing is everything.

Specific Ways to Promote Your Production

The following is a checklist of specific ways to "sell" a production. Don't try to use all of the examples for every production; select the ones that adapt best to the type of play or musical you are presenting, and that have the greatest chances of succeeding in your area. The list is limited; it is not inclusive. Use it as a springboard to free your own imagination. You might come up with a great idea that has never been tried before. That's how sell-outs happen.

Posters.   The most popular form of advertising is "window cards" or posters. A standard size is 14 inches by 22 inches, but some are larger. Don't make them too large or stores will not display them. Posters can be simple or complex, stenciled or printed, and in one or more colors. You can design them yourself or purchase ready-made ones from the publishing houses when you order your scripts. To cut down on costs, you might negotiate with art teachers in the local schools to allow students to design posters as an all-class project and then display the best in the windows of local stores. Or, you might hold a contest for the best logo and have one of the stores donate a gift certificate or prize.

You can give a lot of information on a poster but we don't advise it. You need plenty of "white space" to draw attention to the most important facts. Make sure you do include the following information:

- The producing organization
- The title of play or musical
- All authors (in musicals: book, music, and lyrics)
- The theater and its location
- Performance dates and times
- A telephone number to reserve tickets (optional)

See Figure 24.2 for an example.

Handbills or "stuffers."   Handbills are cheap throw-aways that should not take more than a few seconds to read. As mentioned, they can be stuffed in grocery bags, handed out at related entertainments (concerts, fairs, openings, etc.), inserted in programs for similar events, put behind windshield wipers on cars, or hand stuffed in mail boxes in selected subdivisions. They can be reduced and handed out as bookmarks at libraries. Also they can be laminated and posted on telephone poles. (Make sure you check local and state laws and collect posted bills after the event is over.) You can have someone with advanced computer graphics design the layout. To save money, put two or three on an 8 ½-by-11-inch sheet of paper, supply the paper, and ask a number of local businesses to run a hundred or more off on their photocopy machines.

Flyers.   Flyers are a bit more sophisticated than handbills. They usually have a more professional look and include more information. Most flyers are mailed to select lists of potential patrons. You might be able to borrow or purchase lists for a minimal cost from similar arts organizations. Flyers are especially effective if you want to encourage mail orders. You can design an order form as part of the layout. You can save a great deal of money if you bulk mail your flyer, but remember to allow at least two to four weeks for delivery. Your local postmaster can give you a more specific timetable.

Postcards. A slightly cheaper mailer is a postcard that announces one or more upcoming productions. Like flyers, postcards can be bulk mailed. You get the best results from postcards when they arrive in homes approximately two weeks before your production opens. Postcard sample layouts, front and back, are shown in Figures 24.3 and 24.4.

Newsletters. A one- or two-page newsletter can give lots of information, not only about the play, but about the cast, the design, and other aspects of your production. Because newsletters are more expensive, mail them first class and only to patrons and highly selective mailing lists. Many schools, home associations, and business, religious, and community organizations have newsletters. They might give you some space to announce your production free of charge. Make sure you inquire among the members of your cast and crews about possibilities in this area.

Table tents and placemats. If one or more local restaurants will agree to cooperate, you might design special table tents or placemats that advertise your play. Sometimes the eatery will underwrite the expense of printing. In any case, make sure you credit them in the acknowledgment section of your program. (See Chapter 26.)

Window displays. Selected local merchants might agree to work up a window display that features your play if you approach them early.

Contests. In addition to a poster contest, you might design a contest that relates specifically to your play. For instance, if you were producing *The Importance of Being Earnest,* you might sponsor a tea-tasting contest or recipe for afternoon teas (cookies, cakes, sandwiches, candies, etc.). In school you might sponsor a contest for the best diary entry. Again, get local merchants (or even individuals) to co-sponsor by offering a gift certificate or prize. If individuals, rather than a business, co-sponsor, they might offer a book or a U.S. savings bond as the prize.

Person-to-person contacts. Door-to-door solicitation (although not as effective as when cookies or other gifts or food items are sold) have also been effective, especially in schools.

Previews or "teasers." If you can schedule enough free time with members of your cast, you might consider taking mini-tours to schools, shopping centers, parks, etc., and putting on "teasers" that advertise your play. Teasers work best when you are producing musicals or costume plays. Think how much we can enjoy, and even be persuaded, to see films by watching trailers of upcoming events. In certain instances, the same can hold true of theater events, especially school productions.

All of these gimmicks take time, timing, and talent to work effectively. Make sure you start planning early, and have a responsible person pay attention to details.

CHECKLIST FOR WHAT TO PRINT ON POSTERS

Use this form to help you decide what information you need to include on your poster.

Name of presenting school or organization:

_____

The title of your play or musical:

_____

All authors (in musicals: book, music, and lyrics):
Check the copyright page of your script for the complete and full information that must be included. You might note that in some instances, the publisher will even insist on type size (e.g., 50 percent, which means that the authors' names must be set in type that is one-half the size of the title).

_____

_____

_____

The name of your theater and its location:

_____

_____

The dates of the production:

_____

The times of performance:

_____

Ticket prices:

_____

A telephone number to reserve tickets (optional):

_____

Use the back of this page to sketch your graphic ideas: images, colors, font types and sizes, etc.

UK
THEATRE

presents Stephen Sondheim's
Tony Award-winning musical

October 6, 7, 8, 13, 14, 15 at 8 p.m.
October 9 & 16 at 2 p.m.

GUIGNOL THEATRE

Fine Arts Building
All seats reserved
Call 257-4929
Singletary Center
Ticket Office

INTO THE WOODS

24.3

Postcard Layout—Example 1

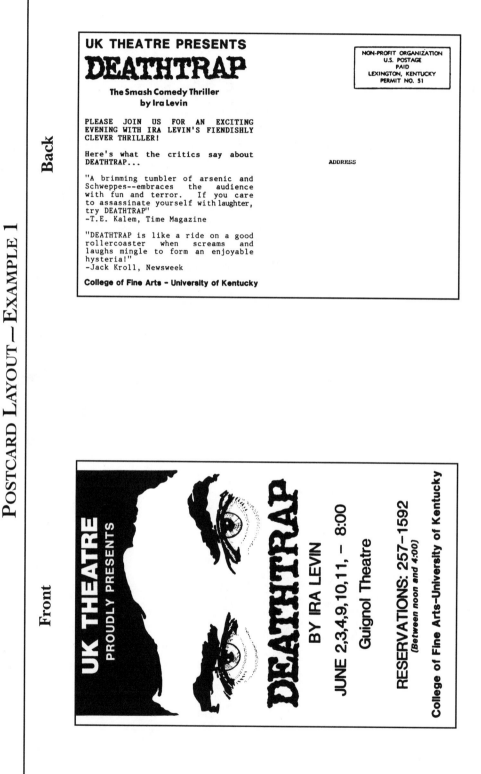

Back

Front

24.4

POSTCARD LAYOUT—EXAMPLE 2

Back

The Gaines Center for the Humanities and the University of Kentucky Equine Research Foundation

CELEBRATION
of the
HORSE

CALENDAR
of EVENTS

Oct. 4 - Nov. 29
"Horses"
Exhibit, UK Art Museum

Oct. 5 - 28
"The History and Romance of the Horse"
Exhibit, Gallery, King Library

Oct. 6
Horse Parade
Midway College Equestrian Team
University of Kentucky
Stoll Field, 12-1 p.m.

Oct. 7
"Don't Upset the Horses"
Vicki Hearne
Lecture, Recital Hall, 8 p.m.
Reception following in UK Art Museum

Oct. 9
"The Horse in Renaissance Literature"
Joan Hartwig
Gallery Lecture, King Library,
12-1 p.m.

Oct. 23
"If Wishes Were Horses: The Horse in Children's Literature"
Anne McConnell
Gallery Lecture, King Library,
12-1 p.m.

Oct. 29 - 31
Drinkers of the Wind
Guignol Theatre, 8 p.m.
$5./$4. students

The Gaines Center for the Humanities
232 East Maxwell Street
Lexington, Kentucky 40506-0344

Front

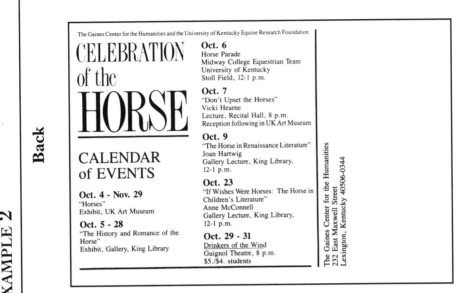

The Gaines Center for the Humanities and the University of Kentucky Equine Research Foundation

CELEBRATION
of the
HORSE

OCTOBER
1-31 1987
an interdisciplinary series of lectures and
UNIVERSITY OF KENTUCKY

25 What You Need to Know About the Media

"You've Got to Be Carefully Taught"

from South Pacific. *Music by Richard Rodgers; lyrics by Oscar Hammerstein II; book by Oscar Hammerstein II and Josh Logan.*

Opened in New York, April 7, 1949; ran 1,925 performances. Mary Martin and Ezio Pinza starred in the original Broadway production.

Deal with the media cautiously; as the song title states, "You've Got to Be Carefully Taught." Entertainment editors and staff have deadlines you must meet, procedures they want you to follow, and unique ways they like to work. You want to keep them interested in what you are doing but not get on their nerves. You have to realize that you are only one very small news item; they must deal with literally hundreds weekly.

THE PRESS

You can get your production mentioned in the local newspaper in several different ways: as a feature story, a paragraph or two in an editor's daily or weekly column, a citing in a "calendar of events," a picture with a caption, a free public service space, a review, or a paid advertisement. You might feel that your production deserves all seven; in reality, the paper will only guarantee one, a paid advertisement. To be successful with the press, you must start early, think big, make personal contact, be alert, write fast, and be very resourceful.

Press Release

Regardless of what kind of coverage you expect, your first step is to prepare a press release. Each newspaper will tell you what it wants to know about your production and your organization. In general, the following information is requested:

- Name of the organization
- Name and author(s) of the play or musical
- Director
- Designers (set, lighting, and costume)
- Date, time and place of the performances
- Ticket prices
- Box office location and telephone
- Brief synopsis of the play
- Brief background of previous professional productions
- Complete cast list
- Contact person and telephone number

A checklist for press releases has been provided at the end of this chapter (Figure 25.1).

Feature Story

You must have an "angle" and be able to convince an editor that your story will have general public appeal before you can expect a major newspaper to give your organization space for a feature story. Don't limit your appeal to the arts editor. Perhaps you can generate interest with someone else. For example, with *The Importance of Being Earnest,* you might interest the foods editor in a cookoff being held at your school or community center for the best menu to serve at an "Afternoon British Tea." Perhaps the educational editor might be interested in relating a story about the winning entries received for a "Cecily Cardew's Diary Writing Contest." Come up with a million ideas; one of them might just get you a feature story.

Special Interest Columns

It's not as difficult to get mentioned in a daily or weekly column. You need to contact the editor directly and talk up your production. Stress the total number of people involved, not just the actors. Talk about long-range objectives and your need to build an audience. Talk about the quality of the play and the learning experience. If the editor continues to be interested, share stories of "incredible moments" that happened at rehearsal. Make the conversation seem casual but be well-prepared. Anticipate questions and have the answers at your fingertips. If you get a question you don't know the answer to, don't make one up. Tell the editor you will find the answer and call back within the hour.

If you have the right angle or a good story, you might end up with a mention in a daily column. Here is another hypothetical example. Let's say you send out a call for authentic props for *The Importance of Being Earnest.* You find a very early copy of your hometown newspaper in a carpet bag that has been loaned. You call and talk to the writer of a daily interest column. The next day the following item appears in the column: "It seems like everyone in town is going through attics trying to help the students at Woodford High find authentic props for their upcoming production of *The Importance of Being Earnest.* Wanda Rodgers, director, called to tell me that she received an old carpetbag the other day that had an almost perfect copy of a May 19 issue of our paper. Would you believe, the year was 1901 and in that issue was a mention of a production of *Earnest* that was scheduled to be done by a local theater group. Isn't it remarkable how some plays never grow old!"

If you think you've got a story and it's newsworthy, follow up on it. If it doesn't work, you've only lost some time. The point to keep in mind is that editors have to fill their columns every day. Your idea might just make their job easier.

Listings

Most major newspapers offer a listing of art events once a week, usually on Sunday. A box near the bottom of the listings tells you what you need to do to be included. Follow the instructions to the letter; instead of mailing your entry in, however, hand deliver it so you can meet the person in charge.

Sometimes newspapers have a policy not to include high school and community productions in their calendar. If this is the case you may need to petition to get the policy changed or find ways around it, for example, explaining that you are directing a "Town and Gown" production since you are using a number of parents and friends as designers and backstage volunteers.

A Picture with a Caption

A picture can be worth a thousand words. Occasionally a newspaper will take a picture of something unusual and write a short caption or even a story to go with it. Here is another hypothetical possibility still using *Earnest* as a source. Let's say that you decide to use antique clothing for all the women because the grandmother of one of the cast members has an attic full of late nineteenth-century clothes in excellent condition. You convince the paper that a picture would be noteworthy because many people are interested in antique clothing. The editor of the community section agrees, and the next week the newspaper runs a large, color photograph of all four actresses posed as their characters in full costume. The example may seem farfetched, but we would argue that if the newspaper needed to fill space, such a picture could appear. Timing is everything.

Free Public Service Space

Some major newspapers give away a limited number of small ads to non-profit organizations as a public service. Call the arts editor of your newspaper to see if your school or organization could be considered for one or more of these ads.

Reviews

As a general rule major newspapers will not review high school plays and many will not review community theater productions. Reviews don't really help to sell tickets unless your production is scheduled to play over two or more weekends. Since reviews can cause a great deal of heartache, it's probably just as well that you don't seek out formal, published reviews from any press.

Advertisement

The only space you can be sure your local newspaper will give your play is space you pay for. All newspapers will be glad to sell you space for advertisements, the larger, the better. The problem is few organizations can afford to advertise, and the return on the investment is questionable. The paper will probably guarantee that your ad will appear in the entertainment section, but they won't guarantee exact placement. In the past we have had ads that were so poorly placed that we couldn't find them the first time we looked. Too many larger ads drew our attention.

RADIO AND TELEVISION

Don't restrict all your attention to newspapers. Local radio stations, and sometimes even television stations, give free public service announcements. Some stations even offer a daily arts calendar. FM stations and some local TV affiliates often include talk shows on their schedules that feature the fine arts. You can even get DJs to give you "plugs" if you are willing to give sets of free tickets to listeners who call in.

The people who work for the media may appear distant, distracted, and disinterested. Often that is because they are overworked and constantly concerned about deadlines. Be courteous and never too persistent. Be realistic in your requests and never late in providing material. Listen carefully and give them exactly what they ask for; no more, no less. Gain their respect, and don't take advantage of their position, and you might be surprised with the support they will give you and your organization when you really need it.

CHECKLIST FOR PREPARING A PRESS RELEASE

Use this page as either a checklist or a worksheet when preparing a press release for your production.

Name of the organization:

_____

Name and author(s) of the play or musical:

_____

Director:

_____

Designers (set, lighting, and costume):

_____

_____

Date, time, and place of the performances:

_____

_____

Ticket prices:

_____

Box office location and telephone:

_____

Brief synopsis of the play:

_____

_____

_____

Brief background of previous professional productions:

_____

_____

Complete cast list:

_____

_____

_____

_____

Contact person and telephone number:

_____

26 What You Need to Know About Programs

"Look at Me, I'm Sandra Dee"

from Grease.
Music, lyrics, and book
by Jim Jacobs
and Warren Casey.

Opened in New York, February 14, 1972; ran 3,388 performances. Richard Gere played Danny Zuko in the London production.

What you need to know first about programs is that they are a giveaway and shouldn't cost much money to reproduce. That doesn't mean they should be flimsy or look cheap—not at all. They should, in fact, be quite substantial and look professional. They are, after all, a reflection of your organization, a permanent memento of the production you have spent weeks working on. Nonetheless, for the majority of your audience, they are little more than a throwaway. It is important, therefore, that you don't commit a sizable portion of your budget to have them printed.

Programs can be a source of income. Just as with every aspect of the production, however, if you want to turn your playbills into a money-making venture, you need to plan ahead and start early. If you do decide to launch a major ad campaign, you shouldn't put yourself in charge. Copy deadlines will fall late in the rehearsal process, probably during the week of final run-throughs. Either your Director of Audience Development and Service needs to oversee this project, or you need to recruit someone who can. You need a real go-getter to do the job right—someone who has gumption and fortitude, a good salesperson, with ready access to a phone and a car, with the patience of Job, and with the ability to stay organized and meet deadlines. Sounds like an impossible profile to fill? Not really, but you need to screen carefully and recruit early or you will end up doing a lot of the work yourself at a time when you can least afford it.

LAYOUT

Before you get bids from printers, you need to decide what you want your program to look like, the size of the piece, and the number of pages. Base this on the amount of information you feel you need to pass on to your audience.

As far as size is concerned, we recommend that you stick to an 8 ½-by-11-inch sheet of paper folded in half. That's a standard size for playbills; they are the least expensive size to reproduce, the easiest to lay out, and the most convenient for audiences to manage.

What you must remember about layout of any size program is that every time you add a sheet, you have added another four pages to your program. If you are not careful and don't plan ahead, you can find yourself with either too much copy and not enough space, or too much space and not enough copy.

We have found, as a rule-of-thumb, that you need a minimum of three pages of program copy for plays, and a minimum of three-and-one-half pages for musicals. If you want to avoid the hassle of launching an all-out ad campaign, you can have one sponsor underwrite the expense of a simple one sheet, four-page program, with their acknowledgment on the back page. You will not have made any money; on the other hand, you will not have added an item to the deficit side of your budget. Consider this point carefully.

PROGRAM COPY

The following is a check list of the information you must include in any size program.

I. **Cover Page**

A. Sponsoring organization

    B. Title of the play

    C. Authors

    (Check the copyright page of the script or your contract for complete and correct listings and point size.)

    D. Dates of all performances (optional)

    E. Time of performance (optional)

    F. Name of auditorium (optional)

II. **Inside and Back Pages**

    A. List of Director(s):

        1. Stage Director

        2. Music Director

        3. Choreographer

        4. Orchestra Director

        (*Note:* Sometimes the Orchestra Director is listed under Production Staff.)

    B. List of Designers

        1. Setting

        2. Lighting

        3. Costume

        (*Note:* Sound, Makeup, Special Effects, Stage Manager, and the Technical Director are usually listed under Production Staff but, on occasion, have been listed in this section.)

    C. Place and Time

    (*Example:* A country road; evening.)

    D. Musical Numbers

    E. Information regarding Intermission(s):

    (*Example:* "Intermission will be fifteen minutes long.")

    F. Cast

    (List either in order of appearance or in an order that the audience will comprehend quickly. *Note:* Triple-check the spelling of names.)

    G. Orchestra

    H. Production Crew:

        1. Production Stage Manager

        2. Director of Audience Development and Services

        3. Stage Manager

        4. Sound Designer

        5. Makeup Designer/Supervisor

        6. Hair/Wig Designer

        7. Special Effects Designer

8. Technical Director
9. Vocal Coach
10. Movement Coach
11. Dramaturg
12. Assistant Designers (Set, Lights, Costume)
13. Assistant Technical Director
14. Assistant Stage Manager(s)
15. Assistant to the Director
16. Light Board Operator
17. Sound Board Operator
18. Master Carpenter
19. Properties Master/Mistress
20. House Manager
21. Box Office Manager
22. Master Electrician
23. Consultants (Makeup, Audio, Movement, Dance)
24. Head Flyman
25. Advertising
26. Program Design and Layout
27. Poster Design
28. Crews (list Running Crews and Construction Crews)

I. Administrative Staff
J. Acknowledgments

(*Note:* List everyone who helps in any capacity. This fosters good will and is invaluable in building your program.)

K. Sponsors/Patrons
L. Special Arrangements

(*Example:* "This play is presented through special arrangement with Samuel French, Inc.")

M. House Rules

(*Example:* "No smoking, food, or beverages permitted in the theater. The use of cameras or recording devices is strictly prohibited.")

Additional Program Material

If you add more pages, you can give your audience more production information that makes for interesting reading before the play begins and during intermission.

- Profiles (brief biographies of actors, directors and designers: a "Who's Who.")
- Program Notes (information about the play)
- Director's Notes (information about the concept you have used)
- Notes About the Author
- Notes About the Producing Organization
- List of Upcoming Events

ADVERTISING

If you decide to solicit advertising, consider the following sources:

- Retailers and service organizations
- Parents of cast members (*Example:* "Break a leg, Kelly McMillan, Love Mom, Dad, Grandma, Wally, and Mary.")
- In-House Supporters (*Example:* "Good Luck from the Freshman Class"; "C'est une vie formidable! Bonne chance! The Dunbar High French Club.")
- Sponsors (*Note:* Sponsors can underwrite a page of a program, the complete playbill, or an entire production.)

PRINTER

Once you have decided on the type of program you want, get bids from a print shop. Try to connect with someone who owns a small business in your community, someone who will give you a discount and preferential treatment. Make sure you are clear about deadlines and understand what is expected of you as far as camera-ready material is concerned.

Typesetting is expensive. Find someone in your school or organization who can do the final layout on a computer using an advanced software program. A checklist and various examples of programs have been provided at the end of this chapter (Figures 26.2–26.8).

You can include drawings and pictures. Black-and-white pencil sketches reproduce nicely, but photographs are not only expensive (because they need to be reduced), but they rarely reproduce clearly.

Remember to solicit help with both layout and advertising. If you recruit the right individuals, you can end up with a very handsome playbill that will not only provide all the information your audience needs to thoroughly enjoy the play, but will also serve as a fine memento for all those involved in the production.

CHECKLIST FOR PROGRAM COPY

Use this page as a checklist when you are preparing the program for your production.

Cover Page

Sponsoring organization

_____

Title of the play

_____

Authors (Check the copyright page of the script or your contract for complete and correct listing and point size.)

_____

Dates of all performances (optional)

_____

Time of performance (optional)

_____

Name of auditorium (optional)

_____

Inside and Back Pages

List of Director(s):
    Stage Director   _____

    Music Director   _____

    Choreographer   _____

    Orchestra Director   _____
    (_Note:_ Sometimes the Orchestra Director is listed under Production Staff.)

List of Designers:
    Setting _____

    Lighting _____

    Costume _____
    (_Note:_ Sound, Makeup, Special Effects, Stage Manager, and the Technical Director are usually listed under Production Staff but, on occasion, have been listed in this section.)

Place and Time (*Example:* A country road; evening.)

_____

Musical Numbers:

_____

_____

_____

_____

Information regarding Intermission(s): (*Example:* "Intermission will be fifteen minutes long.")

_____

Cast (List either in order of appearance, or in an order that the audience will comprehend quickly. *Note:* Triple-check the spelling of names.)

_____

_____

_____

_____

_____

Orchestra:

_____

_____

_____

_____

Production Crew:
   Production Stage Manager _____

   Director of Audience Development and Services _____

   Stage Manager _____

26.1 continued

Sound Designer _____

Makeup Designer/Supervisor _____

Hair/Wig Designer _____

Special Effects Designer _____

Technical Director _____

Vocal Coach_____

Movement Coach _____

Dramaturg_____

Assistant Designers (Set, Lights, Costume)

_____

_____

_____

Assistant Technical Director _____

Assistant Stage Manager(s) _____

Assistant to the Director _____

Light Board Operator _____

Sound Board Operator _____

Master Carpenter _____

Properties Master/Mistress_____

House Manager _____

Box Office Manager_____

Master Electrician_____

Consultants: (Makeup, Audio, Movement, Dance)

_____

Head Flyman_____

© 1995 by John Wiley & Sons, Inc.

Advertising _____

Program Design and Layout _____

Poster Design _____

Crews (Running Crews and Construction Crews)

_____

_____

_____

_____

Administrative Staff

_____

_____

Acknowledgments (*Note:* Make sure that you list everyone who helps in any capacity. This fosters goodwill and is invaluable in building your program.)

_____

_____

_____

Sponsors/Patrons

_____

_____

Special Arrangements (*Example:* "This play is presented through special arrangement with Samuel French, Inc.")

_____

_____

House Rules (*Example:* "No smoking, food, or beverages permitted in the theater. The use of cameras or recording devices is strictly prohibited.")

_____

_____

_____

26.1 continued

Additional Program Material

If you add more pages, you can give your audience more production information that makes for interesting reading before the play begins and during intermission. Here are some suggestions for items you might want to include:

Profiles (Brief biographies of actors, directors and designers: a "Who's Who")

Program Notes (Information about the play)

Director's Notes (Information about the concept you have used)

Notes About the Author

Notes About the Producing Organization

List of Upcoming Events

SAMPLE PROGRAM LAYOUT—UNDER MILKWOOD

OUTSIDE

Faculty and Staff, PERFORMING ARTS CENTRE
DR. JAMES W. RODGERS, *Chairman*

Harriet Berg, *Instructor. Dance Movement*
Kathy Hopkins, *Graduate Assistant. Creative Dramatics*
Michael Huesman, *Technical Director*
Michael Krause, *Associate Professor*
Suzanne Mahoney, *Acting Costumiere*
Dominic E. Missimi, *Director of Theatre, (on-leave)*
Nancy Missimi, *Costumiere (on-leave)*
Marjorie Muffit, *Publicity Director*
David Regal, *Guest Artist in Residence. Term I & Term II*
Shepperd, Strudwick, *Guest Artist in Residence. Term II*
Thelma Sullivan *Secretary*
Harold Thrasher, *Designer*

THE PERFORMING ARTS CENTRE

THE THEATRE - Season I
THE TEMPEST by William Shakespeare
February 3, 4, 5, 6, 10, 11, 12, 13, 17, 18, 19, 20
CHILD'S PLAY by Robert Marasco (Detroit Premiere)
March 9, 10, 11, 12, 16, 17, 18, 19, 23, 24, 25, 26
LYSISTRATA by Aristophanes
April 6, 7, 8, 9, 13, 14, 15, 16

U. OF D. CONCERT SERIES
November 13 DONOVAN $5.50, $4.50 $3.50
November 20 DIONNE WARWICKE $6. $5. $4.

DETROIT METROPOLITAN DANCE PROJECT
Dr. James W. Rodgers, Executive Director
February 24-26 MERCE CUNNINGHAM COMPANY
March 5-12 CARLA MAXWELL & CLYDE MORGAN

For information about any of the above. please write or call:
THE PERFORMING ARTS CENTRE. U. of D.. Det. Mich. 48221 • Phone: 342-1000.

INSIDE

The Performing Arts Centre
University of Detroit-Marygrove College
presents

UNDER MILK WOOD
by DYLAN THOMAS
Directed by DAVID REGAL
Lighting by DAVID HARTMANN
Costumes by SUZANNE MAHONEY

CAST OF CHARACTERS

First Voice .... Gary Eberle
Second Voice .... Lee O'Connell
Captain Catt .... Marc McCulloch
First Drowned .... Tom Nugent
Second Drowned .... Byron Grady
Rosie Probert .... Patty Morouse
Third Drowned .... Alan Shinkman
Fourth Drowned .... Joe Farinella
Fifth Drowned .... Bill McDonald
Miss Myfanwy Price .... Kathy Hopkins
Mr. Mog Edwards .... John Guinn
Jack Black .... Alan Shinkman
Waldo's Wife .... Jeannine Andree
Mr. Waldo .... Bob Beaupre
First Neighbor .... Yvonne Doolittle
Second Neighbor .... Liz Garrett
Mrs. Ogmore-Pritchard .... Kathy Hopkins
Mr. Ogmore .... John Dwyer
Mr. Pritchard .... James Stahl
Utah Watkins .... Bill McDonald
Mrs. Utah Watkins .... Debbie Mims
Ocky Milkman .... Joe Farinella
Mrs. Willy Nilly .... June Snow
Mae Rose Cottage .... Cathy Blaser
Butcher Beynon .... Marc McCulloch
Gossamer Beynon .... Debbie Mims
Reverend Eli Jenkins .... James Stahl
Mr. Pugh .... John Dwyer
Mary Ann Sailors .... Dena Margolis
Dai Bread .... Tom Nugent
Polly Garter .... Marianne Ilg
Nogood Boyo .... Byron Grady
Lord Cut-Glass .... Bob Beaupre
Lilly Smalls .... Jane Hamara

Mrs. Beynon .... Jeannie Andree
Mrs. Pugh .... June Snow
Mrs. Dai Bread One .... Patty Morouse
Mrs. Dai Bread Two .... Yvonne Doolittle
Willy Nilly .... Tom Nugent
Mrs. Cherry Owen .... Dena Margolis
Cherry Owen .... John Guinn
Sinbad Sailors .... Joe Farinella
Mrs. Organ Morgan .... Dena Margolis
Organ Morgan .... Nick Snow
Bessie Bighead .... Liz Garrett

Staff for UNDER MILK WOOD

Assistant Director .... Kathy Bieke
Properties .... Rosemary Gant
Lighting .... David Hartmann, Paul Androkovich
Sound .... Marc McCulloch, Kathy Bieke
Crew .... Jane Linahan. Jane Hamara.
David Kenny, Courtney Morgan
House Manager .... Mary Boyer
Photographer .... Brendan Wehrung

Student Staff for the PERFORMING ARTS CENTRE

Walter Kempski
Joe Rutherford
Greg Menke
Kathleen Vance
Mary Boyer
Cathy Blaser

Marc McCulloch
David Hartmann
James Stahl
Dominic Kline
Sharon Ryszka
Sue Bania

SAMPLE PROGRAM LAYOUT—DEATHTRAP

OUTSIDE

UK THEATRE
1988-89 SEASON!

AH, WILDERNESS!
By Eugene O'Neill
A delightful and tender comedy by America's
premiere writer.
OCTOBER 6,7,8,13,14,15 at 8:00

MISS JULIE
By August Strindberg
A battle between the sexes and the classes.
OCTOBER 27,28,29,30, and NOVEMBER 1,3,4,5,
at 8:00

**JOSEPH AND HIS AMAZING
TECHNICOLOR DREAMCOAT**
By Tim Rice and Andrew Lloyd Webber
A modern musical fantasy of the biblical tale.
NOVEMBER 17,18,19 and DECEMBER 1,2,3 at 8:00

MY SISTER IN THIS HOUSE
By Wendy Kesselman
The story of four lonely women whose lives
become dangerously and tragically intertwined.
FEBRUARY 16,17,18,23,24,25 at 8:00

BILOXI BLUES
By Neil Simon
A Tony Award Winning, autobiographical comedy!
This play begins where BRIGHTON BEACH MEMOIRS
left off.
APRIL 13,14,15,20,21,22 at 8:00

FOR INFORMATION CALL: 257-1592
FOR TICKETS CALL: 257-4929
(Between Noon and 4:00)

UNIVERSITY OF KENTUCKY * COLLEGE OF FINE ARTS

UK THEATRE
PROUDLY PRESENTS

DEATHTRAP

BY IRA LEVIN

JUNE 2,3,4,9,10,11, – 8:00

Guignol Theatre

College of Fine Arts–University of Kentucky

INSIDE

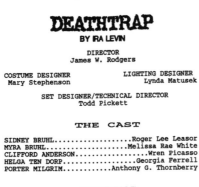

BY IRA LEVIN

DIRECTOR
James W. Rodgers

COSTUME DESIGNER   LIGHTING DESIGNER
Mary Stephenson   Lynda Matusek

SET DESIGNER/TECHNICAL DIRECTOR
Todd Pickett

THE CAST

SIDNEY BRUHL.................Roger Lee Leasor
MYRA BRUHL....................Melissa Rae White
CLIFFORD ANDERSON.................Wren Picasso
HELGA TEN DORP.................Georgia Ferrell
PORTER MILGRIM...........Anthony G. Thornberry

SETTING

The action takes place in Sidney Bruhl's Study,
in the Bruhl home in Westport, Connecticut.

ACT I

Scene 1: An afternoon in October
Scene 2: That evening
Scene 3: Two hours later

ACT II

Scene 1: Two weeks later, morning
Scene 2: A week later, night
Scene 3: A week later, afternoon

THERE WILL BE ONE TEN MINUTE INTERMISSION.

PRODUCTION

STAGE MANAGER.......................Dave Dees
PROPERTIES MASTER/DESIGNERS.........Dave Dees,
.... Todd Pickett, Frank Moles
LIGHT BOARD OPERATOR.............Sully White
SOUND BOARD OPERATOR.......Jenni Lynne Rodgers
MASTER CARPENTER...................Frank Moles
SCENIC ARTIST.....................Todd Pickett
HOUSE MANAGER...................Elisabeth Ford
BOX OFFICE MANAGER.................Sarah Bowen
BOX OFFICE ASSISTANTS.............Cindy Bowen,
........Elisabeth Ford, Pati Marks, Betty Waren
PROGRAM EDITOR........................Pati Marks
PUBLICITY DIRECTOR..............Elisabeth Ford
SCENE CONSTRUCTION.............John Holloway,
........Frank Moles, Sully White, Lisa Blevins,
...............................Judy Walker,
.... Navada Shane Morgan, Amy Berry
COSTUMES.........Melissa White, Brian Holman
WARDROBE MISTRESS..............Ronda Jo Castle
WARDROBE CREW....................Laura Finch,
.... Elizabeth Cornett, Gail Wilborn
FLY PERSON.................Navada Shane Morgan
PROPERTIES........................Judy Walker

SPECIAL THANKS

John Holloway, Pat White, Sherri Hancock,
Antique Mall at Todd's Square, Missy Holloway,
KET, Joe Marks, John Whitehead

Please do not eat, drink, smoke or use cameras
or recorders in the theatre. Leave beepers
with the House Manager. Thank you.

DEATHTRAP is produced with permission of
Dramatist Play Service, 440 Park Ave., New
York, New York 10016.

SAMPLE PROGRAM LAYOUT — TIES THAT BIND

OUTSIDE

WHO'S WHO

BETTY L. BLANTON - (Grace) - A graduate of the University of Louisville Betty also received a Bachelor of Divinity from the Lexington Theological Seminary. She was ordained to the Ministry by Translyvania Presbytery in 1967. Betty served churches in Gainsville and Jacksonville Florida and was interim minister of several churches in Kentucky. Now retired and living in Lexington, this is Betty's acting debut.

GEORGIA FERRELL - (Lilly) - Georgia did both her undergraduate and postgraduate work at the University of Montana. Georgia has had a very active acting career including performances at Newberry College, Bigfork Summer Theatre, with Georgetown Players and in recent years with many theatre groups in Lexington. She has appeared as the lead in many productions including; Madame Arcati in Blithe Spirit, Martha in Who's Afraid of Virginia Woolf, Amanda in The Glass Menagerie, and Big Mama in Cat On A Hot Tin Roof, and Juno in Juno and the Paycock.

MARIE HENDERSON - (Maybell) - Marie recently completed her Master's degree in theatre at the University of Kentucky. While attending U.K. she appeared in productions of Black Coffee, The Lion the Witch and the Wardrobe, Chicago, and others. Besides acting, Marie especially likes to design and construct theatrical masks, and also enjoys the business end of theatre. By day she sells college textbooks-by night she sells theatre tickets--and once in a while she likes to be in a play.

CAROL SPENCE - (Sarah Jane) - Carol is a graduate of the Pennsylvania State University with a B.A. in Speech Communications and an M.A. in Theatre from the University of Kentucky. She has played a variety of roles including; Sissy in Come Back to the 5 & Dime, Jimmy Dean, Jimmy Dean, Veronica In Veronica's Room, and the psychiatrist in Agnes of God. Carol is on of the founding members of Actors' Guild of Lexington and is currently the Producing Director of the company.

KENTUCKY EXTENSION HOMEMAKERS PRESENT

TIES THAT BIND

BY DR. JAMES W. RODGERS
CHAIRMAN, UK THEATRE DEPARTMENT

GRACE / LILLY / MAYBELL / SARAH JANE

UK SINGLETARY CENTER FOR THE ARTS, LEXINGTON, KENTUCKY

INSIDE

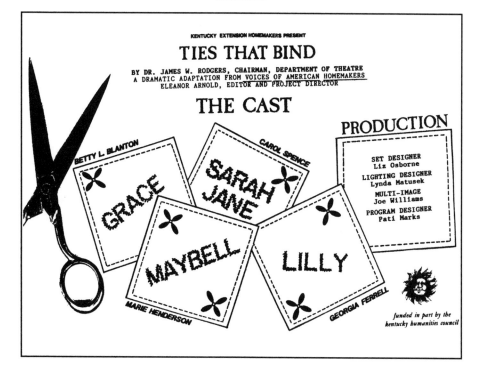

KENTUCKY EXTENSION HOMEMAKERS PRESENT

TIES THAT BIND

BY DR. JAMES W. RODGERS, CHAIRMAN, DEPARTMENT OF THEATRE
A DRAMATIC ADAPTATION FROM VOICES OF AMERICAN HOMEMAKERS
ELEANOR ARNOLD, EDITOR AND PROJECT DIRECTOR

THE CAST

BETTY L. BLANTON — GRACE
CAROL SPENCE — SARAH JANE
MARIE HENDERSON — MAYBELL
GEORGIA FERRELL — LILLY

PRODUCTION

SET DESIGNER
Liz Osborne

LIGHTING DESIGNER
Lynda Matusek

MULTI-IMAGE
Joe Williams

PROGRAM DESIGNER
Pati Marks

funded in part by the
kentucky humanities council

SAMPLE PROGRAM LAYOUT—WE BOMBED IN NEW HAVEN

OUTSIDE

Department for the Performing Arts

Calendar of Events

THE IRON BUTTERFLY — **Sunday, November 1**
U. of D. Memorial Building, 8:30 p.m. — $5.00, $4.00, $3.00

PAUL TAYLOR
DANCE COMPANY — **Friday, November 6**
Detroit Institute of Arts, 8:30 p.m. — $5.50, $4.00, $2.50

MASTER CLASS with
PAUL TAYLOR DANCE CO., Monday, November 9
U. of D. Memorial Building, 4:00 p.m. — $2.50

TIS PITY SHE'S A WHORE — opens November 12
Theatre 113, 8:30 p.m., Sunday at 7:30 p.m. — $2.50

LEONARD COHEN — **Friday, November 20**
U. of D. Memorial Building, 8:30 p.m. — $5.00, $4.00, $3.00

LAURA NYRO — **Friday, December 4**
U. of D. Memorial Building, 8:30 p.m. — $5.00, $4.00, $3.00

For information concerning all Theatre and Town and Gown
events call 342-1000, extension 339. Tickets are available for
all events at the Performing Arts Box Office in the Student
Union Building.

THEATRE 113

INSIDE

Department For The Performing Arts

Faculty and Staff

JAMES W. RODGERS	Chairman, Department of Performing Arts
DOMINIC E. MISSIMI	Director of Theatre
ROBERT CLYMIRE	Assistant Director of Theatre
MICHAEL HUESMAN	Technical Director
NANCY MISSIMI	Costumer
MARJORIE MUFFIT	Publicity Director
THELMA SULLIVAN	Secretary
JEANETTE LINAHAN	Box Office

Student Staff for the University Theatres

HAROLD THRASHER	Designer
STEPHEN GUNTLI, MICHAEL KLIER	Technical Assistants
MARSHA HARDY	Lighting Supervisor
MARY BOYER	House and Properties
KATHLEEN VANCE	Sound and Properties
MARY JO ALEXANDER, CATHY BLASER,	
SUE MAHONEY, GRETCHEN SNOW	Costume Assistants
ROSALIND BROWN	Departmental Secretary
BARBARA MURPHY	Publicity Assistant
NEIL THACKABERRY	Coordinator, Stage II

We Bombed In New Haven

by JOSEPH HELLER

directed by JAMES W. RODGERS

settings by *Harold Thrasher and Michael Huesman*

lighting by *Marsha Hardy*

Cast of Characters

The Major	Jim Scott
Captain Starkey	A. Neil Thackaberry
Sergeant Henderson	Michael Donohue
Corporal Bailey	Richard DeWees
Corporal Sinclair	Sidney Skipper
PFC Joe Carson	Anthony Hayes
Private Fisher	Michael Klier
Ruth	Susan McDonald
Hunter	J. Michael Sparough
Golfer	A. J. Miceli, S.J.
Young Fisher	Tim Kiernan
Starkey's Son	Greg Menke
Pat	Pat O'Leary
Tony	Tony Arnone
Jack	Jack Clanton
Dominic	Dominic Kline
John	John W. Frencher

SAMPLE PROGRAM LAYOUT — A WINNIE-THE-POOH CHRISTMAS TAIL

OUTSIDE

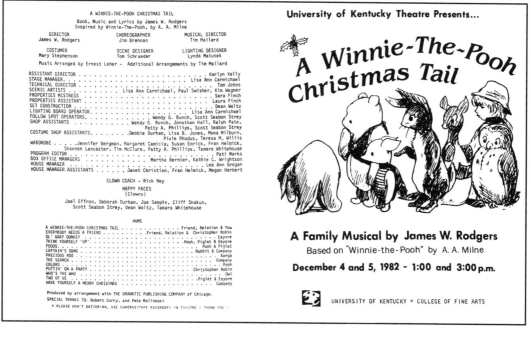

INSIDE

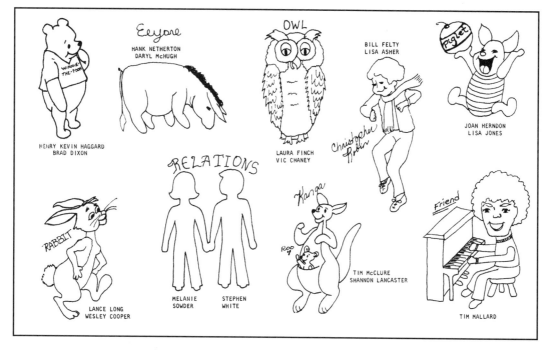

SAMPLE PROGRAM LAYOUT (8 ½″ x 14″)—INTO THE WOODS

OUTSIDE

UK THEATRE

proudly presents

INTO THE WOODS

Music and Lyrics by
STEPHEN SONDHEIM
Book by
JAMES LAPINE

GUIGNOL THEATRE

October 6, 7, 8, 13, 14, 15 at 8 P.M.
October 9 & 16 at 2 P.M.

Original Broadway Production by
Heidi Landesman, Rocco Landesman, Rick Steiner
M. Anthony Fisher, Frederic H. Mayerson, Jujamcyn Theaters
Originally produced by the Old Globe Theater, San Diego, CA.

KC/ACTF XXVII

Kennedy Center American College Theater Festival XXVII

Presented and produced by
The John F. Kennedy Center for the Performing Arts
Supported in Part by
The Kennedy Center Corporate Fund
The U.S. Department of Education
Ryder System

This production is entered in the Kennedy Center American College Theater Festival (KC/ACTF). The aims of this national theater education program are to identify and promote quality in college-level theater production. To this end, each production entered is eligible for adjudication by a regional KC/ACTF representative, and certain students are selected to participate in KC/ACTF programs involving awards, scholarships, and special grants for actors, playwrights, designers, and critics at both the regional and national levels.

Productions entered on the Participating level are eligible for inclusion at the KC/ACTF regional festival and can also be considered for invitation to the non-competitive KC/ACTF national festival at the John F. Kennedy Center for the Performing Arts in Washington, DC, in the spring of 1995.

The KC/ACTF is a program of the Kennedy Center Education Department, which also includes youth and family programs, professional development opportunities for teachers, and performances for school groups, the Kennedy Center Alliance for Arts Education, the Performing Arts Centers and Schools Program, performance enhancement events, national and community outreach initiatives, the Kennedy Center Internship Program, and the National Symphony Orchestra education program. The Kennedy Center also works closely with Very Special Arts, an educational affiliate of the Kennedy Center.

Last year more than 800 productions and 17,000 students participated in the American College Theater Festival nationwide. By entering this production, our department is sharing in the KC/ACTF goals to help college theater grow and to focus attention on the exemplary work produced in college and university theaters across the nation.

SPECIAL THANKS...

BOB ANDREWS
SAM AND HARRIET BALL
TRISH CLARK
PAUL LAURENCE DUNBAR HIGH SCHOOL
JOE FERRELL
SAM GRAPER
MARIE HENDERSON
CLIFF JACKSON

Specialty Costumes by The Lexington Costume Company

ORCHESTRA

Conducted by
PHILLIP MILLER

Violins...CHAD BEAUCHAINE
ALLISON JOHNSTON
Violas...RON DILLARD
JENNIFER TEAL
Cello...HOPE COTTRILL
Contra-Bass...JOE TACKETT
Piano...NAN McSWAIN
Flute...BARB BUEHNER
Clarinet...PETER MONSEN
Bassoon...JENNIFER COLLINS
Horns...DAVID SHELTON
SHERRY HOLBROOK
Trumpet...JARED SCARBROUGH
Percussion...TERALYN SCHWAB

MUSICAL NUMBERS

ACT ONE
"Into The Woods"
"Hello, Little Girl"
"I Guess This Is Goodbye"
"Maybe They're Magic"
"I Know Things Now"
"A Very Nice Prince"
"Our Little World"
"Giants In The Sky"
"Agony"
"It Takes Two"
"Stay With Me"
"On The Steps
Of The Palace"
"Ever After"

ACT TWO
"So Happy"
"Agony"
"Lament"
"Any Moment"
"Moments In The Woods"
"Your Fault"
"The Last Midnight"
"No More"
"No One is Alone"
"Children Will Listen"

© 1995 by John Wiley & Sons, Inc.

SAMPLE PROGRAM LAYOUT (8 ½″ x 14″)—INTO THE WOODS

INSIDE

INTO THE WOODS

Music and Lyrics by STEPHEN SONDHEIM
Book by JAMES LAPINE
Originally Directed on Broadway by James Lapine

Directed by
JAMES W. RODGERS

Musical Direction by
EVERETT McCORVEY

Conducted by
PHILLIP MILLER

Costume Design by
MARY STEPHENSON

Costumier
A. J. PINKNEY

Lighting Design by
JEFF FIGHTMASTER
Assisted by Clifton Grimm

Make-Up Design by
RUSSELL HENDERSON
Assisted by Kris Deskins

Scenery Design by
BARBARA ROGERS
Assisted by Lisa Cordonnier

Sound Design by
MICHAEL LAVIN
Assisted by Susan Ruth

Technical Director
JOHN HOLLOWAY

CAST

Narrator...JUSTIN SMITH
Cinderella...CORRIE JO SMITH
Jack...MIKE FRYMAN
Jack's Mother...TINA TOBER
Baker...JOHNATHAN STEPPE
Baker's Wife...ANNA HESS
Cinderella's Stepmother...JENNY FAIR
Florinda (stepsister)...TESSA MOODY
Lucinda (stepsister)...MELISSA DRISCOL
Cinderella's Father...TIM HUESMAN
Little Red Riding Hood...KELLY TEMPLE
Witch...CATHERINE CLARK
Cinderella's Mother...PAULA HUMPHRESS
Mysterious Man...DENNIS GILBAR
Granny/Giant...DAWN E. A. COON
Rapunzel...CATHERINE HAMBLIN
Rapunzel's Prince...JEFFREY TIEMANN
Steward...BO LIST
Snow White...HEATHER LADICK
Sleeping Beauty...HADLEY COMBS
Woodspersons...JIMMY GISH
        MELISSA GROSECLOSE
        MARK ISON
        LAURIE WARNECKE

Stage Manager
TOM McCORMICK
Assisted by Shalom Anwyl

Rehearsal Pianist
NAN McSWAIN

Into the Woods is produced by special arrangement with
and all authorized performance materials are supplied by
Music Theatre International, 545 Eighth Avenue, NY, NY 10018

There will be one 15-minute intermission

PRODUCTION STAFF

Charge Painter...ASHLEY JONES
Scenic Artists...KELLY FULKERSON
        TONY HARDIN
        NINA JOHANSSON
        KARA WOOTEN
Costume Shop Assistants...KELLY FULKERSON
        LAUREN HITT
        JODEEN HOBLITZELL
Costume Technicians...LORI ADCOCK
        KIM DIXON
        MELANIE-SHA ONKST
        DAVID SENATORE
        KIMBERLY THOMSON
House Manager...STEVEN O'DEA
Properties Master...KAREN HORNBERGER
Scene Shop Assistants...LISA CORDONNIER
        TONY HARDIN
        BARBARA TOMECEK

CREW

Deck Carpenters...JESSE ROBBINS
        ERON WERONKA
        LORI WOODYARD
Deck Electrician...CHARLIE CALVERT
Fly Persons...TRACY McMAHON
        MIKE MOLLOY
        TRACY O'ROARK
Follow Spots...CHAD DOSSETT
        HEATHER SCHAPIRO
Lighting Console...MELIA GRAHAM
Makeup...SCOTT MATHER
Properties...STEFFANI SHREVE
Sound Console...SUSAN RUTH
Wardrobe Master...DAVID SENATORE
Wardrobe...KELLI COMBS
        JAMIE ENOCH
        KARA GRAHAM
        LAUREN HITT
        MELANIE HOUSE
        KARL LINDSTROM

27 What You Need to Know About Audiences

"Bea-u-ti-ful People of Denver"

from The Unsinkable Molly Brown.

Music and lyrics by Meredith Willson;

book by Richard Morris.

Opened in New York, September 26, 1960; ran 532 performances. Tammy Grimes and Harve Presnell played the leads in the Broadway production; Debbie Reynolds played Molly in the film version.

In this chapter we are going to discuss how to treat your audiences like "Beautiful People of Denver." It is critical that you do so. They have given up time and money to see your play. If they are hassled in the lobby before the production, their negative attitude could carry over into the auditorium and ruin their appreciation of the play. We have observed too many occasions when this has been the case. Don't let this happen. With a clearly drawn set of policies, a careful selection of personnel, good training, and some organization, you can be assured that your audience will be treated fairly and courteously.

PERSONNEL AND POLICIES

Box Office

If you have regular box office hours, sellers should work straight through on days of performances. If not, they should arrive at least two hours before the performance (by 6:00 P.M. if you have an 8:00 P.M. curtain). We stress that the box office staff should be very courteous and take care of errors as quickly as possible. Don't dwell on the mistake; fix the problem. Also, don't rush patrons, even if a line is forming. At all times, be pleasant and professional.

House Manager

House Managers should arrive at the theater at least one and one-half hours before curtain. They need to check the temperature in the auditorium and make sure that the lobby, rest rooms, and the house itself have been cleaned. They should check the box office for any messages. They need to have a list of telephone numbers (physical plant, fire department, police) for emergencies.

The House Manager should know how to handle crowd control if the fire alarm goes off in the theater. Additional responsibilities fall under separate headings throughout this chapter.

Ushers, Ticket Takers, Cloak Room Staff, and Concession Operators

The front-of-house staff should arrive at approximately the same time as the House Manager (6:30 P.M. for a 8:00 P.M. curtain). They should all dress appropriately, as if they were hosting a party. It is best if they are given badges or some other clear mark of identification. They also should be equipped with flashlights.

Everyone on staff should greet patrons with a smile.

Ushers and Ticket Takers should familiarize themselves with the seating plan and stuff programs with any inserts before the audience arrives. The House Manager should hold a brief meeting with Ushers. They should be shown the location of the rest rooms and water fountains.

The ticket system should be explained including the color of the tickets for that evening's performance.

The House Manager should go over all House polices on smoking, the use of beepers, cameras, and tape recorders—our recommendation is that all of them be forbidden in the theater.

Ushers need to know the length of the performance, the approximate times of intermissions, and how to handle latecomers.

The House should open at approximately one-half hour before curtain. Ushers and Ticket Takers should stay at their posts until at least fifteen minutes into the performance.

Latecomers should be held in the lobby until scene breaks or appropriate breaks in the play's action. If possible, seat them in the back of the house until intermission.

Ushers and Ticket Takers are usually given permission to watch the show, but they should return to their posts during intermission. After performances, they should stay and pick up programs before they leave.

Ticket Takers need to turn in all stubs immediately, before they sit down to watch the show.

The coat room needs to be secure or staffed during the performance.

Curtain

Never try to hold the curtain more than five minutes. Even if you have a sellout and are trying to seat latecomers, it is best to start the performance after a five-minute delay. The rest of the audience gets frustrated and angry. We have known people who wanted their money back because of long delays.

Pre-Curtain Speeches

Some theaters have their House Manager give a short welcoming speech before the play begins. They acknowledge co-sponsors for the evening's performance; announce the next production; point out exits; state policies regarding smoking, cameras, beepers, and recording devices; correct any errors or additions in the program; and make any other appropriate announcements.

If you use this pre-show option, make sure the House Manager is rehearsed and coached. It is embarrassing and makes a poor impression when the person doing the announcement is ill prepared. The announcer should be pleasant, the message should be short and to the point, and the delivery should be clear and distinct.

Intermission

Intermissions run from ten to twenty minutes in length. Our recommendation is to keep them short. Ushers should be prepared to direct patrons to the smoking area, rest rooms, concession stands, and drinking fountains.

The House Manager should give a clear five-minute warning during intermission. Some theaters flash the lobby lights; others call out the warning; still others play a fanfare over the PA system. Whatever system you use, make sure that it clearly communicates to all patrons in all areas, including rest rooms and out-of-doors, that the curtain will go up in five minutes.

Concessions

Make sure that you have an appropriate number of people to handle concessions. We suggest that you limit the offerings to two or three items. Have plenty of change and an extra supply of napkins. Post selections and prices clearly to avoid confusion. Remember, you probably need to take care of all people interested in refreshments in approximately five minutes.

We suggest that you sell T-shirts and other memorabilia at a location other than the concession stand. People like to browse around these items and think about purchases before they make them.

Lobby Displays

If you don't have a gallery off your lobby, it's nice to set up a display for patrons to look at before the performance and during intermission. If you don't have a picture program, you could display an 8-by-10-inch glossy of each member of your cast with their names (and sometimes the roles they play) marked clearly below. You can also work up displays that announce your next play or relate to the play you are presenting. For example, if you were producing *The Importance of Being Earnest,* you might have a picture display on the life and works of Oscar Wilde, a history of the period, or a collage of pictures with captions from professional productions. Keep reading material at a minimum; the emphasis should be on pictures, not on text.

Protocol During Curtain Calls

Have a clear policy about flowers being given across the footlights at curtain calls. Our strong recommendation is to not allow it.

The House Manager also needs to know the policy regarding patrons going onto the stage after performances, and actors coming out into the House to greet family and friends in costume and makeup. Again, our recommendation is actors should get out of costume and makeup immediately after curtain call so the wardrobe staff is not held up.

Other Considerations

- You need to provide a secure place to hold cameras, beepers, and tape recorders.
- You need to develop a system to contact doctors in the audience who might receive emergency calls during a performance.
- Your theater should be prepared to seat wheelchair patrons without fuss.

Epilogue
DIRECTORY

28 Acting/ Directing Terms

"Life on the Wicked Stage"

from Show Boat.
Music by Jerome Kern;
lyrics and book by Oscar
Hammerstein II.

Opened in New York, December 27, 1927; ran 572 performances. The part of Joe was written for Paul Robeson, who played the role in London and in the 1936 film version. Helen Morgan made the role of Julie La Verne famous.

beat: specific moment in an actor's speech.

business: activity performed by an actor during or in place of a speech; for example, lighting a cigarette, knitting, mixing a drink.

cheat: move that does not attract attention to itself while managing to keep the actor in view of the audience. Director may say, "Cheat right" or "Cheat open."

closed turn: turn made away and with the actor's back to the audience, usually considered a poor movement. The opposite, an open turn, is most often preferred.

counter (also **dress**): as one actor moves, another actor shifts his/her position to balance the composition of a scene.

cover: standing in front of another actor or distracting during another actor's piece of business.

cross: movement of an actor from one position on the stage to another.

cue: signal (line, piece of business) to an actor or stage technician that the next line or stage function is to occur.

director's concept: central idea, metaphor, that forms the basis for all artistic choices in a production.

emotional memory: technique of acting first used by Stanislavsky, by which actors relate to their characters' emotions by recalling the details surrounding some similar emotions from their own personal experience.

ensemble: sense of "family" unity developed by a group of performers during the course of a play; the willingness of actors to subordinate themselves to the production as a whole.

focus: controlling the audience's attention. A director may have to ask an actor not to steal focus with excessive movement on another actor's line.

give stage: director's request that an actor take a weak position so another actor can have focus.

given circumstances: according to Stanislavsky, those aspects of character that are beyond the character's or actor's control: age, sex, state of health, and so on.

magic "if": Stanislavsky's term for the actors' technique to imagine themselves as one with the situations they play.

objective: Stanislavsky's term for the goal toward which a character is striving. The super-objective (also called *spine*) is the life goal that determines how the character responds in any situation.

•

open: actor is to turn front and face the audience.

open turn: actor is to turn toward the audience.

pacing: rate of performance. Speed is not the only factor of pacing; equally important are intensity, precision, clarity, and frequency of new impressions.

projection: actor's technique for making voice, movements, and gestures clear to all parts of the house.

share stage: placing actors so all have equal focus and emphasis.

Stanislavsky method: a system of acting created by the Russian director and actor Constantin Stanislavsky, in which the actor finds and expresses the inner truth of the character by defining the character's objectives, developing a subtext for every moment on stage, exploring the character's emotional life through emotional memory and improvisation, and applying the magic "if" during rehearsal and performance.

static scene: scene with little movement and no drive; to be avoided at all cost.

strike: in two words, to remove; in rehearsal, perhaps a prop, like a glass or a chair; after a production, the entire set and all the properties from the stage area.

subtext: in the Stanislavsky system of acting, the thoughts that accompany the lines, implied but not spoken in the text. The actors invent the subtext appropriate to their characters and situations to help achieve the sense of immediate truth.

tableau: moment in which a living picture is created on stage and held by actors without motion or speech.

tag line: final line of a scene or act, or the exit line of a major character. When it is the final line of an act it is also called a *curtain line.*

take five: slang term used to indicate that you are going to take a break from working for five minutes. Quite often the break is ten, rather than five, minutes.

take stage: director's request that an actor move into a more prominent position on stage; also that the actor needs to expend more energy in the scene.

tempo: general rate of playing a scene. Tempo depends on cue pickup, the rate lines are read, and the overall energy level of the performance: the intensity.

throw away: underplay a moment in a scene; deemphasize a line reading or a piece of business.

top: pick up the energy, the pace, and the volume of a scene: one actor tops the other thereby building tension and emotional impact.

turn in: actor is to face upstage, away from the audience.

turn out: actor is to face downstage, toward the audience.

upstage: area on the stage area farthest away from the audience. The term dates back to the days when the stage was raked away from the audience so that actors had to literally walk upstage.

29 Odd Names for Technical Things

"Drop That Name"

from Bells Are Ringing. *Music by Jule Styne; lyrics and book by Betty Comden and Adolph Green.*

Opened in New York, November 29, 1956; ran 924 performances. The film version (1960) starred Judy Holliday and Dean Martin and was directed by Vincente Minnelli.

The following is a listing by category of not-so-obvious stage terms beginning directors should know. You will need to become familiar with many other terms as you continue to work on plays and musicals, but we have restricted our list in each section to the most basic.

GENERAL THEATER TERMS

acting edition: softbound copy of the script which often contains the stage directions, sound and light cues, prop lists and costume descriptions from the prompt script of the world premier production. It is important to note that this added information was not provided by the playwright.

Actors Equity Association: 165 West 46 Street, New York, New York 10036. Founded in 1912, this organization serves as a labor union for professional actors.

box set: realistic, interior setting made of flats to simulate the three interior walls, and sometimes a ceiling. The audience views the play through the imaginary fourth wall.

Broadway: that area of New York City on and adjacent to the street named Broadway where the commercial theater of the United States is concentrated.

claque: persons who are hired by performers (or their representatives) for the express purpose of starting and sustaining applause for them. Claques may be instructed to start applause on the entrance or exit of a performer, or to cheer, whistle, or otherwise seem to show enthusiasm for the performance, in the hope that other audience members will believe the performance to be better than it is. Thoroughly discredited as a practice in live theater (except on opening nights), claques are still employed in grand opera.

commercial theater: theater produced with the primary goal of making money for investors.

flat: frame constructed of 1-by-3 boards, covered with canvas, painted, and used most often for interior or exterior walls of a building in a stage setting.

greenroom: traditional name of the room in which actors gather to wait for entrances. Although many are not painted green today, it is thought that the equivalent room in London's Drury Lane Theater was green—hence the name.

motif: recurring thematic element or a pattern of repetition of design elements in a work of art.

off-Broadway: smaller professional theaters (with a capacity of less than 299 seats) around and outside the central New York theater district on Broadway and around Times Square. Originally noted for their experimental nature, these theaters have become, for the most part, as commercial as their Broadway counterparts.

off-off-Broadway: very small professional theaters with a capacity of under 137 seats, often subsidized, which are often set up in lofts, warehouses, or churches and are usually characterized by their experimental scripts and styles of production.

regional theater: also called resident theater. A term applied to permanent nonprofit professional theater companies that have established roots outside the major theater centers. Besides bringing first-rate theater to their region, they often have programs to nurture local talent and to encourage new plays of special regional interest.

repertory: set group of productions that a theater company has prepared for performance. Also, the practice of alternating performances of different plays of the repertory.

road company: company of performers who travel with a show that they present in essentially the same way it was originally created in a theater center such as New York.

royalties: payments made to authors (and their representatives) for permission to reproduce, in text or in performance, their artistic products (plays, designs, etc.).

simultaneous staging: stage arrangement in which more than one set appears on the stage at once, often with a neutral playing area (*plateau*) in front that can be used as part of whichever set is being used at the time.

special effect: technical effect—usually spectacular—found in a play, television program, or film. These can vary from the relatively simple gunshot or the flying of a character to a vast flood or thermonuclear war. The more elaborate special effects may be beyond the capacity of most theater technicians; in this case, a specialist—a special effects artist—may be employed.

thespian: actor; after Thespis, the first Greek dramatist.

typecasting: selection of actors based upon their physical similarity to a certain dramatic type or upon their reputation for specializing in that kind of role.

AUDITORIUM TERMINOLOGY

apron (forestage): stage area in front of the main curtain.

asbestos (fire curtain): first specially treated curtain, hung immediately behind the proscenium. Usually held by a fused link which will separate automatically in case of fire and lower the curtain.

balcony: second tier of seating.

continental seating: an arrangement of audience seating without a center aisle.

control booth (light booth/projection booth): small, glass-enclosed room at the back of the auditorium; used to house light and sound equipment. The stage manager often runs the show from the control booth.

curtain line: imaginary line at which the act curtain meets the floor.

FOHs: lighting instruments placed in the auditorium.

follow spot: large lighting instrument (usually a carbon arc or an electric spotlight with a high-intensity beam) mounted with special equipment so that an operator can direct the beam in narrow or wide flood focus in any direction and thereby accompany an actor in his/her various movements over the stage. Used mostly in musicals.

footlights (foots): row of low-wattage lamps providing general illumination and usually circuited in several colors.

front of house: lobby and the auditorium area of the theater.

house curtain: full drapery that separates the stage from the audience. This curtain is rigged to move up and down or open from side to side.

house lights: all the lights in the auditorium except the "exit" lights. These lights usually dim and are controlled from the light booth.

mezzanine: lower section of the second tier of seating.

orchestra: main floor seating area of the auditorium.

pit: area immediately below the stage which is usually lower than the auditorium level. Used primarily by the stage orchestra.

proscenium arch: wall forming a picturing frame separating the stage from the auditorium.

BACKSTAGE TECHNOLOGY

backstage: stage area beyond the acting area.

batten: long iron pipe that stretches across the stage and upon which scenery or drops are hung.

catwalk: narrow metal platform suspended above the stage to permit ready access to the ropes, the lights, and the scenery hung from the grid.

counterweight system: device for balancing the weight of scenery, allowing it to be easily lowered or raised above the stage by means of ropes or wires and pulleys.

cyc (cyclorama): white or blue tautly stretched canvas drop or plaster dome across the back wall of the stage which when lit simulates the sky.

down right: acting area closest to the audience and on the right side of the stage as you face the audience (the actor's right).

DRC: down right center (stage position).

fly loft (flies): space above the stage where scenery may be lifted out of sight of the audience.

gelatin (gel): color medium made of dyed animal material. It is used to change the color in any stage lighting instrument.

gobo: metal cutout that creates a simple pattern when placed on the aperture of an ellipsoidal reflector spotlight.

gridiron (grid): framework of steel affixed to the stage ceiling, used to support rigging necessary for flying scenery.

legs (tormentors): curtains or flats placed on either side of the stage just upstage of the curtain line. Legs serve to mask the wings from the view of the audience and vary the width of the playing area.

light bridge: long, narrow platform suspended by adjustable lines directly behind the house curtain and asbestos.

lines: steel wires or ropes attached to batten and running up to the gridiron and back down to the fly gallery, used to raise and lower scenery and drops.

offstage: areas of the stage not in view of the audience.

pin rail: fixed beam of steel, placed in the fly loft or on the stage floor at one side of the stage, to which are attached the lines that are used to raise and lower scenery or drops.

prompt corner (Stage Manager's Desk): downstage left or right stage from which the stage manager "calls" the show.

stage right: actor's right; the audience's left.

teaser: curtain hanging above and across the stage just upstage of the house curtain and downstage of the tormentors. Used to mask the flies and adjust the height of the stage opening.

trap: opening in the stage floor, normally covered, which can be used for special effects, such as having scenery or performers rise from below, or which permits the construction of a staircase which ostensibly leads to a lower floor or cellar.

up-left center: that part of the playing area farthest from the audience and just left of center as you face the audience (the actor's left).

wings: offstage areas right and left stage.

work lights: lights used solely for illuminating the stage when it is not being watched by an audience, as at rehearsals and when scenery is being shifted.

30 Theater Spaces

"There's Gotta Be Something Better Than This"

from Sweet Charity.
Music by Cy Coleman;
lyrics by Dorothy Fields;
book by Neil Simon.

Opened in New York, January 29, 1966; ran 608 performances. The musical was directed and choreographed by Bob Fosse and starred Gwen Verdon.

The following is a list of possible spaces to produce theater in. A number of them can be adapted by schools and community theater organizations and simulated in a large open hall.

MAJOR SPACES

arena stage/theater-in-the-round: theater space where the audience sits on all four sides of the auditorium and watches the action in an area set in the middle of the room.

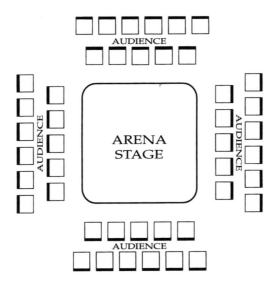

black-box theatre: flexible room for theater performances where the audience seating and playing areas can be rearranged in any way that suits the needs of the individual production.

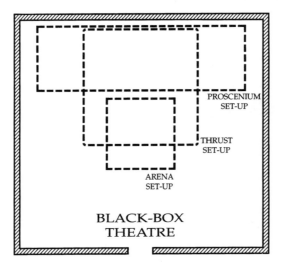

proscenium stage: picture-frame acting area with all of the audience sitting and facing the stage.

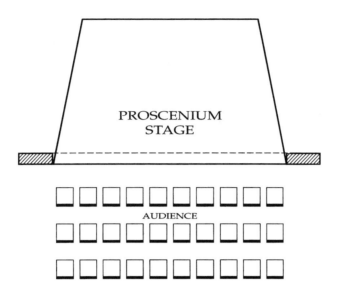

stadium stage: theater space where banks of seating face each other and design elements are simulated on end walls.

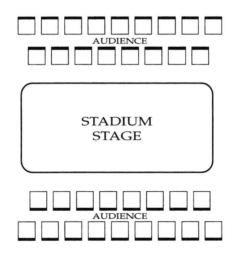

thrust stage (open stage/apron stage): wraparound theater space where the stage extends out into the audience and the spectators view the action from three sides. The main advantage to this setup is that more of the audience can be closer to the actors. Scenically, it can be less expensive to mount a theater piece on a thrust stage than on a proscenium stage.

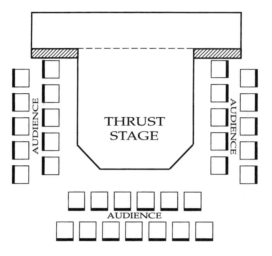

ALTERNATIVE SPACES

environmental theater: contemporary theater space in which the audience space and the playing space are intermixed, so that the audience finds the action occurring all around them and may even have to choose where to look as they would in real life.

found space: acting/audience space that was designed for another purpose. Productions in the streets, bus terminals, gymnasiums, parks, and the like are said to use *found space.*

platform stage: stage raised above the audience area, which is placed at one end of a room.

promenade theater: theater space where there is no designated seating space but where the audience moves to whatever position allows them to follow the action, which is also moving. It is designed to create a feeling of drama as a community experience.

street theater: open-air spaces where acting troupes try to attract audiences, often for the purpose of social activism.

31 Stages of the Production Process

"Perpetual Anticipation"

from A Little Night Music.

Music and lyrics by Stephen Sondheim;

book by Hugh Wheeler.

Opened in New York, February 25, 1973; ran 601 performances. Harold Prince directed, and the musical won both the New York Drama Critics Circle Award and the Tony Award for best musical.

The following are stages you need to follow once you have selected a play or musical and set the dates for your production.

auditions: competitive tryout for a performer seeking a role in a theater production. The process may include interviews, cold readings from the script, the presentation of a prepared audition piece, improvisations, or any combination of these.

casting: difficult task of matching the actors who auditioned for the production with the roles in the play or musical.

orientation: initial gathering of the cast to explain policies, hand out rehearsal schedule, make introductions, discuss directing approach, and explain the concept of the production. On some occasions the costume and set designers show renderings or models of their work.

read-through: cast reads through the play to clarify meaning and pronunciation and to gain greater insight into character development and interpretation.

blocking rehearsals: emphasis on these rehearsals is placed on stage movement, which is either overseen or dictated by the director.

line rehearsals: actors are expected to be "off book" and line perfect when these rehearsals are called.

working rehearsals: process of exploring, then setting and practicing, the artistic decisions inherent in the play.

run-through (walk-through): rehearsal in which the actors perform long sections of the play (an act or the entire play) without interruption, usually to improve the sense of continuity and to gain a better understanding of the shape of the whole.

polishing rehearsals: rehearsals that concentrate on pacing: the perfection of timing (the overall rate and speed in handling lines and business) and tempo (the rhythm) of a production.

dress parade: point in the rehearsal period at which some directors require that all costumes be ready to be seen, often a specific rehearsal during which actors don their costumes and appear on the stage for consideration by the director, the costume designer, and others of the artistic leadership.

paper tech: informal sessions scheduled with the set, lighting, and sound designers to discuss specific cues and desired effects. The stage manager should be present at these sessions.

dry tech: extended rehearsal, without actors, devoted to setting (and, if time allows, practicing) the various technical elements of the production (lighting, sound, flying, set changes, trapping, and so on).

wet tech: extended rehearsal, with actors, devoted to the integration and practice of all technical elements (light, sound, special effects, and set and prop changes).

dress rehearsals: final rehearsals in which all visual elements of production, including costumes, are used. A rehearsal process typically includes three dress rehearsals, each rehearsal striving to duplicate, insofar as possible, an actual performance.

preview performance: special performance aimed at helping the director to judge the response of the audience once the play is open to the public. Usually, audience members are especially invited to preview performances; however, some commercial theaters attract preview audiences with reduced admissions.

32 A List of Theatrical Forms

"*Try to Remember*"

from The Fantasticks.
Music by Harvey Schmidt;
lyrics and book
by Tom Jones.

Opened in New York, May 3, 1960; still running as of 1994. Longest running musical in American history.

DRAMA

Drama is a serious form of theater that takes a thoughtful, sober attitude toward its subject matter. It puts the audience in a frame of mind to think carefully about what it sees and to become involved with the characters on stage.

tragedy: play that treats, at the most uncompromising level, human suffering. Modern tragedy involves ordinary people, rather than the nobility of classical tragedy, and is written generally in prose rather than verse. The common men or women probe the same depths and ask the same questions as their predecessors: Why do men and women suffer? Why are cruelty and injustice in the world? And perhaps most fundamental of all: What is the meaning of our lives? Examples: *Hamlet, Macbeth, Othello,* and *King Lear,* by William Shakespeare; *Long Days Journey Into Night* and *Death of a Salesman* by Arthur Miller.

heroic drama: period play written in verse. In contrast to tragedy, it is marked by a happy ending, or an ending in which the deaths of the main characters are considered a triumph and not a defeat. Example: *Cyrano de Bergerac* by Edmond Rostand.

domestic drama: addresses the problems of ordinary, middle- and lower-class people in a serious but nontragic manner. Example: *The Diary of Anne Frank* by Frances Goodrich and Albert Hackett and *The Miracle Worker* by William Gibson.

melodrama: suspenseful, plot-oriented drama featuring all-good heroes, all-bad villains, simplistic and naturalistic dialogue, soaring moral conclusions, and bravura acting. Only when taken to extreme is melodrama laughable. Mysteries and problem plays are two types of drama that fall under this category. Examples: *Dracula* by Hamilton Deane and John L. Balderston and *The Mousetrap* by Agatha Christie.

thesis play: serious treatment of social, moral, or philosophical ideas. These plays make a one-sided presentation and employ a character who sums up the lesson of the play and serves as the author's voice. Example: *Our Town* by Thornton Wilder.

COMEDY

Comedy is a play with a mixture of humor and pathos, that celebrates the eternal ironies and struggles of human existence, and ends happily.

farce: play that aims to entertain and provoke laughter. Its humor is the result primarily of physical activity and visual effects, and it relies less on language and wit than do so-called higher forms of comedy. Violence, rapid movement, and accelerating pace are characteristics of farce. Example: *Arsenic and Old Lace* by Joseph Kesselring.

domestic comedy: play that explores the contradictions and eccentricities both within and between individual characters. Example: *Life With Father* by Howard Lindsay and Russel Crouse.

satire: play that ridicules social foibles, beliefs, religions, or human vices, almost always in a light-hearted vein. Example: *The Importance of Being Earnest* by Oscar Wilde.

33

A List of Contemporary Plays for Beginning Directors

"Let Me Entertain You"

from Gypsy.
*Music by Jule Styne;
lyrics by Stephen Sondheim;
book by Arthur Laurents,
based on Gypsy Rose Lee's
autobiography.*

Opened in New York, May 21, 1959; ran 702 performances. Ethel Merman, Angela Lansbury, Tyne Daly, and Bette Midler have all played the leading role.

COMEDIES

Arsenic and Old Lace, by Joseph Kesselring (farce); 11M, 3W; 1 int.; contmp.; DPS; even though this has older characters, they are eccentric enough to be played by any age.

Charley's Aunt, by Brandon Thomas (farce); 6M, 4W; 2 int.; 1 ext.; 1892; SF; the drawback here is that this requires three sets but they can be simplified. Even though the script was written nearly one hundred years ago, it still plays well.

Cheaper by the Dozen, based on the book by Frank Gilbreth and Ernestine Gilbreth Carey. Dramatized by Christopher Sergel (comedy); 9M, 7W; 1 int.; early 1900s; Dram. Pub.; large cast includes some young children. Still a crowd pleaser.

Father of the Bride, by Caroline Francke (comedy); 11M, 7W, extras; 1 int.; contemp.; DPS; a number of small roles.

The Foreigner, by Larry Shue (comedy); 5M, 2W; 1 int.; contemp.; DPS; requires a trapdoor; a sure-fire audience pleaser.

It's a Wonderful Life, adapted by James W. Rodgers based on the film by Frank Capra and the story by Philip Van Doren Stern (comedy); 12M; 10W, 2 boys and 2 girls; unit set; 1945; Dram. Pub.; heart-warming classic requiring few sets and props; one leading male role and several rich supporting roles.

Life With Father, by Howard Lindsay and Russel Crouse (comedy); 8M, 8W; 1 int.; 1880s; DPS; requires two young boys; all the family have to have red hair; set requires a large dining table on stage and lots of props.

The Matchmaker, by Thornton Wilder (farce); 9M, 7W; 4 int.; SF; 1880; French; four sets and lots of props; the sets can be stylized.

The Nerd, by Larry Shue (comedy); 5M, 2W; 1 int.; contemp.; DPS; the major male character role includes one very long monologue.

Seventeen, by Booth Tarkington (comedy); 8M, 6W; 1 ext.; early 1900s; French; a real sleeper; good for teenager actors.

Story Theatre, by Paul Sills (fable); 5M, 3W; bare stage; contemp.; SF; casting can be flexible; music can be added; wonderful vehicle for improvisational acting.

You Can't Take It With You, by Moss Hart and George S. Kaufman (comedy); 9M, 7W; 1 int.; 1930s; DPS; many people on stage at the same time; some special effects; grandfather role is pivotal.

MYSTERIES

The Bad Seed, adapted by Maxwell Anderson from W. March's novel (thriller); 7M, 4W, 1 small girl; 1 int.; contemp.; DPS; requires advanced actors.

Dracula, by Hamilton Deane and John L. Balderston from Bram Stoker's novel (horror story); 6M, 2W; 3 int.; French; this is one of several versions carried by all three major publishing companies. The casts vary in size and set requirements.

Haunting of Hill House, adapted by F. Andrew Leslie from the novel by Shirley Jackson (supernatural); 3M, 4W; 1 int.; DPS; requires some special effects.

The Mousetrap, by Agatha Christie (melodrama); 5M, 3W; 1 int.; SF; contemp.; French; longest running play in London; should be played with some humor.

Murder Has Been Arranged, by Emlyn William (melodrama); 4M, 5W; 1 int.; contemp.; SF; fairly straightforward, well-written script.

Ten Little Indians, by Agatha Christie (suspense drama); 8M, 3W; 1 int.; SF; contemp.; French; needs to be played with style.

SERIOUS PLAYS

A Christmas Carol, from Charles Dickens' classic. All three major publishing companies carry one or more versions; flexible cast and sets.

Crimes of the Heart, by Beth Henley (drama); 2M, 4W; 1 int.; DPS; male roles are supportive; excellent vehicle for females; requires Southern accents; delicate balance between humor and serious subject matter.

Diary of Anne Frank, by Frances Goodrich and Albert Hackett (drama); 5M, 5W; 1 int.; WW2; DPS; mature actors required.

The Diviners, by James Leonard, Jr. (drama); 6M, 5W; unit set; SF; 1930s; French; no major problems; winner of the American College Theatre Festival.

Flowers for Algernon, by David Rogers based on a novel by Daniel Keyes (drama); 10M, 17W can be reduced to 8M, 9W; unit set; contemp.; Dram. Pub.; no special problems.

I Remember Mama, by John van Druten, adapted from K. Forbes' novel (play); 9M, 13W; unit set; 1900–1910; DPS; dialects required; strong vehicle.

The Miracle Worker, by William Gibson (drama); 7M, 7W; unit set; 1882; SF; complicated fight scene; young Helen is blind, wild and does not speak.

Our Town, by Thornton Wilder (drama); 17M, 7W, extras; bare stage; 1900 costumes; SF; for all ages.

Picnic, by William Inge (drama); 4M, 7W; ext. set; two porches; contemp.; DPS; advanced actors.

Steel Magnolias, by Robert Harling (drama); 6W; 1 int.; contemp.; DPS; Southern accents; much humor; no males.

To Kill a Mockingbird, dramatized by Christopher Sergel based on the novel by Harper Lee; 11M, 6W, extras; unit set; 1930s; Dram. Pub.; requires black and white actors; three major roles are children who can be portrayed by adults.

Twelve Angry Men/Women/Citizens, adapted by Sherman L. Sergel (from the TV play by Reginald Rose) (drama); 15M, W, or mixed cast; 1 int.; contemp.; Dram. Pub.; flexible cast; a sure-fire "potboiler."

Key to Abbreviations

M—Number of men's roles
W—Number of women's roles
int.—interior set
ext.—exterior set
contemp.—contemporary costumes
SF—Samuel French, Inc.
DPS—Dramatists' Play Service
Dram. Pub.—The Dramatic Publishing Company

34 More Terms About Parts of Plays

"Losing My Mind"

from Follies.
Music and lyrics by
Stephen Sondheim;
book by James Goldman.

Opened in New York, April 4, 1971; ran 522 performances. The musical was probably suggested by the demolition of the great Ziegfeld Theater.

aside: unspoken thoughts of a character delivered directly to the audience with the other characters on stage but unable to hear what is being said.

climax: highest point of dramatic tension in a script. Usually the crux of the play, when the major conflict can proceed no further without beginning the process of resolution.

comic relief: inclusion of a comic line or scene in an otherwise serious play to provide relief from tension.

dénouement: final scene of a play when the plot is unraveled and the play is brought to a tidy conclusion.

epilogue: speech or short scene that sometimes follows the main action of a play.

exposition: units in the script in which the playwright supplies background and past information necessary to the complete understanding of the play.

flashback: theatrical convention in which the audience is able to see scenes from the past through the eyes of one of the characters in a play.

French scene: division in a scene or act of the play framed by the entrance or the exit of a major character.

monologue: uninterrupted speech delivered by one character in a play to other characters who are at least present, if not listening.

plant: work, object, action, or idea deliberately set in to the action of the play by either the playwright or the director so that the audience is led to expect some further development from it later on.

prologue: speech or a short scene preceding the main action of the play that sets a mood and defines or defends the script.

reprise: in musicals, a repetition of a song or dance with some variation.

scenario: outline of the play.

scene: division of an act, usually denoting a change in time or place. Can also be the descriptor for the locale of a play.

soliloquy: inner thoughts of a character spoken alone on stage to explore the character's private thoughts. Often lyric in style and highly emotional.

theme: central ideas or thoughts of a play that synthesize the audience's experiences.

35 Players in a Commercial Theater Organization

"The Little Things We Do Together"

from Company.
Music and lyrics by
Stephen Sondheim;
book by George Furth.

Opened in New York, April 26, 1970; ran 705 performances. Dean Jones and Elaine Stritch starred in the Broadway production.

The following list defines the roles of specialists used in a commercial theater venture. Note the number of duties the director assumes in a school or community theater production.

producer: practical visionary of a theater company (like a chairman of the board or president of a corporation) whose primary responsibility is to secure rights to the script, establish the budget for the production, raise money, lease an appropriate theater space, and draw together the artistic leadership. Working with the producer is a *legal counsel* and an *accountant*.

playwright: person who writes or adapts properties known as plays; in most traditions, the first and most creative artist of all those who collaborate to make theater. It is the playwright's property that stimulates the impetus for a full-fledged production. In musicals, the writers include the writers of the music, the lyrics, and the book.

general manager: oversees all nonartistic parts of the production. Under the producer's guidance, the general manager draws up the budgets and works directly with agents and lawyers in drawing up contracts for actors and the leasing of the theater. He also handles all negotiations with the various theatrical unions.

investor (angel): financial backer for a commercial production. Because of the high cost of mounting a commercial production ($2 million for a "straight" play and $5 million to $8 million for a musical), producers look to corporate funding rather than to individual investors.

general press agent: individual responsible for the promotion of the production: press releases, ad placement, poster distribution, radio and TV spots, interviews, etc. This individual works very closely with the producer and is usually held responsible for the longevity of a production.

director: in modern theater, the major interpretive figure, the artistic visionary whose job it is to bring to life the playwright's script. The director's primary objective is to provide artistic meaning to the theater experience. The director might have a number of professional assistants to work with him/her: *casting director, movement coach, speech consultant (vocal coach)*. In musicals, the music director and the choreographer are also major interpretive figures.

dramaturg: member of a theater company who acts as a script consultant on a production. He/she is a sort of reader-cum-literary editor to a permanent theatrical company; his/her prime responsibility is the selection of plays for production, working with authors (when necessary) on the revisions and adaptation of their texts, and writing program notes, etc., for the company. During the production process, he/she works with the director to clarify background detail and interpretation of the script.

actors: individuals who, within the performance contract, enact characters or situations other than their own, using as the materials of the art their own body and voice. The term "actor" applies to both women and men.

designers (scenic, lighting, special effects, sound, costume, makeup): architects of a production; they provide the practical and artistic environment for a play or musical. The best of these highly skilled artisans knows how to deal effectively with limitations.

stage manager: member of the artistic leadership of a theater company who accepts full responsibility for the integrity of a production once it is open to the public. The stage manager normally "calls the show" (i.e., gives commands to execute all cues during performance) and accepts responsibility for maintaining the artistic integrity of the production throughout the duration of its run.

running crews: all the skilled employees who run the show including flyman, production electrician, production soundman, production propertyman, wardrobe supervisor, wig master, union stagehands, etc.

critic: someone whose verbalized responses to the play or script are thought to enrich the experience for others. The response can take the form of newspaper articles, television reviews, or public talks.

35.1

PLAYERS IN A COMMERCIAL THEATER ORGANIZATION

Producer

Play/Musical
(Playwright or Music, Lyrics, and Book Writers)

General Manger

| Investors (Angels) | Agents/Unions/Lawyers | | Theater Owners | General Press |

Director

Dramaturg

Movement Coach (Combat/Fight)		Vocal Coach (Dialect)		
Choreographer	Music Director	Actors	Stage Manager	Designers
Dance Captain	Rehearsal Pianist		Assistant Stage Manager	
	Singers			
	Musicians			

| Scenery | Special Effects | Lighting | Sound | Makeup | Costume |

Props

Hair/Wigs

— Technical Director —

Scene Shop

Costume Shop

Running Crews

| Stagehands | Flyman | Production Electricians | Production Soundman | Wig Master | Wardrobe Supervisor |

36 A Selected Reading List for Beginning Directors

"Who Can I Turn To?"

from The Roar of the Greasepaint - The Smell of the Crowd.
Book, music and lyrics by Leslie Bricusse and Anthony Newley.

Opened in New York, May 16, 1965; ran 232 performances. Anthony Newley and Cyril Ritchard stared in the Broadway production.

The following is a highly selective list of books for beginning directors; ones that we feel will complement what we have shared with you in this book.

DIRECTING

Brook, Peter. *The Empty Space.* London: MacGibbon & Kee, 1968.

Coger, Leslie Irene and Melvin R. White. *Readers Theatre Handbook.* Glenview, Illinois: Scott, Foresman and Company, 1982.

Corrigan, Robert W. *The Making of Theatre: From Drama to Performance.* Glenview, Illinois: Scott, Foresman and Company, 1981.

Guthrie, Tyrone. *In Various Directions.* New York: Macmillan, 1965.

Leiter, Samuel L. *From Belasco to Brook: Great Stage Directors of the Century.* New York: Drama Book Specialists, 1981.

Rosenberg, Helene S. and Christine Prendergast. *Theatre for Young People: A Sense of Occasion.* New York: Holt, Rinehart and Winston, 1983.

Spolin, Viola. *Improvisation for the Theatre: A Handbook of Teaching and Directing Techniques.* Evanston, Illinois: Northwestern University Press, 1963.

_____. *Theater Games for Rehearsal: A Director's Handbook.* Evanston, Illinois: Northwestern University Press, 1985.

Wills, J. Robert, ed. *The Director in a Changing Theatre: Essays on Theory and Practice, with New Plays for Performance.* Palo Alto, California: Mayfield, 1976.

ACTING

Adler, Stella. *The Technique of Acting.* New York: Bantam Press, 1988.

Albright, Hardie. *Acting: The Creative Process.* 2nd ed. Encino, California and Belmont California: Dickenson Publishing Co., Inc., 1974.

Chekhov, Michael. *To the Actor.* New York: Harper & Brothers, 1953.

Funke, Lewis. *Actors Talk About Theatre.* Chicago: The Dramatic Publishing Co., 1977.

Guthrie, Tyrone. *On Acting.* New York: The Viking Press, 1971.

Hage, Uta and Frankel Haskel. *Respect for Acting.* New York: Macmillan Publishing Co., 1973.

Harrop, John and Sabin R. Epstein. *Acting With Style.* Englewood Cliffs, New Jersey: Prentice-Hall, Inc., 1982.

Lewis, Robert. *Method or Madness?* New York: Samuel French, 1958.

Lewis, Robert. *Advice to the Players.* New York: Harper and Row, 1980.

Olivier, Laurence. *Laurence Olivier on Acting*. New York: Simon & Schuster, 1986.

Ross, Lillian and Helen Ross. *The Player: A Profile of an Art*. New York: Limelight Editions, 1984.

Shurtleff, Michael. *Audition*. New York: Walker and Company, 1978.

DESIGN

Bay, Howard. *Stage Design*. New York: DBS Publications, 1974.

Bellman, Willard F. *Scene Design, Stage Lighting, Sound, Costume and Makeup: A Scenographic Approach*. New York: Harper & Row, 1983.

Burdick, Elizabeth B., et al., eds. *Contemporary Stage Design*. Middletown, Connecticut: Wesleyan University Press, 1975.

Burris-Meyer, Harold, Vincent Mallory and Lewis S. Goodfriend. *Sound in the Theatre*. rev. ed., New York: Theatre Arts Books, 1979.

Corson, Richard. *Stage Make-up*. 5th ed. New York: Appleton-Century-Crofts, 1975.

Ingham, Rosemary and Liz Covey. *Designer's Handbook: A Complete Guide for Amateur and Professional Costume Designers*. Englewood Cliffs, New Jersey: Prentice-Hall, Inc., 1983.

Jones, Robert Edmund. *The Dramatic Imagination*. New York: Meredith, 1941.

Kenton, Warren. *Stage Properties and How to Make Them*. 2nd ed. London: Pitman Publishing, 1978.

Motley. *Designing and Making Stage Costumes*. London: Studio Vista, 1964.

_____. *Theatre Props*. New York: DBS Publications, 1976.

Pilbrow, Richard. *Stage Lighting*. New York: DBS Publications, 1979.

ORGANIZATION AND MANAGEMENT

Ashford, Gerald. *Everyday Publicity: A Practical Guide*. New York: Law-Arts, 1970.

Drucker, Peter F. *Management: Tasks, Responsibilities, Practices*. New York: Harper & Row, 1974.

Farber, Donald C. *From Option to Opening*. 3d ed. New York: Drama Book, 1977.

Langley, Stephen. *Producers on Producing*. New York: Drama Book, 1976.

_____. *Theatre Management in America*. New York: Drama Book, 1974.

Reiss, Alvin H., ed. *Market the Arts!* New York: FEDAPT, 1983.

_____. *The Arts Management Handbook*. New York: Law-Arts, 1970.

Stern, Lawrence. *Stage Management: A Guidebook of Practical Techniques.* Boston: Allyn & Bacon, 1974.

Wolf, Thomas. *Presenting Performers.* Cambridge, Massachusetts: New England Foundation for the Arts, 1977.